FEE–PAYING SCHOOLS AND
EDUCATIONAL CHANGE IN BRITAIN

T0347394

THE WOBURN EDUCATION SERIES

General Series Editor: Professor Peter Gordon

FEE-PAYING SCHOOLS AND EDUCATIONAL CHANGE IN BRITAIN: Between the State and the Marketplace

TED TAPPER
University of Sussex

RoutledgeFalmer
Taylor & Francis Group

LONDON AND NEW YORK

First published in 1997 in Great Britain by
THE WOBURN PRESS
Reprinted 2004
by RoutledgeFalmer
2 Park Square, Milton Park, Abingdon,
Oxon, OX14 4RN

Transferred to Digital Printing 2004

Copyright © 1997 Ted Tapper

British Library Cataloguing in Publication data
Tapper, Ted
Fee-paying schools and educational change in Britain :
between the state and the marketplace. – (The Woburn
education series)
1. Education and the state – Great Britain 2. Education –
Economic aspects – Great Britain 3. Educational change –
Great Britain
I. Title
379.4'1
ISBN 0-7130-0197-6 (cloth)
ISBN 0-7130-4030-0 (paper)

Library of Congress Cataloging in Publication data
Tapper, Ted.
  Fee-paying schools and educational change in Britain :
between the state and the marketplace / Ted Tapper.
    p. cm. -- (The Woburn education series)
  Includes bibliographical reference (p.   ) and index.
  ISBN 0-7130-0197-6 (hardback) 0-7130-4030-0 (paper)
  1. Private schools–Great Britain–Finance. 2. Public
schools, Endowed (Great Britain)–Finance. 3. Education
and state–Great Britain. 4. Educational change–Great Britain.
I. Title.
II. Series.
LC53.G7T37   1997
371.02'0941–dc21   96-37181
                                                        CIP

All rights reserved. No part of this publication may be reproduced
in any form or by any means, electronic, mechanical, photocopying,
recording or otherwise, without the prior permission of
The Woburn Press.

This book is dedicated
to the memory of
my brother John William Tapper

Contents

Abbreviations

AHPS	Association of Headmasters of Preparatory Schools
CEE	Common Entrance Examination
CTCs	City Technology Colleges
DES	Department of Education and Science
DFE	Department for Education
DFEE	Department for Education and Employment
DGJC	Direct Grant Joint Committee
FAS	Funding Agency for Schools
GBA	Governing Bodies Association
GBGSA	Governing Bodies of Girls' Schools Association
GMS	Grant Maintained Schools
GSA	Girls' Schools Association
HMC	Headmasters' (and Headmistresses') Conference
IAPS	Incorporated Association of Preparatory Schools
ISAI	Independent Schools Association Incorporated
ISIS	Independent Schools Information Service
ISJC	Independent Schools Joint Council
LEAs	Local Education Authorities
SHMIS	Society of Headmasters and Headmistresses of Independent Schools
UCAS	Universities and Colleges Admissions Service
UCCA	Universities' Central Council on Admissions

Preface

The primary aim of this book is to examine the changing pattern of access to private schooling in England, in particular to the independent secondary schools. Although there is a strong historical focus to the book, much of the analysis concentrates upon contemporary political struggles. The purpose is to examine the possibility of creating a more unified educational system. Can the fee-paying and maintained sectors of schooling be merged into a new and different whole? Is it possible to create a fused system of secondary schooling, or is the inevitability of selected access to differing kinds of educational resources an irremovable obstacle to such ambitions? The educational system is the focus of considerable policy debate which will intensify as the next general election approaches. This book provides a context for this debate as well as proffering its own advice.

Although the book has definite policy concerns, it is also intended to be a scholarly work. Indeed, part of its purpose is to bridge the gap between scholarship and policy analysis which I believe has been apparent in much of the contemporary analysis of the educational policy-making process. I have developed my long-standing interest in the process of educational change by drawing upon the work of Margaret Scotford Archer (1979) and Randall Collins (1971). This theoretical work builds upon the previous research that I have undertaken with my colleague, Brian Salter. The changing pattern of access to private schooling is examined historically which, besides providing a test of the theory, also encourages a fuller appreciation of the contemporary issues. Access to private schooling is subject to the pressures of both the state and the marketplace. It is these pressures which help us to understand the changing nature of the private sector (see John Rae's *Public School Revolution*, 1981), and which should be co-ordinated – as the final chapter of this book insists – to bring about a steady interpenetration of the two sectors of schooling in the future. There has never been a truly independent sector of schooling and the future should work to ensure the erosion of both the maintained and fee-paying sectors as we know them at present.

I want to thank Clive Griggs for his contribution to this book. Although he disagrees strongly with many of my interpretations, he has given unstintingly of his time to make a sustained and constructive critique. For this I thank him. I have also greatly appreciated the consistently shrewd comments of David Palfreyman. It is impossible to maintain a research interest over a long period of time without the support of many people. I thank all those, too numerous to mention individually, for helping to sustain my efforts. I hope they feel suitably rewarded.

1

Understanding Educational Change in the Fee-paying Sector

In recent years there has been considerable interest in the extent to which the character of private schooling, and in particular of the public schools, has changed. In his perceptive *The Public School Revolution*, John Rae argued that between 1964 and 1979 the schools responded successfully to a number of challenges which enabled them to rebut ten popular, but negative, myths (Rae, 1981). Rae recognised that, by concentrating upon a limited historical period, it was possible to make changes that were essentially evolutionary in nature appear revolutionary. However, it was *the pace of change* between 1964 and 1979, and his contention that 'existing attitudes and practice' had been overturned, which he believed justified describing the changes as revolutionary, or rather as 'to a greater or lesser degree revolutionary' (1981, 177).

Walford has described the changes in somewhat more cautious terms, arguing that they amounted to 'a revolution in chains' (1986). Along with Heward (1988), he has advanced the argument that the schools have adapted steadily to changing circumstances. Moreover, there are constraints which make it difficult for the schools to be unduly innovative: the problem of converting for different purposes what are in some cases ancient monuments, the conservatism of old boys and governors (although Walford found many of the latter surprisingly progressive), and the inevitable difficulty of restructuring the traditional allocation of resources.

To decide between the two evaluations would be to take on a difficult and not especially fruitful task. What is required is a careful consideration of both what has changed and the pace of that change. An examination of the pace of change gives rise to problems of measurement and evaluation, while any consideration of what has changed has to take into account both the purposes of the schools as

1

well as how they are structured to perform those purposes. It is possible that the fee-paying schools have retained the same social purposes while revolutionising their means of fulfilling those purposes. In my previous work I have suggested that we need, first, to understand what has changed within the schools, and then to evaluate the impact of those changes upon the social role of the schools (Salter and Tapper, 1981, 157–88; 1985, 127–54). This, I believe, is a more constructive approach than becoming mired in a semantic debate about the pace of change.

The two most significant developments in recent years within the fee-paying schools have been an intensification of the stress upon examination success (which would suggest a more demanding school environment), coupled with a marked relaxation and widening of the schools' broader socialising practices (which would suggest a more liberal environment). Most commentators have reflected upon these trends, but there has been little analysis of their impact upon the social functions of the fee-paying schools. This is a complex question because of the wide variety of such schools, the problem of defining their traditional goals, and the probability that different kinds of observers will establish their own particular yardsticks. Much of the sociological literature has centred upon the schools' socially selective recruitment patterns, and the special learning environments that have evolved within them. For many sociologists the schools perform the crucial functions of the selective recruitment and socialisation of an elite or ruling class. However, those engaged in the running of the fee-paying sector would be more likely to argue that what their schools have to offer is a worthwhile educational experience which has to be judged on its own merits. While the schools may have broader social consequences, their primary purpose is to sustain a high-class education within the context of a sympathetic environment.

If schooling is an end in itself, then the 'public school revolution', or 'revolution in chains', would represent an attempt to offer an improved educational experience. However, even those who are keenest to stress the pedagogical claims of the fee-paying sector could scarcely deny that it also has social consequences, although precisely what these are may be disputed. The new public school model may, in sociological terms, simply reflect the fact that elite recruitment and socialisation need to be accomplished in a different manner, one that is more in tune with the demands of the contemporary social order. In effect we have new wine in an old bottle. Sociologists, therefore, will stress the purposeful interaction of educational means and social ends;

while a more narrow perspective would claim that pedagogy is the purpose of schooling and its social ramifications are not the responsibility of the schools.

As this book is written by a political sociologist, inevitably it will adopt a sociological perspective. The intention is to construct a theoretical position centred upon the interaction of the institutional needs of the schools and their social role. The theory is designed to account for the process of educational change, which is yet another concern that has been buried by the mountain of descriptive detail enveloping previous interpretations of the public school revolution. While there has been much reflection upon the admission of girls to the former boys' public schools, the broader social composition of the fee-paying sector as a whole has *not* changed substantially in recent years. In concrete terms fee-paying schools are still the preserve of the middle classes: this persists as the major constraint upon the idea of a 'public school revolution' (a point strangely overlooked by Walford).

The important issue is what kind of public school revolution could possibly occur without such a change? At first glance, the answer would seem to depend upon the changing needs, perceived or real, of the British middle classes, and the ability of the schools to respond to those needs. Looked at in this way, if there has been a revolution it has been a bourgeois revolution in which the private schools have changed in order to maintain their established role in the process of social reproduction.

In a passage worthy of considerable elaboration, Rae has written:

> Independent education is a service industry; if a school cannot attract customers it will go out of business. The aim of those who manage the schools' affairs is to provide an educational service that parents will want to buy at a cost that they can afford (1981, 163).

The central premise of this book is that educational change in the fee-paying sector is driven by those institutional forces which seek self-preservation. For private schools the key to institutional survival is the ability to attract a continuous and sufficiently large supply of fee-payers to cover their costs. If it seems that the schools are unable to survive by their appeal in the marketplace, then they will turn to the state for help. In effect this has meant persuading the state that it should be responsible for paying the fees of pupils who, without such support, might be less inclined to purchase an education in the fee-paying sector. Thus, educational change, institutional

3

self-preservation and marketplace/state pressures form an intimate bond.

Having set the scene for this chapter, my first substantive task is to examine the most important theories of educational change. As others have done this in some depth, my goal is more narrowly defined: how do these broad theories of educational change help us to understand the more refined problem of change in the fee-paying schools? What can be adapted from them to support the idea that the key to understanding change in this sector is the struggle for institutional survival? Although the schools need fee-paying pupils if they are to survive, it is important to realise that parents and the state will be persuaded to pay fees for particular reasons. Therefore, the interpretation of change must also be sensitive to the pressures upon those who purchase private schooling. In the case of the state these pressures are essentially political in nature, whereas parents are persuaded by a combination of economic and social forces. Change, therefore, is an interactive process among the schools, the purchasers of their product and the evolving character of state and society.

THREE THEORIES OF EDUCATIONAL CHANGE

The major theories of educational change have had very ambitious concerns: to determine the origins of state systems of education and to account for uneven patterns of national development. Two of the theories, functionalism and Marxism, have been built upon the premise that schooling performs core social functions: as society changes so schooling comes under pressure to assume new functions or to perform the traditional functions in a different manner. The third theoretical stream, which owes its intellectual origins to Max Weber and has been most fully developed by Margaret Scotford Archer, is more concerned to understand the process of change rather than posit a shifting relationship between schooling and society in which the former responds to the changing needs of the latter. In other words, the focus in the Weberian tradition is more upon how change occurs, that is the process of change, rather than upon the pressures for change.

While the Weberian perspective does not deny the possibility of a central dynamic for change (Archer (1979, 3) recognises the constraints of what she terms cultural and structural factors), its focus is upon the stages of educational development and the interplay of the various actors and groups within those stages. Moreover, Archer is keen to highlight the important role of individuals, and so stresses their ability to generate and transmit educational ideas, as well as their skills in the manipulation of political power. For Archer, 'education has the characteristics it does because of the goals pursued by those who control it' and 'change occurs because new educational goals are pursued by those who have the power to modify previous practices' (1979, 2).

In view of the fact that the focus of this book is upon the fee-paying sector of schooling, the theory of educational change developed in this chapter has a more restricted scope than those of the macro-sociologists. While, as a political sociologist, I cannot fail to concur with Archer's recognition that political struggle is at the centre of the change process, the stress is upon the institutionalisation of power rather than the role of individual actors, important as their input may be. Just as we do not make history in circumstances of our own choosing, neither do institutions. Central to the idea that institutional self-preservation is the key to understanding the process of educational change is the further proposition that change is negotiated within, and between, layers of institutions, of which the institutions of the state increasingly form the key layer. While all this may be true, there is a danger of replicating the major weakness of the Weberian position, at least as developed by Archer: that is, of constructing a theory of educational change which results in sophisticated descriptions of a process but leaves us wondering what sets the process in motion or brings it to a halt (assuming, of course, that it is ever brought to a halt).

The pressures for survival, reflected concretely in the fee-paying sector by the demand for places and school budgets, suggest a structural context (to use Archer's phrase) within which change will occur. But the school is reacting – or not reacting – to declining or increasing demand for its services. While this may stimulate the schools into action, the obvious further question is how the increased/decreased demand is to be explained. If the structural context is confined simply to the institutional needs of the school we are in danger of merely stating the obvious. In order, therefore, to broaden the book's central theoretical premise, the macro-sociological review will attempt to discern those wider structural variables – that is, those economic, social and political pressures – which influence the demand for places in the fee-paying schools.

Responding to Societal Needs: Some Functionalist Themes

Although Giddens has attempted to correct Parsons's 'sympathetic misinterpretations' of Durkheim by claiming that the great French sociologist was as much concerned with change and conflict in society as with consensus (Giddens, 1972, 39), it none the less remains true that Durkheim did think in terms of the functional needs of society of which the maintenance of a dominant moral order was paramount. Moreover, the primary social purpose of schooling was the inculcation of this moral order:

> There is no people among whom there is not a certain number of ideas, sentiments and practices which education must inculcate in all children indiscriminately, *to whatever social category they belong* (Durkheim, 1956, 69; stress added).

and

> Education is, then, only the means by which society prepares, within the children, the essential conditions of its very existence ... (and) education consists of a methodical socialisation of the young generation (1956, 71).

While Durkheim is clearly espousing a general sociological principle, that social harmony is underwritten by a dominant moral order, the demands he made of the French educational system resulted from particular historical circumstances. The old moral order was crumbling as the pace of industrialisation and urbanisation intensified in France. The influence of the Catholic Church, which formed the traditional moral backbone of the nation, was in decline. The nation needed a new moral code as the basis for social order in a rapidly changing society, and it was the responsibility of the centralised state system of schooling to ensure that this was successfully transmitted to future generations of Frenchmen and women.

Of course Durkheim was conscious of the fact that demands would be made of the individual '... by both the political society as a whole, *and by the particular milieu for which he is specifically destined*' (Giddens, 1972, 204; stress added). The histories of the public schools, as well as the more contemporary sociological studies of 'life in public schools', have made much play of the development of a well-defined value system, and the evolution of internal school codes for the transmission of those values. These are the elite/ruling class recruitment and socialisation themes which have abounded in the sociological literature, and, in theoretical terms, have been most interestingly analysed by that other prominent European theorist, Gaetano Mosca.

Mosca argued that elites were defined by their group conscious-ness, coherence and sense of conspiracy (Meisel, 1958, 4). It has been widely argued that one of the key functions of the public school in the nineteenth century was to provide an institutional setting in which the interests of the landed aristocracy and the emerging bourgeoisie could be reconciled. There is a body of opinion that the reconciliation of interests was concluded in a manner which ensured that aristocratic values pervaded the ensuing class compromises (Coleman, 1973), and that this has been to the long-term detriment of Britain's economic performance (Wiener, 1981, 11–21; Barnett, 1986, 214–21). Be that as it may, the central point is that potential conflicts generated by fundamental changes to the class structure were allegedly defused by the class accommodation that occurred within the public schools.

In Mosca's terms the public school performed the function of securing a significant measure of group consciousness, coherence and sense of conspiracy between two classes that in several other European nations were set on a collison course. If Barnett and Wiener are correct, perhaps the nation ensured social stability while forsaking the entrepreneurial spirit. And, unlike Barnett and Wiener, there are many who would say that a good bargain was struck.

The changes, therefore, that occurred within the nineteenth-century public schools were dependent upon their need to recruit a new clientele, one with its roots firmly planted in the bourgeoisie. In the long run the public schools could not hope to survive, or at least to remain centres of great influence, without allying themselves to those class interests that were expanding their influence both economically and politically. While Bamford has provided evidence that the schools founded in the early years of the Victorian era catered to a different clientele from the older foundations, by the latter half of the century the newer foundations were attracting the sons of the gentry, while elements of the bourgeoisie were filtering into the ancient public schools (1961; 1967, 17–38). The interpenetration of the two great classes had begun in earnest: the schools as a socialising force were intimately involved in the building of the class consciousness, group coherence and what must have appeared to many outsiders as the closed conspiracy of the world of public schoolboys.

While the schools, new and old, may have needed an expanding social base in order to survive, the memoirs of headmasters suggest that they were circumspect in their choice of pupils. Headmasters had to be sensitive to the interests of their traditional clientele; to have opened the floodgates to emerging social groups could have destroyed a school's prestige, weakened its important connections, and undermined the recruitment of pupils from the ranks of the gentry and aristocracy. As the work of Bamford demonstrates, an evolutionary process of change was set in motion. Moreover, it has always been impossible to understand the internal hierarchy of the fee-paying schools without an appreciation of their differential class base. Class accommodation may be integral to the history of the fee-paying schools, but no more so than an internal hierarchy following in part the lines of social class.

While it is easy to draw upon a functionalist perspective to explain the general line of development within the nineteenth-century world of the fee-paying schools, it is much more difficult to pursue the same line of analysis in terms of the contemporary public school revolution. Although the class base of the fee-paying schools is undoubtedly broader than many of their critics are prepared to admit, there is no analysis that suggests we are experiencing the unfolding of another period in which the class composition of the schools is undergoing a steady transformation. Indeed, such an analysis is conspicuous by its absence from the work of both Rae and Walford. The argument is that faced with a series of challenges – Labour Party policy, inflation and youth culture – the fee-paying sector has responded pragmatically in order to sustain its market share of pupils.

If the essence of the functionalist case is that schooling responds to the changing needs of society, then we have to discern those needs and, in the tradition of Archer, understand how the fee-paying schools responded to meet them. In this respect the only significant change appears to have been the almost universal decline in the position of the classics within the school curriculum, accompanied by a widespread expansion of the sciences – natural, applied and social. This shift in the balance of the curriculum has been accompanied by a much more pronounced emphasis upon the academic accomplishments of the schools. While these developments can be analysed in relation to changing societal pressures, many of the other changes can best be understood in terms of more narrowly defined institutional requirements (such as the admission of girls to the boys' public schools) or simply as responses to new social mores (the growing unease about corporal punishment or the possible negative effects of a boarding education upon family life and the welfare of the child). Clearly these are concerns of a different order from the nineteenth century's need to reconcile the conflict of interests between an expanding bourgeoisie and a declining aristocracy.

Durkheim's functionalism is centred upon the relationship between schooling and the necessity for society to be infused with a shared moral code if social order is to prevail. However, other functionalists have drawn the link beween the development of an industrialised economy and the emergence of national systems of schooling: as the needs of the economy change, in particular as there is a demand for differing kinds of skills, so the educational system is reshaped accordingly to supply them. This is what Collins has called 'the technical-function of education' which he sees 'as a particular application of a more general functional approach'. That is 'the functional theory of stratification' stemming from the work of Davis and Moore (Collins, 1971, 1004). The essence of Collins's argument is that the evidence fails to support the key propositions of the technical-function theory, although it is consistent with what he terms a conflict theory of stratification which he identifies as owing its intellectual origins to Max Weber.

While the work of Archer and Clifford-Vaughan has demonstrated that, in spite of a slower pace of economic development, the rate of educational change was faster in nineteenth-century France than in Britain (1971), and Green has claimed that Prussia developed a national system of education before it was overtaken by the industrial revolution (1990, 120–30), it is evident that in Britain the nineteenth-century public school was influenced enormously by economic change, if only because of the manner in which it reshaped occupational opportunities. And while Green may be correct to argue '... that the development of public education systems can only be understood in relation to the process of state formation' (1990, 77), as he himself recognises, state formation is a continuous process which is intimately related to the pattern of a nation's economic development.

Integral to the value system of the nineteenth-century public school was the idea of public service, and it is difficult to imagine that the call for colonial officers would have been quite so pronounced without the need to man an empire which served a trading nation. What has to be explored, therefore, is how the link between economic development and educational change can be established. Although the functionalist focus upon the apparently ever-increasing demand for more refined human capital as the motor for change may be misguided, this may simply mean that the relationship between schooling and economic change has to be drawn along different lines.

Therefore, consistent with the tradition of Durkheim, the sociological literature has viewed the public schools as agents of elite recruitment and socialisation which, in the nineteenth century, meant that they were vital to maintaining social order by forging the class accommodation between the bourgeoisie and the aristocracy. In turn, this was crucial to their survival as institutions of national importance. However, while Durkheim's functional perspective helps us to make sense of institutional behaviour, what still needs to be explained is the behaviour of the individuals involved – that is, those parents who for the first time were sending their children to the public schools, or alternatively, those families who were switching their allegiances from the old to the new foundations. We will need to see whether Collins's conflict theory of stratification, which like Archer's work owes much to the Weberian stress upon individual social action, can offer not only a credible explanation of this behaviour, but also whether in the process it can draw the links between economic development and educational change more convincingly than the technical-function theory.

Serving the Needs of Capital: Some Marxist Themes

Just as there are different strands within functionalist theory, so there are different variants of Marxism. But for all the internal cleavages within Marxism there is a broad measure of agreement around certain fundamental propositions: liberal democratic societies continue to be governed politically by a ruling class; the paramount function of this ruling class is to serve the interests of capital; although the state may exercise a measure of relative autonomy, it will align itself with ruling class interests on key issues and in crisis situations; and while the dominant ideology of capitalist/liberal democratic societies is best described as an evolving hegemony, constructed out of a myriad differing social concerns, it is shaped primarily by ruling-class interests which it serves to sustain over time.

Futhermore, the major camps within Marxism construct the relationship between state, society and schooling in broadly similar terms. In his much publicised essay 'Ideology and Ideological State Apparatuses' (1984), Louis Althusser has argued that social order in liberal democratic/capitalist societies is maintained by the combined efforts of 'ideological and repressive state apparatuses'. Like Durkheim, he has claimed that the educational system is the most important part of the ideological state apparatus in advanced industrialised societies. In pre-industrial France social order was dependent upon a close interaction of the family and the church; in the modern world the axis between the family and the school achieves the same purpose – once again the parallel with Durkheim is too obvious to ignore.

Although Miliband's approach to Marxism is very different from Althusser's, he has analysed the social functions of schooling in very similar terms (1969, 239-61). Moreover, the distinction between both these Marxist strains and Durkheim's functionalism follows the same line of argument. Miliband has written:

> Durkheim once stressed the need which society had of socialisation through education in terms of the transmission of 'fundamental values', what he called 'essential principles'... he was no doubt right; societies do need to transmit 'fundamental values' and 'essential principles'. The point however is that the values and principles which are generally deemed 'fundamental' and 'essential' are those which are sanctioned by the dominant forces in society (1969, 243).

For both Miliband and Althusser the values perpetuated by the ideological state apparatuses are determined essentially by the ruling class and serve the primary function of sustaining the interests of capital. Of course, with respect to the English public schools, if we give due weight to Durkheim's observation that socialising experiences will reflect specific class destinies, then it is possible to draw parallels between the Marxist and functionalist perspectives. However, while there may be a broad measure of agreement about society's need for a consensual moral code, Marxists would argue that in class-based societies this could not be constructed from the bottom upwards. For those functionalists in the tradition of Durkheim, schools have no choice but to attempt this alleged impossibility, for the value consensus has to be shared, not imposed.

Whereas the technical-functionalists (to use Collins's less than elegant label) have seen changes in the *technical* relations of production as the motor force of educational change, the Marxists have stressed the importance of the *social* relations of production. Not surprisingly, given the stress that Marxism places upon social class in its analysis of capitalist society, the school has the function of ensuring that individuals acquire the attitudes and behaviour appropriate to their class role in society. In Miliband's words: 'In the first instance, education, as far as the vast majority of working-class children are concerned, performs an important *class-conforming* role' (1969, 241; stress added). And, although he accuses him of 'ideological obfuscation', Miliband turns to the major structural-functionalist, that is Talcott Parsons, to support his proposition. In a parallel vein, Althusser has argued that pupils are destined for differing niches in the labour market and so will be exposed to appropriate kinds of schooling (1984, 29-30).

However, it is one thing to hypothesise that schooling is organised in a manner designed to create harmonious social relations of production, but quite another to show exactly *how* schooling performs that function, and then to go beyond that analysis and substantiate the relationship. The clearest Marxist perspective of the linkage is to be found in the work of the American sociologists Bowles and Gintis. In their *Schooling in Capitalist America* they write:

> The educational system helps integrate youth into the economic system, we believe, through a structural correspondence between its social relations and those of production. The structure of social relations in education not only inures the student to the discipline of the work place, but develops the types of personal demeanour, modes of self-preservation, self-image, and social-class identifications which are the crucial ingredients of job adequacy. Specifically, the social relations of education – the relationships between administrators and teachers, teachers and students, students and students, and students and their work – replicate the hierarchical division of labor (1976, 131).

On this basis, the modus operandi of fee-paying schools are explained by the occupational destinies of their pupils which, if nothing else, offers one way of making sense of those tedious studies of the social origins of supposedly elite groups (stockbrokers, doctors, army and naval officers, MPs, cabinet ministers, judges, etc.). Obviously new forms of schooling would reflect general changes in the social relations of production or, if the focus is directed at innovations within a particular school, a new relationship between that school and the labour market.

The viability of the theories of educational change embedded in functionalist and Marxist theories ultimately depends upon an understanding of the individual learning process, which is, to say the very least, problematic. If schooling is to respond effectively to the changing needs of society, then schools have to be potent agents of socialisation. It is scarcely meaningful to credit schooling with an integral role in the change process unless it can deliver the goods. The danger is that the socialised person becomes a passive agent in the learning process and we are presented with an over-socialised interpretation of how individuals acquire their social behaviour.

Wakeford, in his *The Cloistered Elite* (1969, 128–51), refers to differing modes of adaptation to life in public schools, and, although in some cases the boys were expressing deep-seated anti-school values, for the most part they were adopting pragmatic strategies for accommodating institutional pressures. The official value system may not have coincided exactly with that held by most boys, but in only a few cases were the respective value systems in outright conflict. However, it is critical to keep in mind that fee-paying schools are very diverse in their character, and may well have quite contrasting value systems, and, moreover, the many very publicised examples of individual rebellion are symbols of a more generally diverse process of personal adjustment to institutional pressures. If schools do fulfil the needs of the wider society, then they do so precariously.

An understanding, therefore, of educational change in the fee-paying sector of schooling could construct remarkably similar interpretations from both Marxist and functionalist theories. Theorists from both camps see schooling as a powerful socialising force which changes its character in response to broad societal pressures. In Marxist theory schools serve the interests of capital, and change in ways that are consistent with capital's evolving needs. As fee-paying schools cater to very particular class interests, the pattern of change within that sector can be understood only by appreciating how that class is able to preserve, or enhance, its privileged position within capitalist society. For Marxists the key to understanding the relationship between capitalism and schooling is capital's needs for a complex hierarchy in its social relations of production. Sooner or later, the changing social relations of production require new patterns of schooling, while a sophisticated bourgeoisie remains attuned to this ever-present prospect. While functionalist theory may want to draw a relationship between schooling and society's (rather than capital's) needs, it also accepts that patterns of socialisation will vary according to the individual's anticipated social milieu. So the peculiarities of a public school education, and how it changes over time, can be explained in terms very suggestive of a Marxist class analysis. Functionalists would tend to stress the wider pressures for social order over the more narrow focus upon capital's needs, but even some Marxists have seen the need to contain the socially destabilising effects of urbanisation as the most important influence upon the development of national systems of education.

Responding to Political Struggle: Some Weberian Themes

Collins has argued that the link between education and social stratification is best explained by 'a conflict theory derived from the approach of Max Weber, stating the determinants of various outcomes in the struggles amongst status groups' (1971, 1002). In effect status groups (which he defines as 'all persons who share a sense of status equality based on participation in a common culture') use the educational system to enhance their advantages in the struggle for scarce resources – wealth, power and prestige. Educational change, therefore, is either a consequence of the emergence of new opportunities to acquire those scarce resources or a change in the means by which access to scarce resources, established or new, is determined. Alternatively, it may reflect the determination of status groups to improve their competitive edge in relation to other groups. In practice all three developments could emerge simultaneously and reinforce one another. After evaluating the evidence, Collins maintained this conflict theory provided a better explanation of the relationship between education and stratification than the technical-function theory (see p.9).

Regardless of whether Collins's central conclusion is correct or not (and it should be noted that he argues for theoretical amalgamation), his work suggests a structural context within which the idea of institutional self-preservation can be placed. To put it concisely, the demand for private schooling is dependent upon parental perceptions of the schools' relationship to the structure of social stratification. As long as a sufficient number of parents perceive a positive relationship, and they are able to afford the fees, then the demand for places in fee-paying schools will be buoyant.

Musgrove (1970, 122–4) has warned against drawing too simple a relationship between the educational system and the occupational structure, in which changes in the latter determine changes in the former. However, stratification pressures are as much about the values upon which stratification is based, and individual perceptions of changing opportunities, as about the actual character of the structure per se. For example, many of the public school foundations of the early Victorian era, although replicating the classical tradition of the ancient foundations, also introduced a 'modern' side to their curricula. To what extent this appealed to parents is hard to discern, but the probability of institutional genuflection to perceived contemporary interests is too evident not to ignore. A public school education may have brought a 'valued status' rather than a livelihood (Musgrove,

14

1970, 124), but even gentlemen had to fill their days and appear to earn their keep.

In the nineteenth century the structure of social stratification in Britain changed steadily. In the first place, the decline of agriculture and the rise of industry and commerce led to a gradual evolution in the character of the occupational hierarchy. Allegedly the values of the public schools subverted the social prestige of those engaged in trade and manufacturing industry, so that consequently even the most wealthy of the *nouveaux riches* struggled to become synthetic gentlemen, adopting an aristocratic lifestyle in order to enhance their social status. None the less, as a source of income and power agriculture was in relative decline, while industry, and those bourgeois occupations it was to spawn in abundance, steadily gained the ascendancy.

The criteria determining entry into occupations also changed so that individuals had to adjust to new rules of the game in order to secure access to many careers. The best-known example is the civil service (the Northcote–Trevelyan reforms of 1853), including the Indian Civil Service, but the armed services and Oxbridge (the removal of religious tests and a drastic easing of the restrictions upon candidates for scholarships and exhibitions) followed a parallel path. Although Coleman (1973) has claimed that the class interests of the aristocracy and the bourgeoisie were accommodated in a manner which meant the dominance of the former's values, it is important not to overstate the case. It is not too far-fetched to argue that the reform of public institutions in nineteenth-century Britain reflected Weber's 'march of bureaucracy', destroying in its wake 'structures of domination which had no rational character in the special sense of the term' (Gerth and Mills, 1958, 244). The bourgeois value of merit, rather than the aristocratic value of patronage, was the basis upon which the new system increasingly functioned.

However, the rationalisation process was circumscribed by the relatively gradual pace of social change. The continuing presence of the monarchy makes it difficult to resist drawing a parallel between the princely service of the Chinese literati and the fact that British public servants were formally in the service of the Crown. Moreover, although meritocratic criteria increasingly determined entry into public service, it was a form of merit that favoured the classical scholar over the technical specialist, which seemed also to suggest the importance of acquiring a particular cultural style. Weber has reflected upon the so-called magical qualities of the Chinese literati (Gerth and Mills,

1958, 426), which finds a distinct echo in the leadership qualities supposedly instilled by the public schools in those destined to serve the nation on the battlefield or on the frontier (Wilkinson, 1964, 125–76).

In response to these changes in the structure of social stratification, and in the criteria governing what can best be described as elite recruitment, assertive status groups in nineteenth-century Britain started to generate educational change. The new middle classes used their economic resources to create alternative schools which would enable their children to maintain or improve the social position of their families. Not yet in a position to infiltrate the ancient public schools, with no state provision of secondary schooling and many of the less prestigious endowed grammar schools in a parlous state, this emergent bourgeoisie created its own public schools, thus stimulating that boom so admirably researched by Bamford.

Of course, an alternative strategy was the exercise of political power, both to reform the ancient public schools and to encourage the direct state provision of an acceptable level of secondary schooling. But that was to come later, after the middle classes had widened and entrenched their political base. Archer has presented this as two broad strategies of change (1979, 89–142). The first she has termed 'a substitutive strategy' in which economically powerful groups created their own schools and educational networks. The second was 'a restrictive strategy' in which the assertive groups used their political muscle to force government action to relax the hold that established dominant groups exercised over the educational system. Change occurred through the dynamics of group political action: a pluralist struggle which was fuelled by ideological confrontations centred upon the nature of schooling (curricula, pedagogy and evaluation) and its relationship to state and society (with particular reference to the role of the churches).

To place the motivations of all those who were instrumental in founding or expanding public schools in the early Victorian years within the above framework would be to parody reality. Nathaniel Woodard, for example, was driven by the desire to create a national network of fee-paying schools, based upon high Anglican principles, that would cater to differing segments of the middle class. He aimed to remove the need for the state provision of secondary education which he believed would result in the imposition of secular values, so destroying what he considered to be vital to schooling – its foundation upon a religious moral code (Heeney, 1969). However, the change process is not simply about the motivations of those determined to create new schools. No matter how strong their endeavours, these would be meaningless without parents who were willing to pay the fees. Founders may feel the need to put their principles into action, but parents are more likely to be persuaded if the end product enables their children to respond positively to the contemporary pressures of social stratification.

The changes which overtook the public schools in the nineteenth century can, therefore, be interpreted in Weberian terms. The dynamic of change was the emergence of a new structure of social stratification, in which the 'rationalising influence of bureaucratisation' (Clifford-Vaughan and Archer, 1971, 230) was probably as important as the impact of industrialisation. The stratification pressures generated a struggle in which newly emergent social groups employed their resources, both economic and political, to assert their interests against the established dominant parties. The consequence was the creation of new foundations, the gradual reform of the ancient schools (strongly influenced by official action), and a changing class base in the schools' clientele. In effect the public schools became part of a process known as social closure in which 'access to rewards and opportunities' is restricted to 'a limited circle of eligibles' (Parkin, 1974, 3).

Therefore, unlike both the functionalists and the Marxists, those in the Weberian tradition do not believe that the process of educational change is driven by societal needs. Rather, the educational system changes because groups have the power – economic, political or both – to bring about developments which they believe are consistent with their own interests. But these interests are defined by the pressures of social stratification, and how groups respond to those pressures will determine their access to status, income and power. Because of the perceived links between schooling and stratification, it is to be expected that a desire for educational change will be central to any response pattern. Thus perceptions of individual interests interact with social changes to bring about new educational forms.

EDUCATIONAL CHANGE AND THE INSTITUTIONAL NETWORK OF PRIVATE SCHOOLING

One of the startling facts about the history of fee-paying schools is the massive fluctuation in the number of their pupils over even comparatively short periods of time. Bamford has collated data for selected schools during the first half of the nineteenth century (1961), and has argued that these variations depended directly upon changes associated with the individual schools: the appointment of a new head, a change of site, or the addition of a 'modern' side to the curriculum. Bamford, therefore, stresses the dependence of their changing fortunes upon random, school-centred inputs, in direct contrast to the macro-sociological emphasis upon long-term socio-economic and political trends. Bamford's interpretation reminds us that the school itself must be integral to any understanding of the change process. Although this remains true, the theory presented here will argue that the individual schools are part of a complex institutional network which increasingly shapes the overall course of their development.

In legal terms most of the fee-paying schools are independent corporate bodies, and have a freedom of action historically unknown to schools in the maintained sector. The key actors in the running of a fee-paying school are likely to be the actively involved governors, heads and housemasters. Indeed, the histories of many schools, as well of the public school system, have placed great stress upon the contributions of dominant individuals. Perhaps the best-known, if over-stated, example is Thomas Arnold, to whom is attributed the accolade not only of rejuvenating the fortunes of Rugby School but also of making a massive contribution to placing the public school system on a more viable basis. Out of the chaotic world of the eighteenth century, several great Victorian headmasters established an orderly public school model, which by the turn of the century had become an integral part of the nation's social life.

The model of the public school that evolved in the nineteenth century appears to have been a very efficient institution. Houses divided large schools into more manageable segments; they formed tangible communities to which pupils could express their loyalty. Besides developing loyalty to the house, inter-house competitions created acceptable channels for the expression of adolescent energies. Thanks to the prefectorial system, schools were able to sustain a semblance of order with comparatively few masters. The complex internal hierarchies and rituals not only controlled the pupils but also gave their lives a meaning which offered them either tangible rewards or the prospect of tangible rewards. This was an institutional context that purposely encouraged group conformity over individual creativity, and seems to have succeeded – in its own terms – admirably. Undoubtedly the character of the schools was evolved internally: an amalgam of past traditions, the peculiarities of powerful heads and masters, and the sheer magnitude of the demands imposed by trying to educate a large number of boys in boarding schools. There were excesses and abuses, and these did not entirely disappear in the wake of Arnold's reforms, but they were not sufficiently damning to persuade those in the nation with most wealth, the highest status and the greatest power that the public schools were unfit places for the education of their children. Quite the contrary, for many parents a public school education was the only sure way of 'making a man of him', or even better, 'a gentleman'.

Underlying the development of the public schools as a viable organisation was the evolution of the values integral to a public school education. In his penetrating *Godliness and Good Learning*, Newsome has argued that the schools in the early Victorian period,

> despite doctrinal differences and rival philosophic systems, can still be regarded as a single class, stamped with an unmistakable mintmark: a combination of intellectual toughness, moral earnestness and deep spiritual conviction (1961, 25).

This Newsome refers to as the ideal of 'Godliness and Good Learning' which by 1870 had given way 'to a new code in which manliness, animal spirits and prowess at games figured as the attributes most to be admired in a boy' (1961, 37). The 1870s saw the spread of Muscular Christianity which ushered in the new ideal of 'Godliness and Manliness'. The new values (Newsome lists: patriotism, moral and physical beauty, athleticism, spartan habits, masculinity and suspicion of excessive intellectualism) were part of a perfect career training package for public schoolboys (notably, for army officers and colonial officials). Moreover, they were also values that would sustain institutional order. Without an effective institutional structure, infused with a meaningful ideology, the schools could not have exercised a measured control over the lives of large numbers of boys. Perhaps the appeal of the ideology of 'Godliness and Manliness' was that it enabled the schools to function more smoothly than 'Godliness and Good Learning'; the apparent link between the schools' values and traditions and their boys' future career paths was an additional bonus.

One of the striking images of public schools is of ancient buildings surrounded by large playing fields. The surrounding land helps to perpetuate the idea that the schools are isolated, self-contained communities living apart from the outside world. However, besides creating the image, the schools had to sell it to parents. Without the resources that parents could provide, over and above fees, few schools were wealthy enough to pursue expensive capital projects, and Mangan has documented how the cult of athleticism was sold to the late Victorian parent (1981). The physical appearance of the schools, along with their organisational characteristics, were part of the marketable package.

Given this context, Bamford is correct to suggest that institutional regeneration was a product of dynamics internal to the individual school. However, it is crucial to remember that while this internal process of regeneration was taking place, the schools – at all levels – were coming under the pressure of public scrutiny. Some schools seemed to be incapable of reforming themselves, and parts of the system were falling into decay. The consequence was the appointment of several Royal Commissions which, for all the political prevarication, had significant consequences for both individual schools and the educational system in general. This pressure, in Archer's terms, restricted the hold that traditional groups exercised over certain institutions (most notably the Universities of Oxford and Cambridge along with their colleges). But its main focus was to ensure more efficient management and greater financial probity (which largely succeeded), and a more relevant curriculum (about which judgements are equivocal). Reform made the schools more attractive to a wider potential clientele. The expanding bourgeoisie could feel confident at buying into the system, and defend those privileges against which previously they would have railed.

Although there was official pressure upon the schools to change, it could hardly be described as taking a permanent institutional form. The state intervened and retreated, it did not exert constant pressure. However, in the nineteenth century the public schools were starting to gel into an educational system with internal hierarchies and concomitant institutional ties. The nine schools which fell within the Clarendon Commission's terms of reference (the commission was set up in 1861 and reported in 1864) formed an obvious stratum within the public school world, and it was difficult to exclude from this first tier those schools – Cheltenham, Marlborough and Wellington – to which the commissioners had frequently referred (Bamford, 1967, 35). In 1889 the *Public Schools' Year Book* was published for the first time. Allegedly because there was a desire to keep its price down, only thirty schools were included in this edition, and: 'Within this limit, the principle of selection has been to admit such schools as the Editors – representatives respectively of Eton, Harrow and Winchester – *regard as belonging to the same genus as their own*, (as quoted in Bamford, 1967, 188; stress added).

Much of this interest in the emergence of school hierarchies, with the appearance of different divisions, has concentrated upon the location of individual schools within the hierarchy, and the criteria which determine those placements. An equally important but certainly more difficult concern is to ascertain the impact of a particular placement upon the way in which a school would conduct its affairs. Although the divisions may not be formal, they could none the less exercise a guiding influence over their members. In his *Tom Brown's Universe*, Honey is much concerned with the development of the public schools as a system, and the rise of what he calls the public school community in the nineteenth century. Honey claims that membership was dependent upon a mutual recognition which was formalised by competition on the playing fields (1977, 273). Common sense would suggest that to acquire and to sustain membership it would be necessary for any one school to act in ways to which other schools of a similar, or of the desired, status already conformed. The bounds of tolerance, as well changes in the membership codes, then become interesting topics for research.

Alongside what can best be described as the development of these informal institutional ties, the nineteenth century also brought the beginnings of a formalised institutional network. The establishing of the Royal Commissions had aroused the fears of many heads, who – like Woodard – would have seen no positive educational role for the state. The Public Schools Commission prodded the heads into action, and the outcome was the founding in 1869 of the Headmasters' Conference (HMC), with Thring of Uppingham and Michinson of King's School, Canterbury, as the early instigators. Within a few years the heads of the major schools were both members of, and the leading lights in, the Conference. The foundation of HMC was followed, admittedly over a protracted period of time, by a plethora of organisations representing either a segment of the market (for example, preparatory schools) or those performing specialised functions (for example, bursars).

More recently, the most active decade in the growth of institutional networks in the fee-paying sector has been the 1970s. Faced with the pressures of inflation and the threats of the Labour Party, the individual bodies steadily created supra-organisations of which ISIS (Independent Schools Information Service) and ISJC (Independent Schools Joint Council) are the most important. Without detailed research it is impossible to ascertain the extent to which the umbrella organisations exert an influence over the individual schools. Certainly the schools continue to reiterate their status as independent corporate bodies, but the emergence of these new overarching bodies symbolises the welding of the disparate parts into a more co-ordinated whole.

On wider policy issues HMC could be very active, as seen in the setting up of the Fleming Committee (Committee on Public Schools, 1943 and 1944) and the extension of the terms of reference of the Public Schools Commission (1968) to incorporate the direct grant schools (see p.118). Also the emergence of the Assisted Places Scheme owed much to the efforts of the Direct Grant Joint Committee (DGJC). The umbrella organisations have on occasion tried to defuse conflict within the system by issuing guidelines, with the explosive question of the admission of girls to boys' schools being a good example. However, institutional influence is invariably more subtle (and more effective), depending so much on personal interaction and the study of good practices. For all that indirectness, it may on occasion be pointed out that schools do not have a permanent position in the hierarchy, and require the support of others to maintain or improve their standing.

Running parallel to the development of institutional networks within the world of fee-paying schools has been a critical change in the way they relate to the wider society. That relationship has been rationalised: conducted on a different basis and on different terms. Historically the leading public schools developed intimate connections with a variety of elite institutions, which could range from the highly formalised (for example, Eton College and King's College, Cambridge, like Winchester College and New College, Oxford, could be seen as different parts of the same foundation) to the highly informal. What bound the parties together within this model was the interchange of key individuals; they were part of the same extended social network. To some extent this was a system kept going by the exchange of patronage, but, more significantly, it created a set of socio-cultural experiences that would bind its members together while excluding those who did not belong to the magic circle. The glue that held the system together was a set of well-developed expressive values.

The steady bureaucratisation of public and private life over the past century accounts for a decline in the promotion of expressive values, accompanied by an increasing emphasis upon instrumental values. For schools the conclusion is stark: they need to ensure that their pupils possess the necessary qualities to compete successfully for entry into prestigious institutions, whether these be in higher education, the public services or private industry. Rather than, as in the nineteenth century, selling to parents a model of the public school, the schools have been forced to adjust to the demands of their institutional network

22

in the realisation that this is the only sure way to guarantee a reliable supply of pupils. Clearly such changes do not affect all schools equally, but they are all part of an institutional matrix increasingly bound together by rational procedures and instrumental values.

The new situation has been brought about by a shift in the relative importance of the different forms of capital – economic, social and cultural – in relation to social stratification. While a public school education may have been important to a member of the gentry because of the social links it helped him to establish and reaffirm, as well as its embellishment of a cultural style, it had no bearing upon his future occupation, for that was already assured. Moreover, although he overstates the case, Musgrove could write: 'The new Public Schools make sense only because a family was already wealthy and because unpaid or ill-paid careers in Parliament, the Army, Church, or at the Bar, brought not a livelihood but a valued status' (1970, 123–4). Accompanied by the growth of the ideology of meritocracy, the links between the fee-paying schools and elite institutions have been increasingly dependent upon the ability of their pupils to demonstrate their personal competence. Moreover, cultural capital is invariably defined in terms of the narrow ability to compete in the examination arena. Just as some schools have such well-established reputations that they can thwart the pressures of the institutional networks to which they belong (although they do so at their peril), so some individuals have sufficient resources of economic and social capital to resist the demand that they demonstrate their personal competence through the acquisition of certified cultural capital, of which examination success is the most important. But again, as with the schools, we are talking about a few exceptional cases, certainly not enough to sustain a school, let alone a system of fee-paying schools.

Of course, the development of a social network and the demonstration of cultural awareness beyond mere examination success continue to retain considerable importance. And certainly there can still be found segments of the social stratification hierarchy which it is almost impossible to penetrate without the prior possession of economic resources. Furthermore, individual schools can resist the dominant external pressures by creating special niches within the fee-paying sector. Inevitably, however, they need to be attuned to the demands of their more restricted institutional network. But the general trend requires that individuals possess a cultural capital increasingly defined by examination success. The schools have little option but to demonstrate their ability to ensure that success, or rather, to create the perception that this is what parents can expect in return for paying fees. Whether the schools actually make much of a difference in enhancing individual performance is, of course, an entirely different matter.

CONCLUSION

This chapter started with the idea of a 'public school revolution': that the changes in fee-paying schools, especially the elite boarding schools, have been so substantial in recent years that they could only be described as revolutionary. The chapter has purposely avoided any serious evaluation of this claim in favour of trying to construct a theory that makes sense of why fee-paying schools should pursue educational change. Whereas the existing macro-sociological theories of educational change focus upon the impact of the broad patterns of economic, social and political development, this chapter has sought to reverse that approach. It has proposed the simple premise that change in the private sector of schooling is determined by an instinct for institutional survival: that the schools are in the marketplace and their long-term well-being is dependent upon their ability to respond successfully to marketplace pressures.

Of course, there is plenty of evidence to show that schools have also ossified and decayed over time, and that in Britain many privately endowed schools went through this depressing cycle. There is the technical point that their endowments may have sheltered them – at least in the short run – from the vicissitudes of the market, but more importantly, it has to be recognised that because a general theoretical principle has been established it does not necessarily follow that all institutions will act accordingly. Indeed, some of the most famous educational institutions were changed in the nineteenth century only because powerful individuals (like Gladstone) saw them as public, not private property, and were determined to regenerate them through government action.

While both the functionalist and Marxist literature on fee-paying schools stress their importance in the process of elite recruitment and socialisation, the theoretical perspective initiated in this chapter would interpret these functions in terms of the needs of the schools, rather than of the wider society. But there remains an obligation to demonstrate a relationship between the schools and their social context. This chapter has tried to establish that link by turning to Randall Collins and his conflict theory of social stratification. While institutional survival is dependent upon attracting a steady flow of fee-paying parents (or scholarship pupils if other parties – such as private benefactors and the state – are prepared to meet such expenditure), we need to know why parents become the customers of fee-paying schools. The argument is that parents see the purchase of education as a sound investment in securing their children's access to the scarce resources of status, income and power. Schools have to create the impression that they can provide an educational experience that is aware of the changing structure of opportunities, and is in tune with the values which ensure access to the most desired of those opportunities.

As schools change – or fail to change – there is an accompanying process of ideological struggle in which political and economic resources are used to determine outcomes. These struggles occur as an intervening force between the evolving patterns of social stratification and the implementation of educational change within the schools and classrooms. It is political struggle, or political inertia, with the accompanying commitment or non-commitment of resources, that determines whether social stratification pressures are actually translated into new forms of schooling. It is the further contention of this chapter that the institutional contexts, within which the ideological and political struggles occur, have evolved in critically important ways over time. In the nineteenth century the individual school was the central focus of action with the change process very much under the control of key individuals, more often than not the powerful headmasters. Furthermore, the attempt to create new schools, even new systems of schooling, owed much to the initiative of determined individuals, such as Woodard, who tirelessly sought the support of rich and powerful benefactors. Even state intervention directed at a particular form of schooling could make its recommendations in terms of individual schools; thus the Clarendon Commission carried out nine separate investigations and made nine different sets of recommendations. It was setpiece intervention, designed to right the wrongs of the world at a stroke.

State intervention helped to stimulate the institutionalisation of the private sector of schooling which evolved spasmodically for the best part of a century after the 1864 Report of the Clarendon Commission. In the 1970s this culminated in the creation of umbrella organisations which were designed both to present united fronts to the external world on the key policy issues and to iron out internal conflicts. In this new context it is probably true to say that bursars and governors are as important as heads. Major policy initiatives coming from within the private sector are channelled along its institutional network, and, in similar fashion, the sector's response to external pressures for change will be constructed within the same institutional framework. Although the individual school remains the site for change, so much of what eventually happens in schools has already been negotiated on a broader front, with the state frequently acting as a key partner in the process.

The schools' influence upon social stratification is increasingly dependent upon their ties with a range of elite institutions. While it is difficult to conclude unequivocally that the public schools are less important than the universities in shaping the values of the social stratification hierarchy, it is true that the relative balance of influence has shifted towards the latter. Of course the general trend may disguise the fact that important pockets of resistance to change can still be found. Moreover, within the universities there may still persist public school networks that continue to have significant social stratification implications. Furthermore, the basis upon which this broader institutional network is held together has changed its character dramatically over time. At one time it would not be too much of an exaggeration to say that it was infused with the expressive values of the world of the public schools. Elite institutions constituted a social network held together by the fact that its members lived within the confines of a shared socio-cultural experience.

Ironically, in the short run, the bureaucratisation of public and private life reinforced this process. The expressive values of the public schools were integral to the character of public institutions, including the civil service. This was a direct consequence of the fact that there was not a full-blown bourgeois revolution in Britain, and thus the values of public service were never fully those of the middle-class functionary. Over time this has changed. The possession of cultural capital, of which examination success is a critical component, has assumed a greater importance in determining access to elite institutions. For example, with respect to higher education, the relationship between the schools and the universities has been rationalised substantially since 1945. Both the procedures and criteria that determine movement from the schools to the universities have become more visible and standardised: a process accelerated by the intervention of the state which led to the creation of more centralised admissions procedures. The values that form the basis of social stratification are increasingly of an instrumental character. The schools either adapt to them or risk forfeiting the parental support that continues to ensure their institutional survival.

2

Whatever Happened to the Poor and Needy Scholars?

Among the many charges directed at the public schools is that although they were intended by their founders to provide an education for poor and needy scholars, they have become schools catering for the children of well-to-do parents who can afford to purchase what has become an expensive commodity. The main focus of this chapter is to examine and evaluate this simple claim. With very important reservations it is a critique that will be broadly accepted. Moreover, it can be demonstrated that this change was, to a considerable extent, officially sponsored. The purpose of the nineteenth-century commissions, which will be examined in this chapter, was to ensure the very survival of the endowed schools that were for so long the sole providers of what would have been considered as a secondary, or higher, education. The state-sponsored reform of the older foundations was accompanied by the creation of new schools. In his *The Rise of the Public Schools*, Bamford writes: 'Between the accession of Queen Victoria and 1869 no less than thirty-one Classical boarding schools were founded and this figure does not include independent day schools or old endowed schools which had acquired new energy and life' (1967, 34). Thus change was generated by the interaction of the state and the market to create a more diversified and viable system of secondary schooling.

Change was necessary to ensure both the survival of many endowed schools and to resist, albeit in the short run, the entry of the state as a direct provider of secondary schooling. However, it is the contention of this chapter that these goals were achieved only by establishing a closer relationship between class reproduction and formal schooling; that is, the reform of the endowed schools placed secondary education on a more explicit class basis. Thus class reproduction and institutional survival became the bedfellows they have remained ever since. But in the process of drawing more closely the links between social class and schooling, so the influence of other social variables, notably religion and local ties, was slowly eroded.

The chapter concentrates upon the reform of those schools which were investigated by two of the great nineteenth-century Royal Commissions: the Clarendon Commission (Commission Appointed to Inquire into the Revenues and Management of Certain Colleges and Schools, and the Studies Pursued and the Instruction Given Therein, 1864), which examined the affairs of what at the time were considered to be the nine leading public schools, and the Taunton Commission (Commission on Schools not Comprised within Her Majesty's Two Recent Commissions on Popular Education and Public Schools, 1868), whose remit incorporated the remaining endowed schools (there were an estimated 3,000 such schools, of which some 2,200 were considered to be providing only an elementary education). The earlier Newcastle Commission (Commission on the State of Popular Education in England, 1861) and the later Bryce Commission (Commission on Secondary Education, 1896) are included to round out the analysis. While the focus of the Newcastle Commission was different – its brief was to examine the state of popular education in England and Wales – it demonstrates a continuity of thinking about questions of access to schooling with the Clarendon and Taunton Commissions. The Bryce Commission, however, clearly indicated that secondary schooling in England and Wales was moving into a different era, one that would be dominated by the direct involvement of the state, and underwritten by the public purse. While there are explicit pointers within the Bryce Commission's report to this shift in thinking about the state's role, equally, on questions of access to secondary schooling, much of the ethos of the earlier commissions was reaffirmed.

It is important to stress at the outset that these commissions had much to say – especially on the content of the curriculum and the governing of the schools – which is overlooked in this chapter. Moreover, for all their influence the commissions issued no more than reports that contained recommendations. Inevitably these were subjected to the ravages of party politics, close parliamentary scrutiny, often intense local dissension and the partisanship of religious differences. Some of this conflict appears in this chapter, but the reader will have to look elsewhere for a detailed analysis. The chapter's purpose is to present the commissioners' prescriptions for the reform of access to the endowed secondary schools, and more importantly, the principles which directed their thinking. On this front, although subsequent political struggles diluted somewhat the thrust of their reform, they were remarkably successful. The result was the regeneration of the endowed schools, but not without affecting adversely many different interests in the short run, and perhaps even those of the nation at large in the long run.

FOUNDERS' INTENTIONS AND THE STATUTORY CONTROL OF ACCESS

The Scholars

Human nature being what it is, it is not unreasonable to surmise that those who provided the endowments to establish schools, both great and small, were motivated by the desire to further their reputations in this world and the world to come. Thus statutes urge scholars to pray for the souls of founders, and impressive buildings have long been seen as fitting memorials to founders' might and benevolence. However, this is not to deny that founders had other considerations besides personal vainglory. First and foremost was the desire to establish an institution to serve society at large, which for much of our history has meant, to all intents and purposes, to serve the established church.

Of Winchester College, Kirby writes:

> Wykeham seems to have begun his great work of providing free education for the sons of people who could not afford to pay for it, as a means of supplying the exhausted ranks of an educated clergy, very soon after he became Bishop of Winchester (1892, 1).

Henry VI's statutes for Eton College contained clauses that would exclude villeins and bastards, not – according to Hollis – out of any prudish morality but because 'the scholars were primarily to be trained for holy orders and therefore it was reasonable to exclude boys against whose ordination there would be a canonical impediment' (1960, 7).

Many of the older foundations fulfilled the wider charitable functions of the church. Not only did they provide an education for poor and needy scholars, but also some statutes required them to offer shelter and sustenance to the old and the infirm. Moreover, some endowments were split between aiding the sick by creating hospitals, and furthering education by establishing colleges. The link between the two functions is symbolised in the name of what remains one of the most generously endowed schools: Christ's Hospital. Over time the colleges came to serve more narrowly defined pedagogical functions while endowment income was disentangled and, on occasion, restructured to the benefit of schooling. The nineteenth-century commissions are very much at the heart of this rationalising process.

From the perspective of this book it is the founders' pedagogical ambitions that are of particular interest. These tended to fall into three interrelated categories. The first was to make free schooling available to either a limited number of scholars or to particular categories of children, usually local inhabitants. The second was to promote what is probably best described as a classical curriculum, usually centred on Latin, Greek and, on occasion, even Hebrew. There is some doubt whether the statutory strictures on curriculum content reflected a wish to promote classical learning or whether these were merely pro forma inclusions; that is, those who intended to serve in the church needed a classical education. When the pace of reform gathered momentum this was to become a critical issue. The third was to provide a close link between university education and secondary schooling. Maxwell Lyte writes:

> To Wykeham is due the idea of a college at the University continually supplied with scholars from a great grammar school, an idea which was adopted not only by Henry the Sixth, but by Cardinal Wolsey, by Sir Thomas White and by Queen Elizabeth (1911, 2).

The link has been strongest between Winchester and New College, Oxford, and Eton and King's College, Cambridge, but there have been several paler imitations.

Although there were broad societal goals, as well as narrower pedadogical purposes, built into the founders' statutes, there was also the intention to assist individuals with their schooling. Founders' statutes, therefore, have much to tell us about access to schooling. Who are the individuals whom the founders deemed worthy of entering their schools? And, of equal importance, who would determine their worthiness? Given that these matters have been recorded in written statutes, the evidence is indisputable but, not unexpectedly, it is far more difficult both to interpret what the founders themselves actually meant by their statutes, and to assess their wider social significance. There are four areas of special concern to this chapter: that the schools should provide a free education for poor and needy scholars, that preference should be given either to those who reside locally or in one of the counties named in the statutes (often one in which the school held endowed property), that the founder's kin should be given preferential consideration, and that those admitted to the school should have reached a certain level of scholarly competence.

In his commentary on Wykeham's Winchester statutes, Kirby notes that there were to be seventy scholars who were expected to be 'pauperes et indigentes' (1892, 70). In view of the fact that in founding Eton, Henry VI followed closely the Winchester model, it is not surprising that his twenty-five scholars were to be 'poor and needy boys of good character' and that no one having an income of more than 5 marks was eligible (Maxwell Lyte, 1911, 581–2). The debates as to how restrictive these requirements were in practice have been extensive. The educational historian, A. F. Leach, has been the strongest advocate against a literal interpretation of the statutes, believing that these have invariably been prejudiced by the historians' contemporary values. The statutes, as legal documents, may well have been conforming to an established code, and it is not easy to ascertain with great precision who was excluded by the 5 marks prescription (Cook, 1917, 104). Leach has asserted that, with the exception of Christ's Hospital and 'the very few Blue Coat charity schools', the poor were *not* the object of charity. Moreover, Eton's original statutes expressly excluded the sons of villeins. The scholars and commoners (see p.36), according to Leach, came from the same class, and indeed many who entered Winchester as commoners subsequently became scholars (1899, 92–102).

More interesting than the opposition to Leach's view (see, for example, Cook, 1917, 536–41), is the fact that the respective claims of different classes periodically gave rise to sharp conflicts. Probably the most famous – and certainly the most quoted – concerns the election of scholars to the grammar school at Canterbury in 1540. To quote the Report of the Taunton Commission:

> 'There were of the Commissioners more than one or two who would have none admitted but sons or younger brethren of gentlemen', urging that 'husbandmen's children were more meet for the plough, and to be artificers, than to occupy the place of the learned sort ...'. To which Cranmer replied '... but yet utterly to exclude the ploughman's son, and the poor man's son from the benefit of learning ... is as much as to say that Almighty God should not be at liberty to bestow his great gifts of grace upon any person ... . Wherefore, if the gentleman's son be apt to learning, let him be admitted; if not apt, let the poor man's child, that is apt, enter his room' (Taunton Commission, 1868, 122; the Report is quoting from Strype's *Memorials of Cranmer*).

What this particular struggle illustrates is the marginalisation of founders' statutes. The conflict centred upon differing interpretations of what form of schooling, or indeed whether any schooling whatsoever, was considered to be appropriate for the interested parties, rather than what were the founder's intentions. It is none the less true that it did prove generally difficult to keep to the founders' prescriptions on admissions, even assuming that these could be clearly discerned. Wilkins has claimed that by the seventeenth century 'Winchester had become a fee college' and even 'the poor and needy scholars' were subject to certain charges, which implies their social origins were scarely humble (1925, 48).

The foundations of first Winchester (1382) and then Eton (1440) were of such magnitude as to rule out the idea that their founders intended them to serve the interests of their particular locations. From the outset these were *national* institutions, founded to serve society at large rather than local needs. None the less, the original statutes of both colleges gave preference to would-be scholars resident in named dioceses or counties. Not surprisingly, given the very general nature of these directions, they appear to have exercised little hold upon the old nomination process and not to have aroused much controversy when the nineteenth-century commissions proposed the removal of such restrictions (entry to Winchester and Eton was reformed before the Clarendon Commission following inquiries into the Universities of Oxford and Cambridge).

Matters were very different when the statutes restricted entry to a specified locale, usually one town. Of the Clarendon Nine the three schools that fall into this category are Harrow, Rugby and Shrewsbury. Of Harrow's statutes the Report of the Clarendon Commission wrote: 'The Founder's main object, as stated in the Charter, was the education of children and youth of the parish of Harrow' (1864, 210). It appears that Harrow remained a parochial school until the middle of the seventeenth century when the increase in the number of non-foundationers began. By the time the Public Schools Commission was appointed, Harrow had outgrown its local roots and the commission reported that: 'None of the farmers or tradesmen of Harrow now send their sons to the School' (Clarendon Commission, 1864, 211).

Rugby was founded:

> ... solely for the purpose of teaching grammar freely 'to the children of Rugby and Brownsover and next of the places adjoining'. ... By the Act of 1777 these words ('next of the places adjoining') first received a definition in the clause which gave the privilege of the foundation to 'all boys of any town, village or hamlet lying within five measured miles of Rugby, or such other

distance as the major part of the Trustees present at any public meeting should ascertain, regard being had to the annual revenues of the trust estate for the time being' (Clarendon Commission, 1864, 234).

Rugby, as the commissioners noted, had experienced an influx of families intent on establishing local residence, if only temporarily, to avail themselves 'of the education given on very easy terms' (1864, 234). As a consequence the school's trustees imposed a two years' local residence requirement before parents were entitled to the privileges of the foundation, and in 1851 the Court of Chancery gave them the power to extend this to four years if they felt demand for places was outpacing their income.

According to the Clarendon Commissioners, in its original charter Shrewsbury School 'is described as a Free School (Libera Schola) by which term is commonly understood a school in which education was to be given gratuitously...' (1864, 303). The Commission had to contend with the struggle between the governors (most of whom were appointed by the Corporation of Shrewsbury) and the headmaster, Dr Kennedy, as to the school's future direction (Shrosbree, 1988, 135–76). This struggle, which had recurred periodically throughout the school's history, centred upon the relationship between the school and the town: the governors wanted the school to retain its local character integral to which was the awarding of twenty-two scholarships that provided a free education to the 'sons of Shrewsbury burgesses', while Kennedy wanted to break the local ties and see the school evolve as 'a national, fee-paying school' (Shrosbree, 1988, 165).

At the time of the Clarendon Commission, therefore, Harrow, Rugby and Shrewsbury were at different stages in jettisoning their respective founders' apparent intentions to establish schools with strong local ties, and, in particular, to restrict scholarships to local boys. At Harrow the links had been terminated, at Rugby they had been substantially eroded, although the school was attempting to regulate the influx of outsiders; and at Shrewsbury the issue had split the school with the head and governors lining up on opposites sides. In due course the commission would report and help to set the subsequent course that all three schools would take.

Given that many of the schools were founded in an age when family connections were critical in defining social status and personal advancement, it is not surprising that founders took the trouble to ensure that their statutes gave special regard to the claims of their kin.

This affected Winchester College in particular. Wykeham's Statutes gave first claim to his kin in the selection of scholars, and apparently at certain points in the history of the college they saw this right as part of the family's bounty. In spite of earlier attempts to limit their numbers (in 1586 the school was said to be 'writhing under the claims of so many Founder's kin'). Warden Bigg observed in 1732 that 'we swarm with them' (Kirby, 1892, 97)! Inevitably, on occasion the consequences were a considerable embarrassment to the school (Firth 1936, 7).

Leach has suggested that the problem of founder's kin was so pressing at Winchester because the College's Statutes did not require the scholars to be admitted strictly by competitive examination. They had to be 'fit' but not necessarily 'the most fit' claimants (1899, 90), and 'quick to study, well-behaved, and grounded in Latin grammar, reading and plain song' (Kirby, 1892, 71). However, the evidence gathered by the Clarendon Commission demonstrated most clearly that, regardless of founders' intentions, by the mid-nineteenth century scholarship entry at the Clarendon Nine schools had very little to do with individual merit. Inasmuch as the scholarship systems at Eton and Winchester had already been overhauled, they were exempted from such strictures. None the less, as the Clarendon Commission observed, before the very recent reforms at Eton, although the forms of an election were observed, 'the examination consisted in construing a passage which the boys had got up beforehand. The effect was what might be expected. "Very stupid boys got in who had no business to get in"' (1864, 67). And until the recent reforms at Eton and Winchester, Westminister had been the only public school 'to which admission was obtained by competition', and that a most idiosyncratic form of competition (Clarendon Commission, 1864, 159–60).

Of the lower-status endowed schools the Taunton Commission claimed that, 'In order to keep the schools to their proper function the founders prescribed the enforcement of a sufficient entrance examination', and 'the neglect of such an examination, combined frequently with the absence of capitation fees, reduces the grammar school to the level of a bad elementary school, or even of an infant school' (1868, 154–5). Be that as it may, there is a considerable difference between 'a sufficient entrance examination' and a competitive entrance examination. What is clear, and this will be developed more fully in due course, is that the Taunton Commissioners were examining the statutes, and how they were interpreted, from the perspective of men living in a society which had come to embrace very different values from those of the schools' founders. Moreover, their interests were also often in conflict with those who had the responsibility for putting those statutes into effect.

It is very evident that until the pressure for reform began to make itself felt in the nineteenth century, scholars at nearly all schools were selected on the basis of patronage: that is, they were nominated by those to whom the Statutes entrusted the responsibility for their selection. At Charterhouse the Clarendon Commission noted: 'The Foundation scholars, are ... nominated, as has been said, by the Governors, who exercise this right in rotation' (1864, 177). And to give another example, at St. Paul's, which appears to have greatly offended the sensibilities of the commissioners:

> The nomination of a scholar, whatever it may have originally been, has now become an affair of simple patronage. 'The scholars are nominated by each Member of the Court of Assistants in rotation, and they are admitted to the School by the High Master under the direction of the Surveyor Accountant' (1864, 190-1).

While this may be perceived as nepotism, it has to be remembered that the schools were located in a social order that was sustained by patronage. Social ties, with the in-built understanding of mutual obligations, were fuelled by patronage. The statutory commitments to founders' kin, the stress upon local connections, the absence of stringently competitive entrance examinations, and the presence of 'poor and needy' clauses even if they were not applied in a narrowly restrictive manner, are all testaments to the fact that the schools had evolved in a world that was disappearing rapidly as the nineteenth century unfolded.

The Fee-payers

In the original statutes of both Eton and Winchester Colleges, their founders made provision for the admission of boys other than the scholars who were to be supported out of endowment income. Rubric XVI of Winchester's Statutes allowed for the entry of ten sons 'of people of station and influence' (Kirby, 1892, 82) provided that they were not a burden on the Foundation. Henry VI's Statutes made parallel provision: 'The sons of noblemen and special friends of the College, up to the number of twenty, shall be allowed to sleep and board in the College, so long as no expense be incurred for them beyond that of their instruction in grammar' (Maxwell Lyte, 1911, 582). In parallel vein, the Taunton Commission, not surprisingly in view of its recommendations, was keen to demonstrate that many founders of the lesser endowed schools did not want to confine them only to local children in receipt of a gratuitous education (1868, 167–78).

The evidence is that at the leading public schools non-foundationers soon outnumbered those scholars on the foundation. The Clarendon Commission gave the following returns for 1861:

	Foundationers	*Non-Foundationers*
Eton	61	722
Winchester	69	128
Westminster	40	96
Harrow	33	421
Rugby	68	397
Shrewsbury	26	106
Charterhouse	45	71

Source: Clarendon Commission, 1864, 8

Whereas both Wykeham and Henry VI had been prepared to permit a few sons of noblemen to reside in their colleges, by 1861 the non-foundationers were fee-paying students, part of their schools but not part of the original foundations. Invariably their growth had been stimulated by the desire to increase the emoluments of the heads, and sometimes the assistant masters, who in effect had the opportunity to become housemasters. While this may have been a necessary development to increase salaries severely limited by outdated statutory boundaries, it is hard to see it as in keeping with the spirit of the founders' wishes. In the world of schooling, if the pressures for change are sufficiently potent, then nothing is sacred, not even the ancient statutes of powerful founders.

THE PRESSURES FOR REFORM

The immediate pressure for the reform of the endowed schools was not the evasions of founders' statutes, but rather their irrelevance to the needs of the contemporary society along with the evidence of gross corruption. In the damning words of Carlisle:

It is painful, however, to relate that many of our numerous and ample Endowments have fallen into decay, by the negligence or cupidity of ignorant or unprincipled Trustees ... . As the property of those benevolent Institutions is, therefore, in several cases lost or sunk; or embezzled, or disgracefully misapplied; or lessened or impaired by gross dereliction of duty, and very great frauds are committed in letting or managing the estates; – it appears absolutely necessary, that such disorder and misapplication should speedily be abolished, by a PUBLIC INVESTIGATION and REFORM of those evils, which is only within the power of Parliament (Carlisle, 1818, XXXV; stress in original text).

The process of investigation had already been set in motion by Lord Brougham's Select Committee on the Education of the Lower Orders in the Metropolis (1816) which was followed by the appointment of Charity Commissioners (Simon, 1960, 94–5). The subsequent commissions of the 1860s (Newcastle, Clarendon, Taunton) mark the high watermark of the state's investigation into educational endowments.

It could be argued that as the schools had been endowed by individual citizens or private corporations the state's right to intervene was fragile. Indeed, as Leach has remarked, both St. Paul's School and the Merchant Taylors' School were able to secure their exclusion from the Public Schools Act, 1868, on the grounds that the endowments of these schools remained the property of the Mercers' and Merchant Taylors' Companies respectively (1899, 6). In effect both these schools, along with their endowments, were managed by a company. However, these were unusual circumstances and, while there may have been political differences on the issue, endowments were widely considered to have been donated to serve a public or national purpose: J. S. Mill referred to them as 'national property' (Mack, 1938, 375). In a private letter, reproduced by the Clarendon Commission, Gladstone wrote:

We are in danger of timidity in dealing with the work of reform, because the abuses which exist are so much bound up with private interests and because (choosing, I admit, the lesser of two dangers) it is our habit in this country to treat private interests with an extravagant tenderness, and to allow constructions of unbounded liberality in cases where we ought to be rather strict. The truth is that all laxity and extravagance in dealing with *what in a large sense is certainly public property*, approximates more or less to dishonesty, or at least lowers the moral tone of persons concerned (1864a, Volume 11, Appendix: Section F; stress added).

Unfortunately Gladstone's letter continues by asserting that only the study of the classics constitutes a truly liberal education – an assertion as much in need of careful substantiation as the distinction between private and public property is in need of detailed analysis. However, once the Victorian parliamentarians had convinced themselves that action was needed, the results, at least with respect to their commissions of inquiry, were highly impressive.

Although the immediate motivation for reform was the abuse of endowment income, these particular concerns occurred within the context of broad social conflicts and changing societal values. Moreover, many of the endowed schools were simply made irrelevant by the pattern of economic and social change. For example, many endowments were far too meagre to sustain viable schools as the value of money declined, and population shifts could mean either that a school no longer had any pupils or that an endowment originally meant for a small town now had to serve the needs of an expanding city. Although the debate about the role of the classics in the curriculum has wide social and political ramifications, the changing economic base of the nation, with its evolving occupational structure, made it more difficult to defend a classical education regardless of what the founders may have desired. It was scarcely worthwhile availing oneself of a free education if it was irrelevant to one's employment prospects. So schools dedicated by statutes to a classical curriculum could find themselves without pupils.

The social conflicts flowed out of three variables: social class, religion and community. The consequence was a range of political struggles, reflecting either the interaction of these differing social forces or, more simply, conflicts specific to any one of them. There were both intra- and inter-class conflicts, the differing demands of Nonconformists and Anglicans, and the pull of local against national interests. In the endowed schools, in spite of statutory clauses that may have suggested a different clientele, the class conflicts centred predominantly upon the interests of differing segments of the middle class. The Taunton Commission, obviously reflecting the spirit of the age, spoke in terms of three grades of secondary schooling defined by school-leaving age and curriculum content, with special attention paid to the position of the classics (1868, 16–21). Not surprisingly each grade of schooling was perceived as appealing to a different stratum within the middle class, and the Commission set this out in very frank terms.

First-grade schools educated the sons of 'men with considerable incomes independent of their own exertions, or professional men, and men in business, whose profits put them on the same level' (1868, 16). Whereas these men had little difficulty in securing first-grade schooling for their sons, the same could not be said of the other class of parents attracted to these schools: 'These are the great majority of professional men, especially the clergy, medical men, and lawyers; the poorer gentry; all in fact, who, having received a cultivated education themselves, are *very anxious that their sons should not fall below them*' (1868, 17; stress added). In other words, these parents believed that their sons needed a first-grade education in order to maintain their social position. In the penetrating words of the commission, 'They have nothing to look to but education to keep their sons on a high social level' (1868, 18). The problem was that a classical education (still a prerequisite for entering Oxford or Cambridge) was increasingly available only in the public schools, and these were the parents who lacked the resources to pay the schools' fees.

There was a coalescence of interests, therefore, between the less financially secure sections of the bourgeoisie and many heads of the endowed grammar schools who wished to secure the social reputations of their schools while preserving a classical education (perhaps with the addition of a 'modern' side). Indeed, even before the Taunton Commissioners reported, schools had gone to the Court of Chancery to change their statutes in ways which would appeal to the sensibilities of such parents. After a long battle Manchester Grammar School was finally permitted in 1867 to admit paying scholars in addition to the 250 boys with free places, and James Bryce, who inspected the school for the Taunton Commission, recommended that no limit should be placed on their numbers (Balls, 1967, 211).

Of course, enhancing the interests of one class invariably meant diminishing the interests of another. Nothing illustrates the point more clearly than the pressures to remove restrictions upon the competition for scholarship places. Balls has argued that the free places in the English grammar schools went disproportionately to the children of lower-middle-class families. This class feared that the Taunton Commission would make proposals to restrict scholarships to the children of genuinely poor families (Balls, 1968, 223). In fact *both* the poor and the lower-middle-class children lost out. The commissioners made no recommendations designed to restrict scholarships to a particular class of persons. Moreover, removing founders' restrictions upon competition for scholarship places became a central part of the process by which a school went upmarket. Loosening the local ties gave the schools more of a national profile, while widening the competition for scholarships inevitably meant those who were better prepared fared best – that is the more middle-class children.

An important element in the class tension was the belief that the state was increasingly meeting the costs of elementary education for the working classes, a feeling which intensified after the passage of the 1870 Education Act, while there was a shortage of acceptable schools within the price-range of many middle-class families. Arnold's *A French Eton: A Middle Class Education and the State* (1864) is undoubtedly the most famous contemporary thesis on the issue. While Arnold favoured a direct financial input from the state, the dominant prevailing opinion – which was to find favour with the Taunton Commission – was the need to reorganise endowments. Given that elementary schools for the working class were increasingly supported from the public purse, there was an argument that their endowments should be redirected to enhance the educational opportunities of middle-class children. The pressure to take such action was intensified by 1891 legislation which 'replaced scholars' fees by a fee-grant from the national Exchequer' in voluntary elementary schools, so raising 'the question of finding some purpose to which those endowments ... can in future be usefully applied' (Bryce Commission, 1896, 11).

Such a move was difficult to justify given that by 1891 the school boards were increasingly developing higher-grade elementary schools which catered to the lower middle class who had lost out in the restructuring of the endowed secondary schools. Moreover, certainly before 1891 it seemed morally dubious to engineer a class transference of endowment income when the local rates, which sustained the elementary education provided by the school boards, did not fall exclusively upon the middle class. Even if such a course of action were possible, it is evident from the tenor of the Bryce Report that this would not in itself have provided sufficient resources to meet an expanding demand for secondary education. Either new endowments had to be found or there had to be substantial intervention by the state.

The pressures generated by the religious and community variables were equally complex in their ramifications. The claim that schools had a statutory requirement to provide either gratuitous education for local children, or that only local children were eligible for scholarships, is self-evidently a defence of local interests. But, as Balls has shown (1968, 220–6), the case for local needs was made more strongly by some social groups rather than others: for example, by those class factions who were actually benefiting from endowment income or, on occasions, by the Anglican clergy who had no wish to lose control of their schools in any reorganisation of endowments.

The Nonconformists may have been pleased by the easing of the religious restrictions which pervaded the educational system, as these were generally biased in favour of the Church of England, but they may have been less happy with the increased competition for scholarship places in local grammar schools if their children had proved successful competitors in the past. The whole issue was further clouded by the fact that endowment reorganisation could lead to the establishment of elementary board schools, resulting in the possible appointment of Nonconformists as school managers (presumably to the displeasure of many Anglicans). In the end, regardless of what the pressures for change were, the commissioners had to exercise their judgement and make specific recommendations. With respect to the reform of endowments, and the more general proposals that would reshape admissions to the endowed schools, the Clarendon and Taunton Commissions advocated the following changes:

1. Endowments should be restructured both to permit their amalgamation and their subdivision (Taunton Commission, 1868, 626).

2. The varying restrictions upon the selection of scholarship pupils should for the most part be removed (Clarendon Commission, 1864, 10–11; Taunton Commission, 1868, 167–70).

3. The awarding of scholarships should be determined by competitive examination (Clarendon Commission, 1864, 10–11; Taunton Commission, 1868, 156–61). Indeed both commissions believed that an entrance examination should be part of the admissions process for all pupils at endowed secondary schools.

4. A school should not use its endowment income to provide a gratuitous education to all its pupils and, regardless of founders' statutes, fee-paying pupils were generally to be encouraged (Clarendon Commission, 1864, 10–11; Taunton Commission, 1868, 144–54).

The grounds for advocating the proposed changes combined an interesting amalgam of pragmatism, a recognition of the demands of powerful groups in the contemporary society, and principle. Clearly it made little sense to retain the original purpose of an endowment if the result was a grossly underfunded school. Furthermore, it is difficult to contemplate that there was a serious possibility either of restricting scholarships solely to 'the poor and needy' or of excluding fee-paying students. The Clarendon Commission, while recognising that the schools it was investigating were founded 'for the assistance of meritorious poverty', continued by reflecting: 'How far either justice or expediency demand that these intentions should be maintained at present is a question on which there may be different opinions' (1864, 9-10). And then, after a brief review of prevailing practices in several schools, reached the terse conclusion: 'We do not think it necessary to recommend any change in this respect' (1864, 10). To have acted otherwise would have invited intense political opposition, so making it difficult to accomplish anything.

It can be reasonably argued that the impulse to act pragmatically served admirably those who had gradually reconstructed the more prestigious endowed schools to suit their own ends. But it was not the intention of the commissioners merely to reaffirm the status quo, for they wanted to remodel the schools in a manner which would inevitably serve particular interested parties. This is especially true of the Taunton Commission, for the Clarendon Nine were already moving under their own impetus in the direction advocated for the less prestigious endowed schools. Although the well-being of the endowed schools may have been their primary interest, such sophisticated individuals were undoubtedly aware of the social consequences of the reforms they were advocating. The Taunton Commission, while recognising that in order 'to bring the poor fully within the range of higher education, the grammar schools were in the main gratuitous' (1868, 122), none the less issued fierce strictures against it: 'The higher education and indiscriminate admission are incompatible' (1868, 146). And, 'To lower the education rather than impose fees, leads in practice to the reduction of the grammar school to the level of an elementary school' (1868, 147). Finally, '... very few of the grammar school endowments can, unassisted by fees, educate more than a limited number of scholars, at least of the first or second grade' (1868, 148).

Not surprisingly, the answer for the Taunton Commission was to end gratuitous secondary schooling. While the imposition of fees might act as a means of resisting 'the lowering of education' what would be the social ramifications? The pedagogical consequences may have been as the Commission predicted, and, given that the Court of

Chancery had already approved a number of such schemes, there was evidence to support the commission's views. However, their reflections on the likely social consequences are by comparison muted. In view of its advocacy of a three-tier grading of secondary schooling, with the differing grades defined in part by the social composition of the schools, it seems obvious what the main social outcome of the abolition of gratuitous secondary schooling would be. It is as if the commission's explicit acceptance of a class-based system of secondary schooling made redundant further reflection upon the social ramifications of its proposed changes. They were all too self-evident.

In spite of the political pragmatism that surrounded the reform of the endowed secondary schools, the various reports of the commissions of inquiry reveal the concern of the commissioners not to be viewed as devious realists merely responding to dominant societal pressures. They wanted to be seen as men of principle who, rather than subverting founders' statutes, were either upholding them, or applying them to changed circumstances, in a manner that was entirely consistent with their spirit. For example, the commissioners argued that poor highways rather than a founder's commitment to a town or county were likely to account for local prescriptions. Of Shrewsbury School, the Clarendon Commission claimed:

> It appears to us clear that the intention of King Edward and of Queen Elizabeth in establishing and endowing the School was to provide for the education, not only of the sons of the burgesses or inhabitants of Shrewsbury, but of the youth of the whole neighbourhood; by which we understand that the *School was to be open to all who could conveniently attend it* (1864, 306; stress added).

With improved highways, and more significantly the coming of the railways, it could be argued that Shrewsbury School was conveniently located for all in the nation who wished, and could afford, to attend it. To follow this logic, the school had *always* been intended as a national school; in the past it was merely rudimentary transport which had prevented it.

While the attack on gratuitous education may have been firmly rooted in pragmatic considerations (the insufficiency of the endowment to sustain an open commitment to free schooling), and a belief in its negative pedagogical consequences (many grammar schools were offering little more than an elementary education) the Taunton Commission wanted in part to base its own opposition on statutory interpretation. We read in its Report: 'But nowhere does there appear any evidence of a desire to save parents paying, who could afford to pay' (1868, 125). This may indeed be true, but the problem as others perceived it was the admission in the first place of scholars whose parents could afford to pay fees – and hang the pedagogical consequences.

Even the desire to see all nine of the Clarendon Schools introduce competitive examinations for scholarships, along the lines of those already in operation at Eton and Winchester, could be legitimised by an appeal to the statutes. At St. Paul's the number of scholars had always been restricted to 153, apparently in memory of 'the miraculous draught of fishes recorded in the last chapter of St. John's Gospel'. The Clarendon Commissioners were prepared to respect 'this quaint but innocent direction' but it was not clear to them that the founder (Dean Colet) 'contemplated or would have approved the mode in which the scholars are now appointed. The nomination of a scholar, whatever it may have originally been, has now become an affair of simple patronage' (1864, 190). And then, in a scholarly footnote, the commissioners tried to substantiate their belief that entry to the school was intended to be by means of an examination which was 'virtually, though not in form, competitive' (1864, 190).

The problem of trying to base the case for a uniform pattern of reform on an interpretation of the statutes was the variation in their terms, and more significantly, the fact that these were, in any case, open to conflicting interpretations. If trustees could be roundly condemned for their abuses, then so could the commissioners, both by those whose interests were directly affected, as well as by those conservative social figures who disliked centrally orchestrated change in general. The result could be a calculation of whose abuses were the most significant – the trustees or the commissioners. The commissioners, therefore, were on much safer ground when claiming their proposed changes were consistent with the national interest. And, of course, the safest ground of all was to propose changes which were sensitive to the balance of power within the country at large, while furthering the national interest!

Although the commissioners' proposals for the reorganisation of endowments generally prevailed, the subsequent battles were often very fierce. Legislative proposals were compromised, the pace of change was slow, the Endowed Schools Commission – set up by legislation consequent upon the Taunton Commission – was investigated in 1873 by a parliamentary select committee and then, after a change of government, incorporated into the Charity Commission. But still the opposition continued, and the commissioners had to endure another parliamentary select committee inquiry in 1886. However, they conducted a robust defence of their activities, and the Bryce Commission concluded that, as a result of their reforms, the endowed secondary schools were in much better shape than they had been earlier in the century. But these had been hard-won gains which tightened the links between social class and schooling in Britain.

NEW VALUES FOR A NEW AGE

While the nineteenth-century reforms were a response to the political pressures generated by social change, they also signify the emergence of a new set of values within which secondary education was to be embedded. While change, and the resistance to it, was fuelled by conflict between self-interested groups competing for scarce resources, it also symbolised a struggle between differing value systems. The Newcastle, Clarendon and Taunton Commissions can be seen as ideological statements which are not only concerned to propose a reform package but also are engaged in a battle of ideas. Although some of the precise policy skirmishes might be lost, if the ideological high ground could be secured, then in the long run change would flow in the direction of the commissions' recommendations. As one would expect, many of the values that underpinned these three commissions had wider significance than the character of formal schooling; in effect they were values that were integral – at least as far as their proponents were concerned – to the efficient functioning of the Victorian social order.

The central value was that of competition: the belief that the distribution of scarce resources should be determined by a competitive struggle between individuals. Scholarships, as a prime example of a scarce resource, would be used most effectively if an open competition, free from as many restrictions as possible, was established. Consequently there were to be no residential disqualifications, no 'poor and needy' clauses, and no bars in terms of previous schooling, and it was even suggested that to limit the competition was demeaning to successful candidates. Of course, it was recognised that if there were no exclusions upon competitors then scholarships could be won by those who had no financial need of them. But to recognise a potential problem does not automatically stimulate preventive action, and the Clarendon Commissioners reported that in Winchester's newly reformed admissions system, 'No boy has yet been excluded from the competition on the ground of comparative affluence, and it does not appear that any inquiries are made respecting the circumstances of the candidates' (1864, 137). Apparently where open competition prevailed the schools relied upon candidates to adopt self-denying ordinances. Inasmuch as it was generally accepted that the competitive rules should be determined by the schools themselves, presumably this potential abuse – at least in spirit – was considered by the Clarendon Commissioners to be very much the lesser of two evils. To stimulate individual competition was, therefore, more important than to defend the claims of the needy.

In a beautiful quotation from a private letter, reproduced by the Clarendon Commission, we discover that the headmaster of Winchester, Dr Moberly, had been against the reform of admissions but had subsequently changed his mind:

> Let me offer my testimony without reserve. The open elections have been excellently successful. In point of ability, good conduct, and general promise, we have lost nothing, and we have gained much. We do not know what it is to have a thoroughly stupid boy a scholar (1864, 137).

Moberly had sought an accommodation between 'the advantages of a very real competition with the responsibility of nomination' but, not surprisingly, had failed to bridge the divide. The debate illustrates both the strength of the values of the old order, and the potency of the new demands. At Winchester compromise had proved impossible; the old had to give way to the new, and personal patronage found itself steadily replaced by impersonal competition.

The attack upon gratuitous secondary schooling was underpinned by the philosophy of self-help. The Newcastle Commission claimed that generally speaking the poor were against free schooling: 'The sentiment of independence is strong, and it is wounded by the offer of an absolutely gratuitous education' (1861, 73), and the commissioners spoke favourably of schemes in which fees were graduated (1861, 74) – shades of the present-day assisted places scheme! Moreover, the commissioners were not convinced that endowment income was an undisguised blessing, for it could 'remove the necessity for self-exertion and the stimulus of competition' (1861, 469). If school-masters' salaries were more dependent upon fees, the endowment income could be more widely distributed and institutions would be reinvigorated. There was a strong belief that many who received free schooling did not deserve it; the idea of the deserving poor clearly implied that there was an undeserving poor. Consequently, it was important to ensure that resources went to those who could show they were capable of making good use of them, and so the need to measure individual merit was convincingly legitimised.

If the stress was upon personal responsibility, then it followed that the commissioners envisaged only a limited role for the state in the provision of schooling. The Newcastle Commission, while containing an internal minority opposition, supported the decision taken in 1839 to make public grants available to elementary schooling (1861, 297), but in its recommendations made no plea for an increase of that input, instead placing a great deal of faith in the reorganisation of endowments, a line which was subsequently adopted by the Taunton Commission. Late in the nineteenth century, the Bryce Commission was still pursuing a similar line with respect to secondary schooling, although it called for new endowments and raised the possibility of transferring elementary school endowments to secondary schooling. Its Report also revealed that 'None of the witnesses who came before us as representatives of associations appeared to have received any mandate in favour of free Secondary Education ...' (1896, 183). However, besides discussing the financial input that secondary schools were deriving from endowments and fees, the Bryce Commission also considered the input of local rates, parliamentary grants, and the grant available for schooling secured by the Customs and Excise Act of 1890 (1896, 307–16).

Clearly, the state was slowly beginning to expand its direct financial commitment to secondary education, and this was a trend that the Bryce commission wished to encourage. On rates the hope was that the commission's proposals would ' ... so stimulate local interest in education as to increase the willingness of people to tax themselves for it ...' (1896, 310). On parliamentary grants the Commission was more coy, perhaps merely following a politically expedient line, and refused to make a positive recommendation one way or the other (1896, 314–16). In spite of this equivocation, opinion had shifted substantially in the forty years since the Newcastle Commission. In the 1850s, as the Newcastle Commission itself makes clear, grants to elementary schools still aroused considerable opposition. By the 1890s the state – through the school boards – was making direct provision for elementary education, and tentatively increasing its financial contribution to secondary schooling.

Could the state's support for secondary schooling be reconciled with the ideology of competition, the rewarding of personal merit, the attack upon institutional waste, the strictures against individual idleness, the keen support for self-help, and the belief in the virtues of fee-paying? Between the Newcastle and Bryce Commissions it is the development of the idea of the educational ladder – a ladder of opportunity for deserving individuals – that formed the basis of the reconciliation. The Newcastle Commissioners, setting the trend for others who were to follow, recognised that sufficiently large endowments could be subdivided to create different grades of schooling, and gave examples of where this had already occurred (1861, 488). Where such a strategy was adopted the Commission wanted a scholarship ladder to be created ' ... for the purpose of raising the most promising pupils from the elementary to the English, and from the English to the classical school', and believed that were this to be done, 'A way will be thus made for merit to rise' (1861, 488). Similar schemes had already been instigated by some of the schools to be investigated by the Clarendon Commission, although their motivations may have been Machiavellian: that is, to remove the local children so that the schools could establish themselves as national institutions attractive to wealthy parents.

With its explicit reference to three grades of secondary schooling, and its encouragement of the expansion of exhibitions to allow selected scholars to transfer from lower to higher grades, the concept of the ladder was implicit in the recommendations of the Taunton Commission (Gordon, 1980, 103). The Bryce Commission adopted the same idea, elaborated it somewhat, and made explicit reference to the ladder analogy:

> As we have not recommended that Secondary Education shall be provided free of costs to the whole community, we deem it all the more needful that ample provision should be made by every Local Authority for enabling selected children of the poorer parents to climb the educational ladder (1896, 300).

Although the Bryce Commission moved only tentatively towards embracing the idea that secondary education should be more generously underpinned by state financial aid, there was widespread support from all quarters, both in the commission as well as in evidence to it, that the number of scholarships underwritten by rates and endowment income should expand. And the Bryce Commission continued the earlier strong support shown for the rewarding of individual merit through competitive examinations. So, in spite of an enhanced public financial input, the state could demonstrate that there would be no slacking in the war against waste and idleness.

Central to the idea of the educational ladder was the belief that access to secondary schooling, if it were to be underwritten by public resources, had to be restricted to the gifted few. Those who wanted to escape this qualification had to follow the fee-paying route. For most of the first half of the twentieth century the idea of the ladder of educational opportunity was central to the political battles over access to secondary schooling: how long and broad the ladder should be, the continuing restrictions on competition (the requirement of elementary school attendance for those who sought free-places or the necessity of a private preparatory schooling for those seeking a public school scholarship), whether entrance examinations should be competitive or qualifying, what form they should take, and what scholarships should finance – fees, educational extras or even maintenance allowances. The battles continued until the idea of secondary education for all triumphed, since when the conflict has centred upon what the forms of secondary schooling should be, and how to determine access to those varying forms.

CONCLUSION

Many of the endowed schools that were investigated by the nineteenth-century commissions, and that still survive today, form part of what is currently referred to as the independent sector. In spite of the fact that the financial well-being of these schools may be heavily dependent upon attracting a sufficient number of fee-paying pupils, if they have endowment income the state has established the means – usually through the Charity Commission – of intervening in their affairs. Of course, in the sense that parliamentary scrutiny permits precious few hiding-places, this may be a mere quibble. However, the commissions were legitimised in part by the assumption that endowment income placed the schools in the public domain: that is, they exist to pursue a public purpose, and the state has the right to intervene should there be sufficient grounds to suspect that the schools are failing to perform that purpose with due care.

What the investigations of the commissions show is the continuity of educational concerns. The Newcastle, Clarendon, Taunton and Bryce Commissions focused upon the efficient management of schools, the relevance of their curricula to the needs of the contemporary society, their competence at delivering their educational services, patterns of access to the various forms of schooling, and how the costs of schooling should be paid for. Their reflection on these issues illustrates a moving picture steadily restructured by the shift from a world centred upon the values of patronage to one increasingly driven by the ethos of individual competition supposedly based on personal merit.

This trend interacted with another critical development: the move from the provision of schooling as the responsibility of parents and society to a widening role for the state. The two trends were brought together by the constant stress upon the need to balance the contributions of fee-paying, endowments and public moneys in the financing of schooling. This was coupled with the sponsorship of an increasingly publicly funded scholarship system which recognised the virtues of individual competition within the context of a selective system of secondary education. The educational ladder would widen the opportunities of those who had demonstrated their ability to make the best use of public money.

The process of politically directed change was driven by the interaction of social and economic forces. While the intensity of local pressures declined, and the religious variable became somewhat less divisive, so the demands of social class became more pervasive. The impact of these changes on admissions to schooling was to establish a closer link between education and social class; schooling became integral to the process of social selection and reproduction. At the same time these concerns were intimately interwoven into the survival of the schools as institutions. Schools such as Harrow, Rugby and Shrewsbury came to the conclusion that their futures were as schools with a national appeal, attractive to wealthy middle-class parents and even to segments of the gentry. The means to the desired end were: the loosening of local ties; the division of endowments; the founding of schools for a purely local clientele; and the creation of a narrow scholarship ladder.

The change process was driven by the interaction of the internal institutional dynamics and the pressures exerted by the broad societal forces. Neither of these two sets of pressures was consistently coherent or always interacted in a manner which pulled in the same direction. While headmasters may have seen the future of their schools as a close association with the Clarendon Nine, governors – possibly with stronger local ties – may have had different visions. Balls has analysed the subtle intermixing of class, religion and locality, and this chapter has presented the possible tensions within the political objectives of the individual social groups. Furthermore, Allsobrook has complicated the picture greatly by showing both the local variation in how the social forces saw their interests, and how their perceptions of what needed to be done could actually change over time (1973, 35–55). However, this complex moving picture has to be set within the context of a steady shift in the dominant societal values. The reports of the commissions were manifestations of the new values, and, over time, the change process was pushed steadily in a direction broadly consistent with those values. Like Allsobrook (1986, 256–65), one may be less than sympathetic to the outcome, but the political potency of the dominant social forces was not to be denied.

Because of the ebb and flow of social and economic change, and the concomitant political pressure it generates, inevitably the change process is complex. Moreover, the shift from a system of patronage to one of competition based on individual merit generated its own problems. These were partly of a technical nature (for example, what form the competition should take), and partly a consequence of the ability of individuals to manipulate the rules to serve their own purposes. While statutes may have recognised the claims of founders' kin, there is little doubt that these were pursued so vigorously as to undermine the broader goal of founding schools for poor and needy scholars. Consequently, we see the intermittent attempts to limit the claims of kin by prescribing upper limits on their numbers. In parallel fashion the move to competitive scholarships, and later free places underwritten by public resources, saw those who had no real financial need of such support ignoring the implied moral constraint upon their participation. So an integral part of the change process is the constant pressure that individuals exert upon the prevailing rules in order to manipulate them to their own advantage. As long as certain forms of secondary schooling are considered to be more desirable than others, this is unlikely ever to change.

The Report of the Clarendon Commission reproduced an extract of a letter from the Provost of Eton College, Dr Goodford, to the headmaster of Westminster:

> The first and most marked effect of opening our foundation to competition has been that it has raised intellectually the standard of boys in College … . The class of boys which the open competition has drawn here, has been mainly the sons of Clergymen, or younger sons of laymen, whose elder brothers would inherit a sufficiency without the aid of a Fellowship;

sometimes a tradesman's son, but not often. Looking down the list of my own division now, which contains 17 King's Scholars I find 12 clergymen's sons, two younger sons, whose brothers are provided for; two sons of naval officers, and one who is a solicitor's son. *I take these to be, as near as may be, the class of persons whom our Founder meant to benefit*; and the leaven of steadiness and diligence which they impart to the rest of the School is most valuable to us (1864, 67; stress added).

If the Provost's observation on Henry VI's motivations is indeed correct, then perhaps there were never any 'poor and needy' scholars except in the very particular sense that, without being able to avail themselves of endowment income, certain families would experience great difficulty in sending their sons to Eton College. More important, however, is the fact that the statutes which embodied the idea of the poor and needy scholar were seen to be irrelevant to the circumstances of Victorian England. Either 'the poor and needy scholar' was merely a prescribed statutory reference with no real meaning attached to it, or it was one manifestation of a broader system of values which the passage of time had made irrelevant.

3

Charitable Status and Access to Private Schooling: A Troubled Relationship

Over time many of the services provided by charitable bodies have become the responsibility of the state, and in certain cases state provision has made charitable activity redundant. None the less, in spite of the seemingly inexorable expansion of the state's intrusion into the provision of educational services, schooling remains a vibrant field of charitable endeavour. Besides enhancing the state's financial input, this has the potential to broaden the diversity of educational provision, and with it the enrichment of pedagogical practice and the widening of parental choice. The charitable status of many private schools recognises that they are providing a public service, and thus their activities are to be encouraged.

In Britain the determination of what constitutes a charitable purpose has been left primarily to the courts. The administration of charities, including – since 1973 – educational charities, resides with the Charity Commissioners. The latter act within the framework established by the courts and are responsible to Parliament through the Home Secretary and the Attorney-General. This essentially judicial framework of control is a manifestation of the fact that charitable bodies are on the boundary between state and society. While the courts are part of the state, and are amenable to both political and administrative pressure, they also have a powerful tradition of independence. Legislative guidance in deciding what is to constitute a charitable purpose is non-existent, while in direct contrast there is a rich body of case law.

In the discussion on the Bill to transfer responsibilities for educational charities from the then Department of Education and Science to the Charity Commissioners, Lord Belstead remarked:

When the present Government took office in 1970 there was a

comprehensive review of Departmental responsibilities and this included the powers exercised under the Charities Act by the two Secretaries of State, and as a result of it the Government concluded that those powers, being essentially judicial in both origin and character, really are not appropriate to the role of a central Government Minister (*Hansard* [Lords], 14 November 1972, Col. 646).

It was subsequently suggested that the real motivation for the transfer was not, as implied by Lord Belstead, a question of propriety with respect to departmental responsibilities, but rather the wish to protect more securely the charitable status of private schooling. Be that as it may, this administrative relocation of educational charities illustrates perfectly the point that there are degrees of incorporation within the state apparatus. The fact that the understanding of charitable purposes is under the control of the courts, and the concomitant administrative responsibilities located on the further shores of the central state bureaucracy, suggest a blurred demarcation of the boundary between state and society. Furthermore, it is a boundary that can shift over time.

To grant charitable status is to award benefits, both tangible and intangible. These are benefits which the state grants in order to encourage society to provide goods and services widely perceived as desirable. Invariably charitable activities are bathed in a glow of public approval which reinforces state sponsorship. In this sense there is an ideological dimension to charitable status, for it singles out those activities which the state considers worthy of approval. With the spread of taxation the rewards for charities have become more concrete, and in recent years much attention has been paid to measuring the financial returns that flow from charitable status. Additionally, the charitable status of independent schooling has acquired an important political dimension. In the past, part of the Labour Party's strategy for undermining the private sector of schooling was to threaten the removal of its charitable status, so generating wide debate as to whether this was either a desirable or feasible strategy. Thus, the idea of what constitutes a charitable purpose has been caught up in the broader political conflict which surrounds the relationship between the maintained and independent sectors of schooling.

While the political opposition to private schooling is wide-ranging, the objection to its charitable status is very specific: that it does *not* confer a public benefit. Central to this argument is the contention that private schooling serves mainly the interests of a relatively narrow segment of British society – that is, those who can afford to pay its fees. Invariably in pursuing this argument, some reference will be made to the irony (to put it mildly) that the nation's most expensive schools, catering to an already socially privileged clientele, are deemed to be charities. It is not the intention of this chapter to explain in detail this irony, for that ground has already been well covered (Gladstone, 1982, 60–5; Moffat, 1989, 192–200; Salter and Tapper, 1985, 95–103). The chapter has the more narrow task of analysing the relationship between admissions to private schools and their charitable status. Although this is a more specific focus than the attempt to unravel the legal tangle upon which the charitable status of fee-paying schools is based, it is a critical issue in the wider debate, and, undoubtedly, the one that has generated the most political controversy. The courts' decisions have both determined how the schools must conduct their affairs if they wish to retain their charitable status, and influenced the wider discussion of what reforms – if any – are needed to preserve their privileged position.

The previous chapter argued that the reform of the endowed schools reflected the transition from a society based on patronage to one in which social relations were increasingly centred on the idea of personal merit and individual competition. The essence of the reforms was the redirection of the institutional purposes of the schools: they became more clearly defined educational institutions (as opposed to institutions in the service of the church), with an elaborate experience of schooling designed to suit the interests of a narrow class segment of the nation at large. This chapter will discern a parallel shift in the preconditions prescribed by the courts in determining the charitable basis of schooling. The general drift of the nineteenth-century Royal Commissions was to remove the restrictions upon the competition for scholarship places. At an earlier date the courts had shifted from a narrow understanding of charitable purposes, centred upon the relief of poverty, to a much broader definition in which schooling itself was deemed to be a charitable purpose. To put it baldly, in fact too baldly, fee-paying schools could have charitable status because of their promotion of learning, and other considerations, while not necessarily irrelevant, were of secondary importance. The current conflict, which is examined in the final section of the chapter, focuses upon whether the definition of charitable status should return to more restrictive criteria, or whether the prevailing expansive interpretation should be retained.

INTERPRETING THE COURT CASES

It is customary to trace the understanding of what constitutes a charitable purpose back to the statutes of charitable uses enacted in the latter years of the reign of Elizabeth I, and in particular to the Charitable Uses Act, 1601 (Jones, 1969, 22–6). While the preamble to the Act did not attempt to define charity, it provided what Gladstone has called an illustrative list of charitable purposes (1982, 46). In 1805, in Morice v. Bishop of Durham, Sir Samuel Romilly ventured the following fourfold classification:

> There are four objects, within one of which all charity, to be administered in this Court, must fall: 1st, relief of the indigent; in various ways: money: provisions: education: medical assistance; etc.: 2dly, the advancement of learning: 3dly, the advancement of religion; and, 4thly, which is the most difficult, the advancement of objects of general public utility (Morice v. Bishop of Durham, 1805, 10 Ves. 522).

Nearly a century later, Lord Macnaghten, following closely the line established by Romilly, formulated what has remained the standard classification:

> 'Charity' in its legal sense comprises four principal divisions: trusts for the relief of poverty; trusts for the advancement of education; trusts for the advancement of religion; and trusts for other purposes beneficial to the community, not falling under any of the preceding heads (Income Tax Special Purposes Courts v. Pemsel, 1891, A.C. 583).

The key consideration is whether 'the advancement of learning' (Romilly), or 'trusts for the advancement of education' (Macnaghten), constitute a sufficient basis for claiming charitable status. Alternatively, are there further conditions that have to be satisfied before the promotion of education/learning can be deemed to be a charitable purpose?

Much of the debate has focused on the relationship between charity and the relief of poverty. A contemporary analysis of the 1601 Statute by Sir Francis Moore demonstrated, according to Gladstone, an 'almost obsessive concern with poverty' (1982, 56). While many of the purposes listed in the preamble to the statute did not 'explicitly refer to poverty', apparently, according to Moore, 'the intention of the statute was to exclude benefit for [sic] those who could afford to pay' (1982, 56). But it was recognised that, inevitably, many charitable services would benefit both the rich and the poor, and the maintenance of bridges and highways is the much-quoted example. However, the benefit to the rich had to be incidental to, rather than the primary purpose of, the charitable trust. In an illuminating observation on Moore's *Reading* of the 1601 Statute, Jones quotes Moore's judgment that 'a trust to erect a mill on private ground where the poor cannot grind their corn free, was not within the statute...' (1969, 30).

Gladstone has argued that for a long period of time the courts retained this refinement (1982, 57). So, in 1700 (Attorney-General v. Hewer, 2 Vern. 387) it was held 'that only free schools came within the ambit of the 1601 Act', and as late as 1767 the Lord Chancellor defined charity as 'a gift to a general public use which extends to the poor as well as to the rich' (Jones v. Williams Amb. per Lord Camden). In spite of these decisions, it has to be recognised that many of the endowed schools had long ceased to cater exclusively for either poor and/or free scholars. While the poor might continue to benefit from free schooling, they were often vastly outnumbered by fee-payers. In such circumstances, the question becomes one of the relative benefit to the poor as opposed to the rich, with, over time, the balance of advantage shifting steadily towards the latter. It is unclear what line had to be crossed before there was a breach in Moore's understanding that the relief of poverty was the object of charity. Moreover, it is possible in certain cases to make a distinction between the original foundation which catered for free scholars (and perhaps aided the poor), and the creation of schoolhouses for the fee-paying pupils. It does not require much imagination, thinking along these lines, to see that foundations such as Eton and Winchester Colleges could retain their charitable status in spite of the comparative paucity of the foundation scholars. In effect the colleges were composed of two schools, which should each have had its own legal status.

Several commentators have regretted the willingness of the courts to alter the preconditions that determined whether a purpose was charitable or not. In the judgement of Gladstone, in Morice v. Bishop of Durham 1805 the court gave the Preamble to the Act of Charitable Uses, 1601 'an authority it had never had before and which, it is submitted, is poor history and, inasmuch as it is irreconcilable with the full range of accepted precedents, worse logic' (1982, 47–8). Moffat has claimed that it was 'the ambiguity in the language of the preamble – there being no specific reference to relief of poverty in relation to schools of learning' that 'left the way open for schools benefiting non-poor persons to be accorded charitable status' (1989, 194). While this degree of flexibility may be disagreeable to some, it is surely one of the reasons for having courts decide these matters rather than Parliament. Parliament would face the problem of drafting tight and coherent legislation, it would be subject to evident political pressures (with the danger that the interpretation of charitable purposes could become a political football), and it would act only at the instigation of the executive with the invariably long delays before reform was forthcoming. This is not to suggest that the courts are a model of speed and cogency, but in some areas their control might be preferable to that of either the executive or the legislature.

The suspicion is that the objection is not so much to the courts' flexibility but the ends to which they have put that flexibility. They have broadened the interpretation of charity so there is a large gap between its commensense meaning (the relief of poverty) and its far wider technical or legal meanings. However, it is difficult to see how the courts could have maintained their control without exercising a measure of flexibility. If they had not proved responsive to societal change, then Parliament would inevitably have intervened. Similarly, the Supreme Court of the United States can sustain its right to interpret the Constitution partly because it has been able to conclude that at different times in American history it has meant different things. Failure to have acted otherwise would have meant either the destruction of the Constitution or a different role for the Supreme Court – or both. It can reasonably be concluded that the British courts have been more responsive to the needs of the most powerful social forces than to the interests of society at large. But this is a criticism of how power is distributed in Britain, and does not sustain the case against judicial flexibility.

The clearest indication that the courts were prepared to embrace a broader interpretation of charitable purposes as the nineteenth century unfolded is illustrated by the case of the Attorney-General v. the Earl of Lonsdale, 1827 (1 Sim. 105). The issue at stake was whether property that had been bequeathed to endow a school should, on the school's closure, revert to the founder's heirs or be devoted to other charitable ends. Part of the case for the defendants was that the original trust failed 'because the school, being for the education of gentlemen's sons, is not a charity'. However, in robust language, Sir John Leach arrived at a very different conclusion: 'The institution of a school for the sons of gentlemen is not, in popular language, a charity; but in view of the statute of Elizabeth, all schools for learning are so to be considered; and on that ground no objection can be made to the trusts of the deed of 1697.' But as Moffat has pointed out there was no 'reference to the charging of fees at the school' and provided the endowment income of the trust was sufficiently large, it perhaps had no need to charge fees (1989, 194). However, Sir John Leach did say that *all* schools for learning are to be considered charities, which would presumably embrace fee-charging as well as free schools. Although the decision may not mark a fundamental break with the past, it does suggest a change of direction.

However, the evidence that a protracted battle between opposing principles was taking place, rather than a mere squabble over technical issues, is illustrated by further reference to the 1891 Pemsel case. The case demonstrates that, even at the very end of the nineteenth century, there remained within the judiciary a sizeable conflict over the relationship between charity and poverty, and between the popular and technical definitions of charity. In his judgment on the case, Lord Halsbury remarked:

> I would say, without attempting an exhaustive definition or even description of what may be comprehended within the term 'charitable purpose', I conceive that the real ordinary use of the word 'charitable' as distinguished from any technicalities whatsoever, always does involve the relief of poverty (Income Tax Special Purposes Courts v. Pemsel, 1891, A.C. 583).

One is reminded of Francis Moore's early seventeenth-century interpretation of the Statute of Charitable Uses. And with reference to the trust upon whose status Halsbury and his fellow Lords had to decide, he concluded that '... purposes appear to be contemplated, having no relation to poverty at all'. Indeed, in the very same case, Lord Bramwell went so far as to argue that 'schools of learning not limited to the poor', and 'so, also, a school for the sons of gentlemen', could not, *according to any reasonable definition of the words*, be said to be "charitable purposes"' (stress added). Lord Bramwell made his case partly on the grounds that the preamble to the 1601 Statute went beyond its title, and that a distinction had to be made between trusts that were charitable in character, as opposed to those that were intended to further benevolent causes.

However, in the Pemsel case the majority of the law lords rejected Halsbury and Bramwell's attempt to limit the understanding of charitable purposes to the relief of poverty, and granted charitable status to the trust which, incidentally, had been drawn up to sustain the missionary activities of the Church of the United Brethren. In effect most of the law lords were persuaded to apply the wide, if technical, understanding of the meaning of charitable purposes. Moreover, in his judgment on the case, Lord Macnaghten had referred to an Act of 1842 in which '... the Legislature considered the purposes of a public school to be charitable, and a public school to be a trust for charitable purposes, just as much as an almshouse or a hospital'. So, in Macnaghten's view, the court's majority decision had the support of Parliament: the judiciary and the legislature were as one on this issue.

While the Pemsel case could be said to have decided this key issue of principle, it would be rash to suggest that the outcome was far from a foregone conclusion. The struggle had emerged repeatedly over the centuries, some judges were prepared to reject precedents because they believed them to be injudicious, and opinions were by no mean unanimous. Such observations must raise the hopes of those who would like to reverse the course of history. However, it seems improbable that the courts will take the initiative, and those hoping for change will need to look to Parliament. But recent evidence suggests that Parliament is reluctant to grasp the nettle; while it has been prepared to regulate charities it has left the definition of charitable purposes in the courts' hands. Were Parliament to construct a definition, it is doubtful if it would be any less controversial, or result in the creation of a more rational system than we have at present.

Although in the legal sense it is consistent with the idea of charity for a school to charge fees, and to cater for the more prosperous members of this society (one requires a late twentieth-century equivalent to Sir John Leach's 'sons of gentlemen'), none the less, the courts require charitable trusts to make their benefits available to a large rather than a narrow segment of society. In effect this is a continuation of Francis Moore's dictum that by definition charities cannot be for the benefit of the rich alone. The question, therefore, is how large a segment of the community has to benefit from a trust before the courts are satisfied that a public benefit is being pursued. In Oppenheim and Tobacco Securities Trust Co. Ltd, 1951, Lord Simonds made the startlingly obvious but nevertheless very apt observation that 'this time a question is asked to which no wholly satisfactory answer can be given'. In effect, this has been a grey area in which the judges have exercised their discretion, according to Lord MacDermott, with reference to the same case, 'on a general survey of the circumstances and considerations regarded as relevant rather than of making a single, conclusive test'. Presumably Simonds's and MacDermott's survey of the circumstances, as well as the considerations they felt to be relevant, differed because they reached contrasting conclusions! This, of course, is precisely the problem when pragmatism, sustained by personal values, prevails over principle.

In *Halsbury's Laws of England* we read:

> An orphanage for the children of deceased railway employees has been held to be a public charity, a 'seaman's mission' for the benefit of seamen in port in the Port of London and the London docks area is charitable, and a statutory body established to promote and improve the standard of training within the whole of one industry in England, Scotland and Wales has been held to be established for exclusively charitable purposes. But a trust for all members of a trade union which was open to all members of the printing industry, but to which not all members of the industry in fact belonged, was held not to be charitable, nor was a society for the relief of the sickness of its own members, who numbered over 400,000, charitable (Hailsham (ed.), 1993, 12–13).

This is a long way from establishing clear principles, and in sharp contrast to the conflict over the relationship between charity and poverty. We are now examining the messy business of drawing boundaries across difficult terrain. Not only are the outcomes, to use Lord Simonds's words, unlikely to be wholly satisfactory, but to the uninitiated they may appear obscure, and to those whose interests are adversely affected, even malevolent.

While the charitable status of private schooling seems to rest securely on the provision of a service that is considered to be a public benefit, its critics have argued that it is hardly a benefit that accrues to a wide segment of the community. Of the overall school population well under 10 per cent are in private schools, and, by a large margin, they come from middle-class homes. However, many middle-class parents choose not to have their children educated privately, presumably because they find the maintained sector satisfactory for their needs. Moreover, although high fees have the obvious effect of excluding most children, the schools would argue that while it is not their intention to discriminate against certain social groups, the education they offer, especially a boarding education, is costly. None the less, it does seem perverse to many people that the historical link between charity and poverty should be so explicitly flouted by the leading public schools, irrespective of how the courts may have decided to interpret the meaning of charitable status. One would anticipate a difference between the legal and commonsense interpretations of language, but in this case it is the apparent *extent* of the difference which causes the problem. The courts may have precedence and logic on their side but they appear to have forsaken common sense. It is the realisation of this glaring gap that has persuaded many within the world of the fee-paying schools of the need to close it by extending and reforming their scholarship and bursary schemes (see p.160).

Although with respect to private schools it may be difficult, if not impossible, to establish a link between poverty and charity, it is true that they do offer an education to some children whose parents cannot afford to pay the full fees. Poverty can be measured in relative terms, and against different yardsticks. Once again we have to grapple with the language of privilege and deprivation, and while there may be few, if any, pupils in fee-paying schools from very poor families, there are obviously many from families who are needy in the sense that they cannot afford the full fees. It is pertinent to note, as Moffat has also observed (1989, 215), that schools participating in the assisted places scheme all have charitable status. Inasmuch as assisted places are awarded on a means-tested basis, the link between educational charities and the deserving poor is recreated in a new guise. Therefore, even though the private schools may cater disproportionately for the privileged, the links to an established tradition of meeting the needs of the gifted, but relatively humble, members of society – upon which their charitable status seemingly once depended – has not been entirely lost. Significantly, assistance is offered not in the language of social class but in relation to personal need and individual qualities. These are the terms of reference within which charities traditionally have worked.

An important additional constraint that the courts have imposed upon charities, and that has implications for the admissions policies of private schools, is that they must be non-profit-making bodies if they wish to avoid the payment of taxes. In his penetrating analysis of the case of Brighton College v. Marriott (1926, AC 192-204), Jones has shown that the Act of 1842, which exempted public schools from paying tax on profits from buildings, rents and lands, was restricted in its focus:

> The law, however, recognised only a handful of schools as 'public'. They were the old endowed foundations known collectively as the 'Great Schools'... . The rest, most notably those public schools founded during Victoria's reign, were ineligible. Many were proprietary schools, founded on the

joint-stock principle, and in every way a business. Some even became limited liability companies. As a class they were highly successful, and a few managed to rival the 'Great Schools'. The exclusive privilege of tax exemption remained, however, beyond their grasp. They were deemed in law to be carrying on a trade, so profits, if any, were liable to tax (Jones, 1983, 122-3).

Jones goes on to document how after a protracted legal battle, fought on behalf of Brighton College between 1914 and 1926, the law was changed. If the primary purpose of a school is to be a profit-making venture then it cannot claim charitable status. However, if the school's primary purposes are charitable (for example, the provision of a sound Christian education) then it may accrue profits (a secondary purpose) as a consequence of its primary purposes.

Invariably the schools that have charitable status devote their income, including their profits, to the pursuit of their primary goals. Indeed, in the case of Brighton College there were legal and statutory requirements to prevent it from applying its income and property to any other purpose than the provision 'of a sound education in accordance with the principles of the Church of England' (Jones, 1983, 123; Jones is quoting from Brighton College's Council Minute Book). Furthermore, a school might refrain from charging fee levels which it knows the market will bear, or, alternatively, it might direct some of its income, including its fee income, towards providing scholarships and bursaries. Either could have the effect of widening the social base of the schools. Were they to lose their charitable status some schools might reduce such commitments: partly because of the loss of income, and partly because they might feel less constrained to act charitably if they were no longer considered to be charities. It is difficult, however, to predict behaviour in such hypothetical circumstances. Moreover, it should be remembered that scholarships and bursaries confer benefits upon the schools, as well as upon the individuals who are awarded them: scholarships because they bring to the school talented pupils, and bursaries because they can minimise the financial loss to the school by supporting pupils whose parents may temporarily find themselves in unforeseen straitened circumstances.

The fee-paying schools, therefore, may be in the marketplace, but, should they have charitable status, their behaviour is constrained by the courts. In effect it is a market managed by the judges who establish the parameters within which the schools have to function. By weakening the relationship between poverty and charity, the courts have relaxed the constraints upon the admissions policies of private schools, but they have not altogether abandoned their regulatory powers. Inasmuch as some schools, under the terms of their foundation statutes, can continue to exist only as long as they remain charitable bodies, these are matters that they cannot ignore. Historically, although charitable status may have given the schools a prestigious legal status, with their activities receiving the seal of official approval, the concrete rewards were more limited. However, in the present era, it is the tangible financial benefits of charitable status that are of primary consideration. Although most schools could survive its loss, it would make life more difficult for them. Moreover, it could reinforce the public perception of them as schools exclusively for the privileged members of our society, and, perhaps more importantly, even change their own self-image.

The willingness of the courts to weaken the link between charity and poverty means that the focus of attention in determining charitable activities has to be directed at the service they offer (that is, schooling itself is the charitable purpose), and, to a lesser extent, how they deliver that service. From the perspective of the private schools the terms of the popular (as opposed to the legal) debate as to what constitutes charitable action needs to be changed. The question is whether the schools are capable of restructuring the arguments in a way that closes the gap between the commonsense and legal under-standings of charity. Alternatively, they can argue that, even in terms of the commonsense understanding of charity, they come closer to fulfilling the criteria than their critics are prepared to admit. The obvious way to build on this claim is through the extension of their scholarships. However, the traditional image of the schools as elite institutions makes this a difficult course of action to pursue. Can the public, therefore, be persuaded that it is right to make the purpose itself, rather than those who benefit from the purpose, the object of charity? As a supporting argument, there is the claim that charitable bodies provide their services more effectively and sensitively than state-run institutions. The critics of the charitable status of the fee-paying schools invariably conclude by suggesting that the legal definition of charity needs to conform more closely to its commonsense meaning. But perhaps what we really need is a new commonsense definition.

In an interesting reversal of the argument that charitable status is part of the private sector's ideological defences, Moffat has suggested that the 'charitable status of private schools can be seen as an integral part of a broad support system for the existing definition of charity'

65

(1989, 217). This may indeed be true, but the solidity of that 'broad support system' would be that much firmer if the public at large could be persuaded that private schools are deserving of their charitable status. The question remains as to whether the public's understanding of what is meant by charity can indeed be changed. If it cannot, then one must question how broad that support really is, or, at the very least, for how much longer it is likely to remain broad.

CLASS REPRODUCTION, SCHOOLING AND CHARITABLE STATUS

In his cross-examination of the Charity Commissioners, which formed part of the parliamentary inquiry, *Charity Commissioners and their Accountability*, Christopher Price raised the question of whether there is '... any way of making educational charities, all of which, almost without exception, were founded for the poor and needy, conform to their original statutes?' (Education, Arts and Home Office Sub-committee of the House of Commons Expenditure Committee, 1975, 40). To which he received the cryptic reply: 'Legislation, I would suggest.' Although Price had drawn an interesting interconnection between charitable status and the needs of the poor as prescribed by founders' statutes, he was undoubtedly aware that Parliament itself had been instrumental in breaking the bonds which he apparently wanted to re-establish. As the previous chapter has shown, parliamentary-appointed commissioners helped to change the purposes of the endowed schools by undermining their established patterns of entry.

There are similarities between the values built into founders' statutes, and those upon which the tradition of charitable purposes was established. The most obvious common elements are the recognition of society's duty to help the poor and needy, and the promotion of schooling as a worthy social goal. In the nineteenth century Parliament created the great Royal Commissions which seriously eroded the restrictions that founders had placed upon the entry of the scholarship pupils into their schools, while it was left to the courts to modify the interpretation of charitable purposes. The outcome of the courts' decisions did not, unlike parliamentary action, directly affect admissions, but it did allow the schools, within the framework of the qualifications discussed above, to retain their charitable status almost regardless of the social composition of their pupils.

The parliamentary-sponsored reforms were a recognition that secondary schooling of the first grade was dependent upon a school's ability to break restrictive local ties, to recruit pupils on a national basis, and to develop pedagogical practices that appealed to the more prosperous segments of the bourgeoisie. The reforms, therefore, broke the established links, or reaffirmed newly emerging links, between the schools and their social base. Hesitantly Parliament concluded that if the endowed schools were to prosper then founders' intentions had to be overruled; that the long-term interests of the schools were more important than founders' prescriptions. Similarly, the shift in the courts' interpretation of charitable purposes meant that the schools could acquire the benefits of charitable status regardless of whom they educated. Schools would be charities because of the functions they performed; their legal status was not dependent upon whom they educated.

The undermining of foundation statutes, which had given rights to poor and needy children, was accounted for by the fact that the schools had assumed a new and enhanced importance in the reproduction of the social order. If they were to perform this changed role then it was necessary to undermine traditional claims; that is, the rights of the schools as ongoing institutions were asserted against the claims of the community at large. In more concrete terms this was a political struggle in which schooling became a valuable resource in the perpetuation of class advantages. In a complementary process, once the link between charity and poverty had been eroded by the courts, then the endowed schools could perform their new role without harming their legal status, that is without losing their institutional privileges. A parallel process was at work in the rewriting of founders' statutes and in the reinterpretation of the meaning of charitable purposes. A shared value system, therefore, came under attack from similar social developments, with the changes taking place over very much the same period of time. But it is important to stress, as the legal and political struggles illustrate, both the longevity and fragility of this process. Cannell's study (1981) demonstrates the point perfectly with reference to the conflict between St. Paul's School and the Charity Commission between 1860 and 1904.

In fact, the court decisions on charitable status were evolving before the reform of founders' statutes instigated by the Newcastle, Clarendon and Taunton Commissions. If the case of Attorney-General v. Lonsdale, 1827 is seen as a seminal development in the history of charitable purposes (notwithstanding Moffat's caution), the courts were ahead of Parliament by some decades – and it should not be forgotten that founders' statutes were also being directly revised by court action *before* Parliament speeded up the process. The courts were responding to changed circumstances sooner than Parliament because they had the right to act, and because action could be instigated by the interested parties. Of course, there was the possibility that other concerned parties would mobilise to prevent change, as the repeated attempts to reform the statutes of Manchester Grammar School demonstrate, but this is an inevitable part of the judicial process. In contrast, for Parliament to act, political sentiment on a wide front had to be generated, and it took literally decades to achieve this. Even then, as the history of the Royal Commissions illustrates, the outcome was far from certain. However, it is important not to underestimate the valiant efforts of the Charity Commissioners as they struggled to implement the spirit of the recommendations that had been agreed by the various commissions of inquiry.

While the courts' redefinition of charitable purposes, accompanied by the limited redrafting of founders' statutes, can be understood in these narrow terms, the significance of contemporary educational developments should not be overlooked. Partly as a consequence of the inability of the established endowed schools to break the hold of founders' statutes, new private schools were established, and subsequently flourished. A combination of legally and politically sponsored change was reinforced by the creation of new foundations as an emerging bourgeoisie channelled its financial resources into schools designed to serve its purposes. Many of the new foundations were first-grade secondary schools charging fees that would undoubtedly exclude the poor. Even if they were not schools for 'the sons of gentlemen', they were undoubtedly schools for the well-to-do.

In the course of examining the redrafting of founders' statutes it was possible to point to many examples of the expression of explicit class interests at work. It is more difficult to discover such overt sentiments in the courts' reinterpretation of charitable purposes. The judicial language refers to precedents, interprets precisely how the judgments of the past are to be understood, and how fine distinctions between seemingly very similar cases are to be made. This is not the stuff of class conflict. But, while we may lack the blood and thunder of, for example, some of the evidence to the commissions, it should not be assumed that the social consequences are any less significant. Indeed, given the steady extension of taxation, the private schools value their charitable status highly. In fact the balance between the interests of fee-payers and free scholars had been decided long before the nineteenth century in favour of the former, and the changes instigated by the commissions were the icing on the cake.

It is not intended to accuse the courts of being motivated by class bias, but rather to argue that the courts – for all their alleged independence – were also part of a social movement which led to the more refined restructuring of English education along class lines. Even if the courts had wished otherwise, and it is obvious from the protracted struggle to break the link between charity and poverty that several judges *did* wish otherwise, it is hard to see how the courts could have acted differently. The commissions that reformed founders' statutes were set up partly because the courts had proved so tardy in the matter. The increasingly dominant political forces wanted Parliament to legislate where the courts had failed to act. In such a context, if the courts had attempted to reaffirm the link between charity and poverty, it is possible that Parliament would have been persuaded to have acted more swiftly. The courts would have been threatening a wide range of educational interests with powerful political connections, and it is difficult to imagine that these would have been easily placated by judicial niceties.

The courts were caught up in the process of making an acceptable form of education available to the new middle classes; this, as the writings of Matthew Arnold show, was a pressing political issue in mid-Victorian England. For the various commissions the resolution of the problem depended upon the creation of differing grades of secondary schools which recruited along class lines and offered appropriate forms of schooling. The role of the courts was to reinforce this process, which they did partly by permitting changes to founders' statutes, and partly by defining schooling in general as a charitable purpose. Thus, after some lengthy struggles, issues of access were resolved, and the schools were left to determine their purposes without the fear of threats to their legal status.

The courts' redefining of charitable status was part of a broad movement for social change which restructured the traditional links between access to education, the legal and social status of schools, and the role of education in the process of social reproduction. While a school's success was determined by its ability to attract a continuous supply of fee-paying pupils, its charitable status ensured institutional advantages that would prove increasingly helpful in a competitive marketplace. While there were schools, such as Brighton College, which prospered without charitable status, it must have been unsettling to concede financial advantages to schools pursuing similar social and pedagogical goals, especially in times of economic crisis. Cementing the links of access, school status and social reproduction were the appropriate pedagogical forms which were defined as much by the broad socio-cultural characteristics of the schools as by their formal curricula. Those who seek to re-establish a relationship between poverty and charity are in effect seeking to restructure the social purposes of schooling. It is not simply a question of access – as no doubt Price would concur – but about the wider role of schooling in present-day society.

TO ABOLISH OR TO EXTEND CHARITABLE STATUS?

Without a new political input, notwithstanding the recent ruling of the Charity Commission on educational trusts (see p.163), the understanding of what constitutes a charitable purpose will not change in the foreseeable future. Cases may reach the courts which require judgements on matters of interpretation, but there will not be a change in underlying principles without legislation. While there has been some disquiet with respect to how certain charities are administered, there is no great pressure for changing the understanding of charitable purposes, and little evidence to suggest that this state of affairs is about to end. Those who have expressed displeasure at the pragmatic and piecemeal fashion in which charity law has been built up over the years may be dismayed, but there is no great ground swell in favour of reform, and presumably if there were, it would be on the political agenda.

If change on a broad front is unlikely, this leaves open the question of whether it is possible to act on the narrow front of the fee-paying schools. At the time of writing the Labour Party is committed to reviewing their charitable status. In the unlikely event of the party promising in its general election manifesto to end this supposed privilege, and given sufficient political will, there is no reason why it should not be terminated comparatively swiftly by a Labour government. However, even with this restricted focus, the hazards are significant.

The legislation would be hotly contested, possibly including a challenge in the European courts (ISIS, 1982, 1991). It would have to be drafted in a manner that hit only the intended targets, for the Labour Party has always maintained that it has no wish to affect adversely the interests of those schools catering for children with special educational needs. Inevitably the Conservative Party would promise to rescind the legislation, with the consequence that charity law would become politically divisive. Perhaps, sooner or later, such a development cannot be avoided, but the ramifications need to be considered carefully. It opens up the prospect of governments of differing political persuasions selecting their own favourite targets with all the institutional uncertainty that this would engender. Obviously, it would be the prerogative of a government contemplating such action to evaluate the overall balance of gains and losses, but no one has suggested that the ending of their charitable status would sound the death-knell for the private schools. Generally speaking, the likes of Brighton College prospered without the benefits of charitable status. If the withdrawal of charitable status meant that the schools became even more socially exclusive, it might make it politically easier to pursue a direct line of action. But these are difficult calculations.

To restrict charitable status to only those fee-paying schools that cater exclusively to children with special educational needs would be to refine the present relationship between charity and schooling. While not recreating the link between charity and poverty, it would suggest that for charitable status to be granted the character of those who receive the service would have to be taken into consideration. The poverty link points to the *social* character of the recipients, whereas the link to special educational needs points to their *personal* requirements. The question then would be to ascertain which personal needs would merit the award of charitable status and which would not. It is difficult to imagine that detailed legislation could be drafted tightly in these terms, and one can envisage the court cases which could arise as the judges were called upon to interpret Parliament's will. An interesting parallel case is the Labour Party's desire to end the current assisted places scheme for academically gifted pupils, coupled with its commitment to continuing support for those with a special talent for the performing arts. The question again would be which personal characteristics deserve state support, and which do not.

An alternative strategy to redefining what forms of schooling are entitled to charitable status would be to vary the benefits that are associated with it. Thus, some schools could be defined in law as charities but have the established financial benefits denied them. This would have the advantage of allowing schools that can exist in law only as charitable trusts to continue (Gladstone, 1982, 145). But the obvious problem remains of determining on what basis the line between the different kinds of charities is to be drawn. If, as Ben Whitaker argued in his Minority Report to the Goodman Committee, charitable status should not be granted to bodies whose benefits are restricted by costly fees (National Council of Social Services, 1976,

146), then this could even exclude a few schools catering to those with special educational needs; they would be denied the accolade, as well as the associated financial benefits, of charitable status.

In the recent favourable political environment the private sector interests have been under less pressure to justify their charitable status. But with the approach of a general election, conjuring up the distinct possibility of another Labour government, the appearance of defensive articles can be expected to proliferate. There are two well-established lines of argument. The first is to stress the assistance that many schools make towards the payment of fees, and the second is to argue that they already contribute positively to their local communities, including the help they give to maintained schools (Devlin, 26 August 1983, 4; ISIS, 1991; Jewell, 20 January 1992, 32). A common theme in these arguments is to urge the extension of both activities, along with the need to publicise them more widely. Although such suggestions may be viewed as mere political expediency, they do imply that morally, if not legally, the provision of schooling is *not* within itself sufficient grounds for the granting of charitable status. The implication is that the schools have to demonstrate their public benefit through the assistance they give to needy pupils, and their positive input into the local communities. It is hard not to recall, with a certain amount of irony, those nineteenth-century conflicts in which the schools fought to loosen their local ties, and to recruit not the community's 'poor and needy' scholars, but fee-paying pupils drawn from the nation at large. Moreover, the usual questions would emerge as to precisely whom the schools are helping, and how deeply embedded are their local roots.

While internally stimulated reform may make good political sense, it also betrays some unease that not all the interests within the private sector are comfortable with its charitable status. Such moves may help the private sector interests to convince themselves that they are actually earning their charitable status, and if they are successful at getting the message across to a broad spectrum of opinion, it may also help to close in the public's mind the gap between the legal and commonsense understandings of charitable purposes. On the one hand, the charitable status of private schools is protected by a broad understanding of charity that the courts have come to support; on the other hand, to thwart possible political interference with the courts' interpretation it is felt necessary to associate the schools with the narrower, more traditional understanding of charity. However, while such manoeuvring is to be expected, the outcome of the struggle will be determined by broader political developments, in particular the realignment of forces within the Labour Party and the restructuring of its electoral image. In political terms the schools' internal reforms are of marginal importance.

While the abolition of the charitable status of private schools would undoubtedly seriously inconvenience much of the independent sector, it would not lead to a radical restructuring of the relationship between the maintained and private sectors of schooling. The most likely prognosis is that such a development would push up costs, probably result in the closure of some schools, and make independent schooling somewhat more socially exclusive. In recent years there have been some interesting suggestions that charitable status could be extended to all schools (Mountfield, 1991). Grant-maintained schools, city technology colleges and the new technology/language colleges either have, or can apply for, charitable status, and even schools ineligible for recognition as charities can establish charitable trusts to augment their funding. Whether such developments are to be welcomed or not, it is a trend that could revolutionise the contemporary system. The charitable status of most private schools ensures that they are not independent of the state's financial tentacles, while to extend charitable status to all maintained schools would inevitably make them increasingly dependent upon funding from society, which – in most cases – would mean direct contributions from the pupils' parents.

Although discounting the argument that there are legal constraints upon using charitable money to meet statutory requirements, Mountfield agrees that there may be political and/or ethical objections (1991, 24). There is a powerful body of opinion that formal schooling should be one of the state's primary social responsibilities. The perceived danger of making schools charities is that governments will try to cut expenditure on education in general so restricting the state's obligations to its citizens. Moreover, it is also likely that inequalities in resourcing between schools would actually increase. If this were to occur, then the effect could be declining educational opportunities in the less well-resourced schools. One of the pressures for expanding the role of the state was to increase the educational opportunities of the more disadvantaged members of society. Alternatively, what could occur is a general rise in educational funding; with an increase in *all schools* coupled with an intensification of the funding differentials *between schools*. What impact this would have on patterns of educational opportunity is more problematic, but undoubtedly it would stimulate political conflict.

Although Mountfield's book adopted an essentially neutral posture, simply asking whether state schools are indeed 'a suitable case for charity', it does suggest a strategy for helping to break the established mould. The issues that have to be addressed are: how best to encourage the enhanced societal input; how to ensure that an increasing societal input does not simply replace a declining public input; and how to minimise the possibility of greater inequalities emerging between schools. While the problems associated with these issues may be formidable, and their resolution unlikely to command a universal consensus, the alternatives are even less appetising: stagnant funding, stringent accountability mechanisms, and more central control. Whereas the politically radical perspective of the past was to deny charitable status to private schooling, a more appropriate radical perspective for the future is to extend it to all schools; to encourage them to develop their institutional autonomy and to become more accountable to society and less dependent upon the state. We will return to these issues in the penultimate chapter.

CONCLUSION

The social forces that led to the redefining of the statutes which founded the public schools also resulted in a broader understanding of the idea of charitable purposes. Whereas the former change was led by Parliament, the latter was, for the most part, under the control of the courts, where it still remains. Both changes were a manifestation of the values of a new age, which in the case of the public schools meant that there was a more explicit recognition of the particular class interests they served, and that, moreover, they could serve those interests without forgoing the benefits of their charitable status.

A series of legal decisions steadily eroded the links between the relief of poverty and the pursuit of a charitable purpose. Thus it is the activity, rather than those who benefit from it, which determines whether or not a charitable purpose is being fulfilled. Of course, the courts have laid down ground rules which constrain somewhat the boundaries within which would-be charities can operate. But how constraining these boundaries really are is a matter for debate. Thus charities have to benefit a sufficiently large segment of the population in order to retain their status, but this has not excluded schools that charge very high fees. And, although charities cannot make the pursuit of profit their primary purpose, they can be profit-making bodies. As the chapter has shown, these decisions were not arrived at without considerable opposition within the judicial profession itself, and, furthermore, the process of change was exceedingly protracted. Even today there remain many learned scholars of charity law who want to re-establish the links between poverty and charity, and are prepared to argue that charitable status should be reserved for those institutions whose activities are aimed specifically at assisting the poor.

It is frequently argued by many learned commentators that the courts' decisions have opened up a sharp divide between the legal or technical meaning of charity and its commonsense meaning. Of course, this claim is dependent upon the idea that ingrained in the consciousness of most people is the idea that charity is indeed directed at the relief of poverty. However, those same learned commentators rarely present evidence to substantiate this claim, and one is left to ponder whether their assertion is not more a comment upon their own personal predispositions and values rather than an accurate observation of what most people actually believe. They may in fact be entrapped in an ideological web of their own making.

More important, however, than ascertaining the general understanding of the idea of charity is to decide how the law of charity should evolve in the future. Should the link between poverty and charity be re-established? Should certain schools (or indeed other institutions) be allowed to retain their charitable status in law but not to reap the associated financial rewards? Are these matters best left to Parliament and the political process rather than to the courts and the judicial process? Because the central theme of this book is that schooling should be more the responsibility of society, and less under the control of the state, this chapter has argued against restricting the definition of a charitable purpose. If there is indeed a gap between the legal/technical and commonsense meanings of what constitutes a charitable purpose, it is the latter, and not the former, which should be changed. If governments should feel compelled to intervene, then the purpose should be to broaden the range of schools which can benefit from charitable status. While it is recognised that this could result in a decline in the public funding of schooling, and even greater differentials in the financial support that individual schools receive, these issues need to be tackled directly rather than used as excuses for preventing schools from becoming more entwined in society and less beholden to the state.

4

Uncoupling the Maintained and Fee-paying Sectors: From 1944 to 1976

Educational historians tend to view the inter-war development of the British educational system negatively. In his influential *Education and the Social Order: 1940–1990*, Brian Simon describes the years from 1918 to 1939 as 'a period of stagnation, both economically and educationally' (1991, 25). In similar vein, the Education Group of the Centre for Contemporary Cultural Studies refers to this as a time in which opportunities were excluded and restricted (1981, 47). In view of the economic crisis which developed shortly after 1918, and the prolonged depression of the 1930s, it is difficult to imagine that the political support for educational progress would have been anything but fragile. In the circumstances it was only to be expected that educational expenditure would not be left unscathed. Not only was there the reining-in of financial commitments but also a subtle shift of values implicit in the renaming of free places in secondary schools as special places.

However, this pessimistic perspective has to be weighed against the steady advance of the idea of free secondary education for all. As Simon himself notes, the proportion of free places in secondary schools expanded in the inter-war years from 30 per cent to 46 per cent; which, strangely, Simon calls a 'slight increase' (1991, 26). By 1938 there were also, according to Simon, some 470,000 children in secondary education, 54.2 per cent as fee-payers and 45.8 per cent as free-place pupils (1991, 28). However, the movement towards free secondary education was both uneven and politically driven. As early as 1914 the Labour Party's educational programme was urging that entry to secondary schools should not be dependent upon the payment of fees (Barker 1972, 25). Moreover, in 1919 Bradford had removed fee-paying from its maintained secondary schools, and by the time of the first Labour government eleven local education authorities were pursuing the same policy (Barker, 1972, 53).

The consensus among educational historians deems that we view the movement towards free secondary schooling as progressive, and thus desirable. But, in undoubtedly what remains the best overview of the development of the British educational system in the first half of this century, Olive Banks has made the following powerful observation:

> The Education Act of 1902 drew the aided grammar schools into closer relationship with the State and local education authorities, which were now free to aid secondary as well as technical education. Most of them indeed, in addition to aiding the endowed grammar schools in their area, went on to provide and maintain their own schools. The whole state system of secondary education which grew up between 1902 and 1944 was indeed based upon a fusion between the aided school with its roots in the medieval grammar school and the maintained school, a creation of the local education authorities and the Board out of the higher grade schools (1955, 223–4).

The question was whether this fusion of the two traditions could be preserved, or was even worth preserving. Inevitably the balance of political forces would determine policy outcomes. Although the promotion of free secondary schooling endangered the fused model, for many it was a price worth paying. None the less, the impact of the expansion of free secondary schooling upon the evolving character of the educational system should not be underestimated.

THE 1944 EDUCATION ACT

The 1944 Education Act was the most important piece of social legislation passed by the wartime National government. Jeffreys has argued that the political parties remained sharply divided during the war years on the direction of social reform, and education was one of the few areas where a measure of consensus could be established (1987, 123-44). While the genesis of the legislation may have been the responsibility of the Board of Education's officials (Wallace, 1981, 283–90), its highly successful political management owed much to R.A. Butler, the Board's wartime President. While part of the explanation of Butler's success may have been the legislation's qualities of consolidation, as opposed to innovation (Jeffreys, 1987, 142), it is none the less justly considered to be one of the key landmarks in the development of the nation's educational system.

The political consensus was constructed around four main issues: the raising of the school-leaving age, the creation of a common code of regulations; the enactment of a different relationship between the church schools and the local education authorities (LEAs); and the promise of free secondary education for all. Although it is possible to dissect the 1944 Education Act into its component parts, perhaps its true significance lies in its general underlying message. That is, it both reflected and espoused the values that would pervade the post-war moral and political order (Ranson, 1988, 3–5).

It may be the wisdom of hindsight that enables legislation, which was in essence a series of pragmatic compromises, to become the symbol of a moral code, but there is no reason why the consolidation of piecemeal innovation should not create a whole greater than the sum of its parts. Moreover, the fact that the spirit of the 1944 Education Act survived for so long has helped to consolidate its status, as has the fact that it has been substantially replaced by an educational landmark, that is the 1988 Education Reform Act, whose origins were so very different. The 1944 Education Act was the product of political consensus and commanded the broad sympathy of the interested parties. In contrast, the Education Reform Act of 1988 has been perceived as the creation of a government driven by narrow ideological considerations, and was vilified by much of what that government would have called the Educational Establishment.

Nowhere is the balance between principle and pragmatism in the 1944 Education Act better illustrated than by the decision to incorporate within it the idea of free secondary schooling for all. Given the Labour Party's well-established commitment to the cause, it was obvious that the party would require its inclusion in any legislation as the price of its support. As early as 1922, R. H. Tawney, the party's leading protagonist on educational matters in the inter-war years, had given the issue prime consideration in his *Secondary Education for All*. The early movement of several local education authorities in this direction meant that legislation would merely confirm a developing trend. As significant, however, was the recognition that the forms of secondary education would vary. Historically secondary education had been understood as an academic education closely associated with the grammar and public schools. It was widely argued that it was neither realistic nor desirable that all pupils should receive this form of schooling. In effect, the official intention was to follow the recommendations of the Spens Report (Board of Education, 1938) and to recognise three forms of secondary schooling – grammar, technical and modern – which would operate under a common code.

In fact, many of the local education authorities had been engaged in reorganising their elementary schools, so that pupils over the age of 11 were placed in senior departments. Moreover, the 1918 Education Act had required the local education authorities to offer free elementary schooling, so the pupils in these senior ranks of the elementary schools were not required to pay fees. Under the reorganisation necessitated by the 1944 Education Act, it was these schools that made up the core of the new secondary modern schools. Obviously, it was politically impossible to require their pupils to start paying fees simply because the schools had been redefined as offering a secondary, rather than an elementary, education. It was equally impossible to insist upon a common code of regulations if some maintained secondary schools were to permit the entry of fee-payers, while others excluded them. Furthermore, it would make little sense to argue that pupils were distributed within the secondary system according to the individual's age, aptitude and ability if some parents were in a position to determine otherwise, thanks to their financial circumstances. The maintained grammar schools, therefore, simply could not be allowed to retain their fee-payers.

Obvious as this decision may have been, its importance should not be overlooked. While within itself it did not signify the end of what Banks called the fusion of the medieval grammar school tradition and the higher grade schools of the local education authorities, it marked a real shift in the balance of influence between those two traditions. Grammar schools were a product of society, run by their own governors, often supported by a trust, in control of whom they admitted as pupils and whom they appointed as teachers, and offering a clearly defined academic education. In effect the schools were autonomous institutions, and while the aided or controlled status that they were offered under the terms of the 1944 Education Act may have preserved some of the vestiges of their autonomy, inevitably overwhelming financial dependence upon the public purse made them more accountable institutions.

More important than the change in the legal status of a limited number of schools was the impact this was to have upon the relationship between the maintained and the fee-paying schools. The reforms of the nineteenth century, invariably carried forward by state action, led to a more clearly defined class-based educational system. The majority of children of school age received only an elementary education, provided by either the churches or the school boards, while secondary schooling was graded according to the interests of different segments of the middle classes and priced accordingly. In concrete terms, the traditions that bound the endowed schools to 'poor and needy scholars', and made the relief of poverty central to the idea of charity, were broken.

The increasing demand for secondary education, coupled with the monopoly that the endowed schools initially exercised over its definition, opened up the possibility of eroding significantly the established class basis of schooling. After 1902 the local education authorities either bought places in the established secondary schools or created models which inevitably reflected in some measure their image. One may not have approved of the selection processes this necessitated – invariably involving the ability to pay fees and/or to demonstrate, by whatever dubious means, individual potential – but it did mean, in Banks's language, more of a fused system, with inevitably a measure of class interchange between the elementary schools, both board and voluntary supported, and the secondary schools, both maintained and aided. If, as a result of the 1944 Education Act, fee-payers were to be excluded from the aided endowed secondary schools, then such schools had two choices. Either they would cut their ties with the local authorities, base their financial futures essentially upon their ability to attract a sufficient number of fee-payers, and in the process inevitably become more socially exclusive; or they would join the maintained sector, presumably as voluntary-aided or voluntary-controlled secondary schools, exclude fee-payers and, although this cannot be said with the same certainty, also become less socially diverse – albeit perhaps more socially representative of their local communities.

The decision, therefore, to extend from elementary to secondary schooling the principle that education should be a commodity free of a direct charge to the consumer led to an intensification of the social polarisation between the private and maintained sectors. In the latter half of the nineteenth century many of the endowed secondary schools had seen their long-term interests as best secured by the structuring of admissions along class lines. In the first half of the twentieth century all but the most prestigious segment of the fee-paying sector had become steadily more financially dependent upon the public purse, and had to adjust to the inevitable social consequences of their financial need for free-place pupils.

The principle of free secondary schooling slowly undermined a period of pragmatic adjustment in the relationship between parents, local education authorities and the fee-paying schools. But in the best English tradition, the principle assumed its importance because of the need to establish a political compromise, and because previous decisions had created a situation in which alternative strategies were difficult, even impossible, to implement. Except perhaps within the political left, it is doubtful if there was much support in 1944 for revamping the educational system on the basis of agreed principles – assuming that these *could* be agreed in the first place. Moreover, and most importantly, it was one thing to agree that there should be free secondary education for all, and quite another to decide how it should be implemented.

THE LIMITS TO PRINCIPLED ACTION

Although it was part of the political consensus that fee-paying pupils should be excluded from the endowed grammar schools that were aided by the local education authorities, some Members of Parliament were prepared to fight a rearguard action on their behalf. In his speech opening the Second Reading of the Education Bill, Butler indicated the government's intention to retain the direct grant list ('to preserve tradition and variety') and saw 'no reason why a clean sweep should be made of fees in this limited class of schools' (*Hansard* [Commons], 19 January 1944). He recognised that to insist on the abolition of fees in the direct grant schools could result in some of them leaving the state system, which would 'accentuate social distinctions and widen existing gaps'. The impression is that on this issue Butler was driven by pragmatic, rather than principled, considerations. If it was wrong in principle to permit fee-paying in locally aided grammar schools, the suspicion is that the direct grant schools were not similarly treated because many more of them could refuse their grant and hope to survive as fee-paying schools. None the less, Butler had offered a window of opportunity to his critics within the parliamentary Conservative Party.

During the Committee Stage of the Bill, Sir John Mellor (Tamworth) argued that those endowed schools which in 1926 had opted for local authority support rather than direct financing from the Board should be allowed to continue to charge fees or given the option of being placed on the direct grant list (*Hansard* [Commons], 28 March 1944). In view of the political consensus that sustained the Bill there was no possibility that they would be permitted to charge fees and remain within the state system. But Butler did offer the prospect of some of them being included in a new direct grant list: '... the direct grant list of the future will have to be worked out, and the Government are willing to give guidance to the Committee and to the country as to the principles which govern them in making up that new list'. In fact Mellor had extracted merely a token concession from Butler, one which had already been publicly offered. In the event, a handful of schools were added to the new direct grant list, while a few that had been on the old list opted for financial independence. However, between 1943 and 1952 the number of schools on the direct grant list fell from 232 to 164, which hardly suggests that the direct grant option was much of an escape route for those schools that wanted to evade the clutches of the local education authorities.

The desire to avoid the acceptance of voluntary-aided or controlled status was partly a question of standing (inevitably such schools would be seen as serving no more than very local interests) and partly a question of institutional autonomy. Butler constantly emphasised that there was nothing about controlled status 'which derogates from the dignity or independence of the school', but there were (and still are) deeply ingrained feelings running counter to such a view ('he who pays the piper calls the tune'), as well as specific aspects of school management to suggest the contrary. In her penetrating study of educational change in one local authority, Saran has claimed that even the conditions attached to direct grant status were disliked by the governors of some schools. The governors of one grammar school and the local authority were at loggerheads over admissions: 'The governors were unwilling to give preference to LEA children over potential feepayers who had done better in the school's entrance examination. On competitive grading alone, argued the governors, less than a quarter of the places would be awarded to ex-primary school children' (1973, 237). The differences were so intense that the governors decided to admit only fee-payers – so much for the soothing reassurances of the President of the Board of Education!

Although in his speech on the Second Reading of the Bill, Butler had committed the government to the continuing admission of fee-payers to the direct grant schools, in fact the issue had been resolved only after a protracted battle. Wallace has claimed Butler personally 'accepted that fees should be abolished in all of the non-boarding schools', but it was the opposition from within his own parliamentary party, the schools themselves, and his permanent secretary (Maurice Holmes) that persuaded him otherwise. On the one hand, there was considerable pressure for the government to embrace the principle that all schools in receipt of assistance from public funds should not be allowed to charge fees. On the other hand, there were those who believed that a school's status and autonomy were intrinsically dependent upon its right to admit fee-payers.

Butler had referred the question of fee-paying in the direct grant schools to the Fleming Committee which issued an interim report advocating its abolition (1943). But the Committee had been hopelessly split on the issue (the recommendation had been supported by 11 to 7 members), and even the majority did not want all the places to be at the disposal of the local education authorities. Perhaps the most pointed opposition to the Committee's recommendation came from the Treasury which was expected, via the Board, to pay grants 'to cover both lost fees, and all capital and development costs' (Gosden, 1976, 352). Gosden maintains that Holmes saw this as 'really an astonishing decision' which was wholly repugnant to Treasury opinion.

The obvious compromise position, therefore, was to allow the schools to continue charging fees, revise the direct grant list, and standardise the terms on which the system operated. In effect this is what happened. In spite of the fact that the revised list of direct grant schools was substantially smaller than the old list, it is still pertinent to ask whatever happened to the principle of free secondary education for all. Clearly there needed to be compromises at the margins in order to ensure the successful passage of the Bill as a whole. Butler was too sophisticated a political operator to admit to anything too crass. He argued that the local authorities would be able to reserve the number of places they required in the direct grant schools to meet their needs (*Hansard* [Commons], 28 March 1944). By implication the places available to fee-payers were surplus to the requirements of the local authority, and thus would not affect the rights of those who wanted free secondary schooling. No wonder Butler is probably best remembered for describing politics as 'the art of the possible'.

The new direct grant list was drawn up after the election of the first post-war Labour government, and the replacement of Butler by Ellen Wilkinson at what was now the Ministry of Education. Not surprisingly, some Members of Parliament lobbied hard to ensure that a particular school in their constituency was either included in, or retained on, the list, and there was considerable expression of outraged indignation when a school's request was refused. Partly in order to disarm her critics, the Minister revealed that the criteria guiding her decisions had been drawn up by the Fleming Committee (which had, of course, been appointed by the exalted Butler!): the school's financial stability, the extent of its non-local character, the nature of the education given, and – most significantly in relation to free secondary education – the views of the local authority (*Hansard* [Commons], 9 November 1945).

In some communities, before the 1944 Education Act, the only secondary grammar school education on offer, other than to fee-paying pupils, would be in the direct grant school. Thus, after 1944 some local authorities were heavily dependent upon buying places in the direct grant schools if they wanted to make a secondary grammar school education freely available to the local community. This was why some schools were refused entry to the new list; all their places had to be available to the local authority if it was to deliver on the promise of free secondary education for all. As long as there were varying kinds of secondary schooling, each thought to be suitable for pupils of differing aptitudes and abilities, this was the only way in which the government could fulfil the promise of the 1944 Education Act. Inevitably, therefore, some schools had to make what was for some of them the unenviable decision of either joining the maintained sector with voluntary controlled/aided status or becoming wholly dependent on fee-paying pupils.

As legislation reflects the pragmatic adjustment of moral codes, so it also represents the concrete expression of different values, not all of them mutually reinforcing. The 1944 Education Act can be interpreted as a government-sponsored attempt to extend educational opportunities, and, more debatably, to ensure a greater measure of equality of opportunity. At the time, social class was perceived as the critical divide in British society, and the 1944 Education Act can be interpreted as the official sponsorship of class change. Besides the tension between the extension and the equalisation of opportunities, there was the parallel friction between those who wanted schooling to create a greater measure of social cohesion as opposed to those who saw it as a means of liberating individual talent. To enable individuals to develop their full potential could lead to less, rather than greater, social cohesion. As the post-1945 years unfolded these stresses and strains were brought to the fore in the context of the struggle for comprehensive secondary schooling.

Although all the values implicit in the 1944 Education Act may not have been mutually reinforcing, undoubtedly the Act did confer upon the state, at both local and national levels, greater responsibility for the organisation of the educational system and consequently for the promotion of social goals and values. While there were political differences about the precise extent and character of the state's role, the belief that it should be enhanced did have a broad measure of support. For example, there were local education authorities controlled by the Conservative Party which felt that they could manage the direct grant schools just as effectively as the schools' governors. The governors often received a more sympathetic hearing from the constituency's MP than their local councillors in the struggle over the direct grant list, which helps to explain some of the vitriol in the parliamentary debates.

In spite of the enhanced role assumed by the state after 1944, Section 76 of the Education Act, significantly described as the 'general principle to be observed by Minister and Local Education Authorities', states:

> In the exercise and performance of all powers and duties conferred and imposed on them by this Act the Minister and local education authorities shall have regard to the general principle that, so far as is compatible with the provision of efficient instruction and training, and the avoidance of unreasonable expenditure, pupils are to be educated in accordance with the wishes of their parents (Education Act, 1944, Ch. 31, Section 76).

The Act itself, therefore, set up the possibility of a clash between parents and local education authorities, duty-bound to acknowledge the wishes of parents, while trying to run an efficient and cost-effective service. Furthermore, an earlier section of the Act (9.1) had given the local authorities the right, subject to the approval of the Minister, 'to assist any such school (that is a secondary or primary school) which is not maintained by them'. A potential clash of interests could occur, therefore, at two different levels: between parents and local education authorities, and between the local education authorities and the Ministry. It was not long before conflict broke out within both levels, and indeed, following appeals from parents to the Ministry, between the two levels. In view of the compromises that had emerged in establishing the new direct grant list, it was not surprising that the direct grant schools should figure prominently in many of the most important conflicts. The 1944 Education Act may have enshrined, with due consideration to the necessary political nuances, the principle of free secondary education for all, but the inevitable tension between selection procedures controlled by the local authorities and parental choice would soon demonstrate the fragility of the new order.

PRINCIPLE AND PRAGMATISM IN THE DEFENCE OF
PARENTAL CHOICE

Although the 1944 Education Bill had been welcomed across the broad spectrum of political opinion in Parliament, there was considerable antagonism – confined mainly to the Labour Party benches – to the retention of fee-paying pupils in the direct grant schools. The argument was that all schools in receipt of public funding should be required to exclude fee-payers or forgo their right to financial support from the state. The logical outcome of this position would be two separately financed systems, one dependent upon fee-payers and the other upon the public purse. And yet, as we have noted, certain local authorities needed – at least in the short run – to supplement their provision of secondary grammar school education by buying places in the direct grant schools. Furthermore, Clause 9 (1) of the 1944 Education Act empowered the local education authorities to give sustenance to any primary or secondary school not maintained by them, subject of course to ministerial approval.

Indeed, there were good reasons why local authorities might want to buy into the independent sector, in addition to the direct grant schools, both to fulfil their statutory obligations as well as to enhance parental choice. On well-recognised social grounds certain pupils could require a boarding education, and few local authorities would have sufficient places in their schools to cater for such demands. Also children with special educational needs owing to, for example, physical or mental disabilities might find more stimulating educational environments in specialised, fee-paying schools. In such circumstances some local authorities might have felt it was to everyone's benefit if they were to place certain children in such schools and to underwrite their fees. The children would, it was hoped, receive a richer education, and the local authority would save on capital expenditure. Interestingly, whenever local authorities have purchased places in the fee-paying sector to meet either the social or special educational needs of children (including those who are highly gifted in the performing arts), it has rarely generated any controversy, in sharp contrast to the purchase of places for the academically gifted.

If it is accepted that, perhaps for essentially practical reasons, the local authorities had to purchase a limited number of places in the private sector (at least in the short term), then a somewhat different financial model can be constructed. On the one hand there would be a maintained sector from which fee-payers were barred, and on the other hand a fee-paying sector from which the state purchased places. The extent of the state's purchase could vary according to the segment of schooling under consideration: extensive in the case of the direct grant schools, but perhaps more limited in terms of the traditional public schools. The state's purchase of these places stimulated one of the central debates in the post-1944 history of the British educational system. Should the purchase be restricted, even abolished, in order to curtail class privilege and educational selection? Or should it be encouraged in order to enhance parental choice and stimulate educational diversity? Inevitably, therefore, besides determining how resources will be used, the purchasing decisions have reflected different value positions. With the slow erosion of the political consensus that enveloped the passage of the 1944 Education Act, this polarisation became sharper over time.

Other than the purchase of places in the direct grant schools, it could be argued that the 1944 Education Act sanctioned only very limited state financial support for independent schooling. However, besides the take-up of places by the local education authorities, central government departments – notably the Ministry of Defence and the Foreign and Commonwealth Office – have been prepared to assist their personnel with the payment of school fees. For employees either serving overseas or liable to overseas service, assistance could be justified as it ensured continuity in the schooling of their children. This can be viewed either as one of the perks of the job or a perfectly reasonable obligation for the state to assume. Moreover, by making parental choice such a key principle, the 1944 Education Act ensured that the state's financial input into the private sector was not completely under the control of either the local education authorities or central government. The Act enhanced the ability of parents to exercise their rights, which occasionally they did; sometimes to the embarrassment of both the local and central levels of government.

The principle of parental choice was reinforced by the Education (Miscellaneous Provisions) Act of 1953. This Act permitted the local education authorities to support a pupil in a non-maintained school where they were 'satisfied that, by reason of a shortage of places in schools maintained by them and schools maintained by other local education authorities', this pupil would not receive schooling that was commensurate with his/her age, aptitude and ability. As with the 1944 Education Act, the local authorities were also allowed to purchase places for those who required what was now described as 'special educational treatment'. Again, in keeping with established practice, the purchase of these various places had to be made 'with the approval of the Minister'.

87

In the late 1940s and 1950s, there was little political pressure to disturb these arrangements, but as Saran's superb study of educational change in Middlesex has shown (1973), they became a matter of intense controversy in the 1960s. It is important to remember that this was not simply an ideological struggle fought between the proponents of comprehensive secondary schooling and the defenders of secondary school selection. Long before comprehensive secondary schooling became a divisive political issue, a range of very practical problems started to influence how the local educational authorities viewed the non-maintained sector of schooling. Local authorities, like Middlesex, were expanding their provision of grammar school places, which naturally meant that they could offer more children of secondary school age a grammar school education. The potential repercussions were critically important. Either the grammar schools would remain highly selective, and the places would be left unfilled, which suggested an inefficient pattern of capital expenditure, or the grammar schools would be required to accept pupils of a wider ability range.

While many may have considered the latter course a positive development, not all the grammar school interests were inclined to agree. What also needs to be kept in mind is the knock-on effect upon the secondary modern and secondary technical schools. Certainly it did not appear to make sense for the local authority to buy places in the direct grant and independent schools while there were empty places in the maintained grammar schools. The latter were deprived of talented pupils while the expenditure of the local authority was increased – a twofold public loss.

But what may appear rational in financial and educational terms may not be politically acceptable. Saran's research demonstrates how articulate parents were able to mobilise in defence of their publicly funded privileges. Middlesex's Chief Education Officer had proposed cutting the county's expenditure upon places in non-maintained schools by lowering the number of pupils it was prepared to assist, and by introducing means-tested support. Subsequently the education officials found themselves under fire from, on one front, local councillors obviously responding to forceful representations from irate local parents, and on another front, a less than sympathetic Ministry which seemed intent on defending the direct grant schools on the grounds that these were part of the state's provision of secondary schooling (Saran, 1973, 193–211).

Of course, what has been termed a defence of privilege can be viewed in a very different light: that is, as a defence of a right which has a statutory basis. However, neither the 1944 nor the 1953 Act gave parents an *unrestricted* right to determine the secondary schooling of their children at public expense. The 1944 Education Act required the local authorities to have due regard to 'the provision of efficient instruction and training', and more importantly, to avoid 'unreasonable public expenditure', whereas the 1953 Act argued that 'a shortage of places' in maintained schools was the key criterion. As always, the language of legislation has to be interpreted, and it would not be surprising if the interpretations were, to some extent, shaped by political considerations. Local education authorities could be expected to balance different requirements and, almost certainly, to arrive at different answers from one another and, furthermore, to change their interpretations over time. For example, the work of Royston Lambert shows how the local authorities adopted contrasting definitions of boarding need with the result that their support for boarding education varied widely (1966, 8–14).

While the 1953 Act clearly stated that the local authorities' purchase of places in the non-maintained schools required 'the approval of the Minister', this appears to have become a perfunctory restraint over time. Saran writes:

> Originally the Minister had to approve arrangements made by LEAs to take up places at non-maintained schools, but Circular 350 (issued on 24 March 1959) gave the general approval required under Section 6 of the 1953 Act (1973, 68).

Again, given the general political climate, this development may not have been too surprising, but as the secondary education became more politicised, so it had potentially very significant ramifications. It could act as a loophole through which the local education authorities evaded central government pressure in the move towards comprehensive secondary education. In 1965/66, out of a total income of £90.9 million the independent schools received £9.2 million by way of direct state support, of which £5.4 million was provided by the local education authorities. The direct grant schools were overwhelmingly dependent on the state's input: £14.0 million (of which £5.7 million came from the LEAs) out of a total income of £21.1 million (Glennerster and Wilson, 1970, 30). The ability, therefore, of the LEAs to erode quite substantially the move towards comprehensive secondary schooling was real enough.

Also within the local authorities battles developed between the political parties, which were reflected in their differing reactions to departmental circulars and their alacrity, or otherwise, in using their statutory powers. It was obvious that the direct grant schools would become enveloped in the struggle for comprehensive secondary schooling. It was also equally obvious, given that the 1944 Education Act had sanctioned a form of association between the maintained and non-maintained sectors built mainly upon selection and the grammar school tradition, that the conflict would also embrace the fee-paying schools and the principle of parental choice.

It was partly in order to overcome these conflicts that the Labour government passed the 1976 Education Act which, in spite of being composed of only ten substantive clauses, took up more parliamentary time than the Act of 1944. Clause 1 in effect laid down the principle of comprehensive secondary schooling by forbidding local education authorities to organise admissions to their secondary schools on the basis of 'selection by reference to ability or aptitude'. The legislation then proceeded to incorporate the usual pragmatic exemption for those deemed to require 'special educational treatment', and perhaps surprisingly, also for those with 'ability or aptitude for music or dancing'. In Clause 5, the Secretary of State clawed back those powers apparently lost as a result of Circular 350 (why the Circular could not have been withdrawn and replaced by one more in line with the government's wishes is a moot point). The Secretary of State was empowered to revoke any previous approvals that had been given, and equally controversially, the LEAs could only exercise their power to purchase places in fee-paying schools 'in accordance with arrangements approved by the Secretary of State'.

In view of the fact that Clause 1 of the Act prevented the local authorities from establishing selective admissions procedures to their secondary schools, it seemed likely that the Secretary of State would block any attempt to funnel pupils into the fee-paying sector, except for those with special needs or talent in the performing arts. To approve additional placements would result in a leakage of talent from the maintained sector into schools that were generally academically selective and also charged fees. It is not only that the decisions of the local education authorities required, as under the terms of the 1944 Education Act, the approval of the Secretary of Education, but also that conditions were being laid down which, with very limited exceptions, prevented local education authorities from purchasing places in non-maintained schools. The outcome would depend upon how broadly Ministers interpreted their authority, but undoubtedly the implicit message of Clause 1 of the 1976 Education Act was that they could use the powers granted them in Clause 5 to prevent placements outside the maintained sector that had been determined by an individual's ability or aptitude.

Although the 1976 Education Act may have curtailed the powers of the LEAs, and in the process somewhat restricted parental choice, it was clearly an attempt by the Labour government to bring into line what it considered to be a few recalcitrant authorities. Moreover, if Saran's study was an accurate guide, parental choice had generally worked against the interests of the maintained schools. It could also be argued that the Act made strategic sense. In 1975 the government had issued Statutory Instrument No. 1198 which initiated the phasing out of the direct grant. The 1976 Education Act represented a complementary central push towards the creation of a universal system of comprehensive secondary schooling. The Secretary of State, Fred Mulley, defended Clause 5 as follows: 'This clause will prevent a local authority from seeking to circumvent Clause 1 and using the take-up of independent places as a means to avoid establishing a fully comprehensive system of secondary schooling' (*Hansard* [Commons], 4 February 1976, Volume 904).

With the wisdom of hindsight, it can be reasonably concluded that the mid-1970s represent the high-water mark of the centrally orchestrated push in favour of comprehensive secondary schooling. The 1944 Education Act had, partly in order to enhance parental choice, sought an accommodation between the maintained and fee-paying sectors of schooling, and much of the political context which had brought about its enactnent had supported diversified forms of secondary schooling, based upon selection by age, ability and aptitude. There would be free secondary schooling for all who wanted it but its character would vary. The 1976 Education Act, along with Statutory Instrument 1198, sought to resolve the prevailing value tensions by dividing more sharply the maintained and fee-paying sectors, and by bolstering non-selective forms of secondary schooling. Principle would finally prevail over pragmatism. Or would it?

The 1976 Education Act generated much heat, though arguably not much light, because of its unequivocal support for the principle of comprehensive secondary schooling and the restrictions it placed upon the LEAs which apparently curtailed parental choice. However, the legislation also had its in-built exemption clauses. There was some scepticism about excluding those with particular aptitudes (why these aptitudes?), and there was also a growing awareness (presaging the Warnock Report, 1978), that perhaps those with special educational needs were best served by integrating them into the general educational system. Moreover, for the resourceful local authority, determined to evade the Secretary of State's will, it was not that difficult to justify the purchase of places in the independent sector. For example, the idea of 'boarding need', and the belief that there was a large untapped demand, had been touted for some years by Royston Lambert (Lambert and Woolfe, 1968, 264–9). To suggest that local education authorities could resort to such ruses may sound unduly cynical, but the embittered political context needs to be kept in mind. The demands of the time were such that the official line of the Conservative Party was not to oppose comprehensive secondary reorganisation in principle, but also to support the retention of secondary grammar schools. Logic and common sense suggest that this had more to do with the political exigencies of the day rather than any desire to form a coherent educational policy. The days of a cross-party educational policy consensus had all but evaporated.

Some of the debate in the House of Lords, at the committee stage of the 1976 Bill, illustrates perfectly the continuing political pragmatism. Lord Vaizey (better known for his contribution to the economics of education than to the Lords) moved an amendment which would have forbidden central government departments from paying, in full or in part, school fees '... unless the school to which the payment is ultimately made shall accord with the general principle established by section 1 of this Act' – that is the section designed to prevent selection by ability or aptitude (*Hansard* [Lords], 7 October 1976). Vaizey went on to claim that the parents of some 25,750 children (of whom approximately 20,000 were in independent schools) received allowances which amounted to about £28.5 million per annum. While Vaizey was not opposed to such payments, his point was

> ... that what is desirable at home is desirable abroad; that is to say, if it is illegal for Kent County Council to pay for children to go to an independent school because that school is independent or selective, then I am all in favour of the children of eminent diplomats getting a broader experience in the comprehensive schools of our nation (Col. 1642).

For the government, Lord Donaldson, who professed to have good friends in the diplomatic corps and armed services, offered no substantive objections to Vaizey's logic (one would have hoped that Vaizey himself would have been alive to the potential increase in capital expenditure necessitated by the need to extend boarding opportunities in the comprehensive schools), and simply rejected the proposed amendment, believing that it had gone 'too far in the other direction', by which he appeared to mean to the political left. Good-naturedly, Vaizey agreed to withdraw the amendment, but in the process made the most telling observation: '... there is humbug on this issue'!

In view of the fact that the Labour government was defeated in the 1979 general election, since when there has been a succession of Conservative governments, it is scarcely surprising that the 1976 Education Act had a limited impact. One of the very early pieces of legislation of the first Thatcher government was the 1980 Education Act which, besides repealing the essentials of the 1976 Act, also rescinded those clauses in the 1944 and 1953 Acts which required the local authorities to seek the approval of the Secretary of State when purchasing places in the fee-paying schools. Thus, Mrs Thatcher's government could pose as the champion of local authority autonomy which, in view of later events, may be thought to have something of a hollow ring about it.

It is feasible that if there had not been four successive Conservative governments, the political manoeuvring would have continued. What the longevity of Conservative government has achieved is to place different educational issues at the heart of the political agenda. In recent years the focus has been upon: the expansion and redefinition of higher education; the creation of the national curriculum; the testing of pupils; the emergence of new kinds of secondary schools/colleges (grant-maintained schools, city technology colleges, and technology/language colleges), and the development of a new relationship between the central bureaucracy (now the DFEE), the local education authorities and the schools in which governors and heads have acquired more authority but also increased responsibilities. All this has occurred within a context in which schools are required to focus primarily upon raising educational standards and serving the needs of the economy. To what extent the rights of parents have been increased is debatable. All four consecutive Conservative governments have been reluctant to give the parental input into the admissions process the very radical cutting edge that, for example, a voucher scheme would ensure.

But we have moved away from what had become almost ritualised confrontations on the question of comprehensive secondary schooling, and, excepting a brief spasm of political vitriol which was generated by the assisted places scheme, the question of the relationship between maintained and fee-paying schools has all but disappeared. It is financial, rather than legal or political, considerations that are likely to determine how many places a local education authority purchases in the independent sector; and the sheer scale of the decline in the size of the armed forces probably poses a greater threat to the fee-paying schools than a Labour government. Although it is dangerous to make political predictions, it is hard to imagine that the old issues can be resurrected, or if they are resurrected, that they could assume the same form. The parliamentary debates on the 1976 Bill seem to belong to a different educational age.

CONCLUSION

Although the educational historians have addressed the question of whether the 1944 Education Act was a conservative measure, they have been far more reticent about defining the nature of conservatism. In spite of his failure to offer any clear defining guidelines, Simon is in no doubt:

> The threat of radical change had been held at bay. The 'New Order' in English education, celebrated by Dent and many others, turned out to be the old order in a new disguise (1986, 43; Dent was the wartime editor of *The Times Educational Supplement*).

And in evident sympathy with Simon, Roy Lowe has written: 'The 1944 Education Act itself was in the longer-term perspective merely a part of an essentially conservative reaction to the traumas of wartime' (1992, 15). In view of the established tradition of educational change in Britain, coupled with the balance of political power within Parliament during the war years, could the Act have been anything other than a cautiously progressive measure? But to label it as conservative is not to demean its qualities, as it is clearly demonstrated by McCulloch's insightful portrayal of the Act as a civic project (1994).

However, while recognising its essentially consolidating character, the purpose of this chapter has been to argue that the 1944 Education Act represented a further stage in the breaking up of the fused model of the English educational system, with secondary schooling as its particular focus of change. Central to this model was the close association between the secondary schooling of fee-paying and free-place pupils. After 1944 the interaction of the free-place and fee-paying traditions was continued on the narrow fronts of the direct grant schools, and the limited purchase of places in the private sector by central departments of government and the local authorities. Such purchases were usually justified on the grounds that some pupils needed a boarding education or had special educational requirements, and were reinforced by the statutory obligation of the local education authorities to take into account the wishes of parents. Failure to act on the proposals of either the Fleming or the Newsom Reports meant that the association between the two sectors remained restricted. Indeed, with the phasing out of the direct grant from the mid-1970s, and the passage of the 1976 Education Act, the two sectors appeared on the verge of a final and complete separation.

Although post-1944 the interaction between the fee-paying and maintained sectors was restricted, none the less the forms it took were the target of prolonged political confrontation. Compromise between the two major political parties had led to the 1944 Education Act, including the maintenance of the direct grant schools, but once the Labour Party embraced the principle of comprehensive secondary education, it was inevitable that the days of the direct grant system were numbered, and the purchase of places in the fee-paying sector would come under close scrutiny. In terms of the number of schools, and pupils directly affected, these were minor issues, but the principles at stake were critical. At the political level, much of the debate centred upon the questions of selection and parental rights. Important as these might be, they emerged within a broader context, that is what the relationship between state and society should be in shaping the character of secondary schooling. In effect two contrasting traditions in the history of British education were working themselves out, not to complement and reinforce one another positively, but in a negative juxtaposition.

In spite of all the changes that have occurred since the Second World War this legacy of the past, exacerbated by the pragmatic political compromises built into the 1944 Education Act, remains unresolved. If a broader and closer association is to be established between the two educational sectors then it has to be a settlement that neither unduly favours one over the other (as the assisted places scheme does) nor seeks to penalise one in the expectation that the other will benefit (as was at least the implied message of the 1976 Education Act). Can the conundrum be resolved? Is it worth trying to resolve?

5

The Fleming Committee, the Public Schools Commission and the Frustration of Good Intentions

The relationship between the state and private schooling in Britain has been essentially pragmatic. In the nineteenth century the church schools were supported by grants from the Exchequer, and the 1870 Education Act legislated for local school boards to establish elementary schools only where there was no adequate provision already in place. The 1902 Education Act brought about both an expansion of maintained secondary schools and an increasing purchase, at the ratepayers' expense, of places in the fee-paying schools. This pragmatic relationship has served both the state and the schools reasonably well. State moneys secured the financial stability of many schools whose existence otherwise would have been precarious. Moreover, by enabling talented children from often humble backgrounds to attend fee-paying schools, the state enhanced the academic status of the private sector. On the other hand, there was a political pay-off from helping such children to attend what were often prestigious local secondary schools. Moreover, buying into an existing system meant that large-scale capital expenditure could be avoided, at least in the short run.

Inevitably pragmatic relationships find it difficult to withstand ideological pressure. As the twentieth century unfolded, there was increasing opposition to the fact that many secondary schools were kept solvent by public money, yet still allowed access to fee-payers. The previous chapter explored how the 1944 Education Act forced the schools to make a choice: either to join the maintained sector (possibly with voluntary-aided or voluntary-controlled status) and end the charging of fees, or to become fully independent institutions in the sense that all their pupils would be fee-payers. Thereafter the pragmatic relationship between the maintained and private sectors was continued on a narrower foundation: local education authorities could purchase places either in response to the special needs of certain children or under pressure from those exercising their right of 'parental choice', the central state was prepared to assist in paying the fees of its personnel liable to overseas postings, and both central government and the local authorities continued to support some 170 direct grant schools.

However, not all the political traffic was in the same direction. There have been two serious official attempts in this century to establish a closer association between the fee-paying schools and the maintained sector: the Fleming Committee which issued an interim report in 1943 and its main report in 1944, and the Public Schools Commission which reported in 1968 (the Newsom Report) and 1970 (the Donnison Report). Both the Fleming Committee and the Public Schools Commission divided their briefs into two broad categories: the independent boarding schools, and the direct grant/independent day schools. The 1943 Report of the Fleming Committee, because it was directed at the narrow question of the future of the fee-payers in the direct grant schools, has been considered briefly in the previous chapter. Its 1944 Report tackled the wider question of the long-term relationship between the state and the fee-paying schools in general. More conveniently, the Reports of the Public Schools Commission had specific targets: the Newsom Report concentrating on the independent boarding schools and the Donnison Report on the direct grant/ independent day schools.

In broad terms, the next two chapters will follow the division established by the Public Schools Commission. This chapter will analyse the political context within which the two inquiries were established. It will compare and contrast how the Fleming Committee and the Newsom Report understood the future relationship between the state and the independent boarding schools, and analyse why their proposals were not implemented. Chapter 6 will focus upon the collapse of the direct grant tradition and its replacement by the assisted places scheme. Both of these chapters examine past attempts to create a different relationship between the state and fee-paying schools. What lessons can be learnt from those attempts? In particular, what political preconditions are necessary if a new relationship is to be realised? These are the concerns of Chapter 7.

THE CONTEXT OF REFORM

Both Fleming's Committee on Public Schools, and the two reports of the Public Schools Commission, emerged within historical circumstances that placed strong emphasis upon the need to extend equality of educational opportunity. The Fleming Committee has to be evaluated in the light of the 1943 White Paper *Educational Reconstruction* which prepared the way for the 1944 Education Act, while the Public Schools Commission was a product of Circular 10/65 which outlined government proposals for the reorganisation of secondary schooling along comprehensive lines. Even if one is unimpressed by the argument that squeezing fee-payers out of grammar schools or encouraging local education authorities to integrate secondary schooling would actually enhance educational opportunities, there is no denying the contemporary strength and political impact of such sentiments.

In the latter years of the Second World War, as well as in the 1960s, the feeling that Britain was about to enter 'a brave new world' was widely (although perhaps not very deeply) felt. The 1940s stressed the need to maintain the apparent sense of social cohesion that had seen the nation through the war, while the 1960s promised a technological revolution that would blow away a stagnant, class-stratified society. In both decades the educational system was perceived as the handmaiden of change – it would bring the nation to the promised land. Inevitably, in both contexts there were questions about where the public schools were to fit into the scheme of things. Many felt that the schools were socially divisive institutions which both caused and perpetuated class stratification. Others claimed they were attached to an outmoded curriculum, while they reaffirmed socio-cultural values that were highly inappropriate for a small nation struggling to compete effectively in a global economy in the latter half of the twentieth century. They had either to change or to go.

Of course high politics and grand social developments inevitably have their seamier sides. As the Fleming Report makes clear:

> Our Committee was set up in response to a request made to the President of the Board of Education jointly by the Governing Bodies' Association and the Headmasters' Conference, both of which had been considering for some time previously by what means the Schools which they represented could be of service to a wider range of pupils (1944, 2).

While the motives of the governors and heads may have been noble, Gosden's more sanguine judgement is hard to ignore:

> In the later 1930s many public boarding schools were faced with falling numbers of pupils, sagging fee income and increasing financial difficulties. The establishment of the Fleming Committee came about not so much in an endeavour to 'democratise' the public schools – even though that appeared to many to be its purpose – but rather out of an attempt to find a politically acceptable way of bringing state-supported pupils, and therefore public money, to the salvation of the financially unstable and threatened boarding schools (1976, 332–3).

Perhaps this was yet another of those situations in which the individuals involved were fortunate enough to discover a convenient marriage between their self-interest and their social duties.

In an excellent overview of the history of HMC between 1919 and 1945, Laurence Le Quesne neatly encapsulates the differing perspectives by means of pertinent quotes from two leading headmasters of the day. In 1939, at the Conference's AGM, Robert Birley – then headmaster of Eton College – put the pragmatic argument concisely and bluntly: 'We are over-capitalised, we have got room for more boys, and to have more boys is the only solution' (Le Quesne, 1970, 10). But the very next speaker, P. H. B. Lyon of Rugby School, remarked: 'I think that all of us in our hearts are longing for the barriers of class and wealth, which at present keep the advantages we have to offer out of the reach of so many of the best boys in the country, to be destroyed.'

Thus, the Fleming Committee, while emerging within the context of the 1944 Education Act, can be seen as an attempt by the schools to preserve their sectoral interests. They needed to explore what compromises they would be called upon to make if, in order to ensure their survival, they were to receive more resources from the state. Could mutually acceptable deals be struck? Or would the terms of exchange be so unreasonable that no bargains were possible? Although the differing sentiments expressed by Birley and Lyon were not mutually exclusive, it does not automatically follow that their respective positions could be bridged.

The events leading to the creation of the Public Schools Commission appear to have been less under the control of the schools. After Circular 10/65, the central issue was whether Wilson's Labour government would have the political will to establish an all-embracing system of comprehensive secondary schooling, or whether it would be politically expedient to tread softly. None the less, it would be wrong to see the schools as completely passive players. Although in the 1960s internal change was under way, the private sector remained in a very defensive frame of mind, and Rae's 'public school revolution' was far from complete. The schools would be making their case to the commission in a political environment that appeared increasingly hostile to them. It was especially important to defend the interests of the direct grant schools, which received most of their income not from their fee-payers but from the state. To this end, the schools were part of an effective lobby which persuaded the Wilson government to broaden the commission's terms of reference: that is, to incorporate the direct grant and independent day schools as well as the independent boarding schools. As a consequence it would be impossible to terminate the direct grant arrangements before a major public airing of the relevant issues.

It would be wrong to see all this low-level political manoeuvring as stemming from the private sector interests alone. Indeed, both the Fleming Committee and the Public Schools Commission can be seen as essentially political exercises, established not to suggest purposeful policies but rather as delaying tactics which would obviate the need for government action. In the case of the Fleming Committee, the then President of the Board of Education came close to admitting as much. Butler referred to the public schools as a first-class carriage which had been placed on a convenient railway siding while the National government got on with the more important business of reforming the maintained sector (1971, 120). The fear was that his prospective legislation would have enough thorny issues to deal with – notably reaching a settlement with the churches – and that one additional major controversy could destroy the whole Bill. His strategy was a great success, for the contemporary parliamentary debates are replete with references to the effect that no action was possible on the public schools until the Fleming Committee had reported.

Again in the 1960s, while many elements in the Labour Party felt that the public schools posed problems which their government should tackle, there was no policy consensus. At one extreme, there were those who believed that if the quality of maintained schooling was steadily improved demand for places in the private sector would steadily decline. The problem would be conveniently resolved, thus undermining the case for potentially damaging political action. At the other extreme were those who called for the abolition of the private sector, although what this meant in precise terms was not always clear. In such circumstances it obviously made sense to remove the issue – albeit temporarily – from the political agenda while proceeding to fulfil more easily attainable, and arguably more significant, parts of the party's educational programme. Once again the tactic of establishing a commission of inquiry presented itself as the convenient stop-gap measure.

It can be seen, therefore, that the reform of the public schools has generated the usual combination of high and low politics, of grandiose visions of Britain's future social order and the tactical political manoeuvring designed to ensure institutional self-interest and government harmony. Even if one accepts that it is naive to see either the Fleming Committee or the Public Schools Commission as clarion calls to action, it should not be assumed that they were no more than convenient tactical devices. As we shall see, the recommendations of the Second Report of the Public Schools Commission (produced under the chairmanship of Professor David Donnison) were followed closely by a subsequent Labour government. However, what the contexts that generated these reports throw into question is the *depth* of the commitment to change. In particular it could be argued that the commissions were created, not because governments lacked policy options or even the mechanisms to resolve policy differences, but because of a failure of political will. Action was too politically expensive. On the other hand, if the motivation of the private sector – with particular reference to its support for the creation of the Fleming Committee – was essentially financial, then one could expect that once market conditions changed the desire for reform would be quickly dissipated.

THE LANGUAGE OF ASSOCIATION AND INTEGRATION

As is to be expected, a committee of inquiry's tone and recommendations are influenced strongly by its terms of reference. Butler, as President of the Board of Education, required the Fleming Committee to act within the following guidelines:

> To consider means whereby the association between the Public Schools ... and the general educational system of the country could be developed and extended... (1944, 1).

To this end the committee made one key recommendation regarding the purchase of places in the independent boarding schools: there would be a new scheme to permit local education authorities to reserve places in boarding schools (a minimum of 25 per cent of admissions in the first instance). These places, both tuition and boarding costs, would be means-tested with parental shortfalls met by the local authorities. The local authorities would receive grants from the Board on their expenditure. Naturally it was expected that the residue of places would be filled by fee-paying pupils (1944, 63–7). For the Fleming Committee, therefore, the key to promoting association was to encourage, with the use of state resources, a continuous and reasonably substantial transfer of pupils from the maintained sector to the private sector of schooling.

The first report of the Public Schools Commission (the Newsom Report) was directed by the following central reference:

> The main function of the Commission will be to advise on the best way of integrating the public schools with the State system of education (1968, vii).

Even if the language is almost equally nebulous (integration compared with association), it is evident that the terms of reference of the Newsom phase of the Public Schools Commission have a sharper edge. However, the Newsom Report conspicuously failed to translate this into more radical proposals. The central recommendation was that, over a period of approximately seven years, each independent boarding school willing to enter a new integrated sector of schooling should fill at least half of its places with assisted pupils from maintained schools (1968, 8). In effect, this was a simple doubling of the percentage that had been recommended by the Fleming Committee. However, the Fleming Committee had seen 25 per cent as a minimum target to be offered in the first instance, as opposed to Newsom's goal of 50 per cent, building up possibly over seven years. Moreover, both reports rejected the argument that places should be awarded on the basis of competitive academic examinations, although the Newsom Report clearly felt the need for a qualifying examination. Again both reports accepted that the schools should be able to reject applicants (so sustaining one of the hallmarks of their independence), but saw rejections as exceptional events which would require monitoring.

The most significant overlap in the two reports was the stress upon the importance of offering places to pupils who needed them. Whereas for the Fleming Committee need was understood in terms of 'the capacity of the pupil to profit by education in the school' (1944, 100), for the Newsom inquiry it was dependent upon individual social and academic circumstances, and it seemed to assume that pupils in such circumstances would automatically benefit from a boarding education (1968, 11). But clearly there would be no point in a child attending a boarding school unless, at the very least, he or she could cope with its demands; hence Newsom's contention that places should be restricted to those with a measure of academic ability.

Both the Fleming and Newsom Reports are, therefore, speaking the language of association. The distinction between the two emerges from their differing implied understandings of the likely consequences of a period of association. Important sections of the Fleming Report (1944, 45–50) were devoted to presenting the advantages of a boarding education. While there is no explicit rejection of the idea that the boarding schools needed to change in response to their potentially wider social intake, equally there is little serious discussion as to whether the schools actually should change. It is as if the blessings of a prized form of education were to be extended to a wider range of the population. To a considerable extent this perspective is dependent upon the committee's narrow understanding of 'need': pupils have a need if they could benefit from the schools' education but are currently denied it by their financial circumstances. The Fleming Committee wanted the state to broaden access by providing the financial resources, but otherwise would leave the schools essentially untouched.

In contrast, the Newsom Report accepted that the culture of the boarding schools would, and indeed should, change as they moved towards accepting an entry composed of 50 per cent assisted places. Presumably it was this belief that persuaded the commissioners that they were laying down terms for integration rather than simply constructing another form of association. However, even on this front they can be accused of sloppy thinking, possibly designed to paper over internal tensions and to enhance their potential political appeal. While boarding school culture must change, the outcome is not so much a new sense of identity for the public schools, but rather that 'integration offers a wider range of things to be done' (1968, 119) – as if additional notes were to be tacked on to a favourite tune.

It can be reasonably argued that the commission could not possibly be expected to deal with the details of integration. However, perhaps it should have considered the central principles which would determine the form of integration, and this it substantially failed to accomplish. However, these are not easy matters to resolve. The schools have generally been of the opinion that they offer a worthwhile educational experience, and too much change could do more harm than good. None the less, much of the criticism of the independent schools has been directed at the character of their boarding education. Was a compromise feasible? Or, from the perspective of the schools, really desirable? The previous chapter made the argument that the strong push towards free secondary schooling to be found in the 1944 Education Act seriously eroded what Olive Banks had described as a system of schooling based upon the fusion of two differing traditions (see, p.77). It is interesting to consider in what sense those traditions were really fused, as opposed to co-existing alongside one another, and, more importantly in terms of the theme of this book, whether it is possible to ensure a meaningful fusion in the future, even if it has failed to materialise in the past.

THE POLITICS OF INERTIA

The one general conclusion as to the impact of these reports on reshaping the relationship between the maintained and independent boarding schools is that they were essentially marked by failure. In the words of Le Quesne:

> When we can see the history of the English public schools in the twentieth century in proper perspective, it seems certain that one of its chief themes must be the repeated attempts to associate formally and more closely with the state system, and one of the chief questions the historian will have to ask himself will be why an attempt so often renewed, and supported (in public at least) by so large a proportion of those concerned and those whose opinions are supposed to carry weight in the community, yet failed, or took so long to succeed – as the case may be (1970, 3–5).

While it is dangerous to suggest an answer to Le Quesne's conundrum that would fit all occasions, a major continuing weakness in the case for a closer association has been its dependence upon the claim that there is a large unfulfilled need for boarding education. Both the Fleming Committee and the Newsom Commission suffered from this delusion.

Assuming the Fleming Committee was correct in its assumption that there was a widespread need for boarding education, the statistics alone would suggest that the public boarding schools were scarcely in a position to meet much of that need. The committee's statistics showed that there were some 6,000 annual vacancies for boys in the public boarding schools, as against an age group population at 13 (the usual age of entry) of about 295,000 boys in England (1944, 56). And yet these places would cost the state considerably more per pupil than those in its maintained secondary day schools. Furthermore, these were costs to be incurred at a time when the nation was faced with the massive reconstruction programme necessitated by the war. No wonder many felt that to incur such an obligation would be to establish grossly inappropriate priorities. Given the Treasury's opposition to the committee's earlier recommendation (see the Interim Report of 1943) that the Board of Education should pay the tuition fees of all pupils in the direct grant schools, it was scarcely likely to support this further commitment of public resources. At least the recommendation of the Interim Report had the merit of being consistent with the principle of free secondary schooling, and could, therefore, expect the sympathy of many on the political left.

With the exception of some minor changes to the direct grant system (see p.114), no policy proposals were instigated on the recommendations of the Fleming Committee. Inasmuch as the boarding schools were not required to participate in a form of association which at least some of them considered to be flawed, the GBA and HMC were, for the most part, satisfied with the outcome. If the financial circumstances of their schools, especially the boarding schools, had continued to remain precarious then it is hard to predict what their reaction would have been. However, this was not the case, and as the Fleming Report itself makes evident, by the end of the war the fortunes of the boarding schools were on the mend:

> For the first two years of the present war numbers again fell at many Public Schools, but, since then, most have recovered and it would probably be true, now, to say that Public Schools as a whole are fuller and more prosperous than they have been for some years (1944, 75).

Le Quesne's figures of entrants for the common entrance examination show that, after fluctuations of between 4,200 to 4,500 from approximately 1925 to 1935, it plunged sharply after 1936, reaching its nadir in 1940–41 when there were only 2,973 entrants. Thereafter it recovered steadily and by 1944–45, the year in which the recommendations of the Fleming Report would have been under consideration, it had reached 4,600 (1970, 9).

Clearly the pressure upon the heads and governors to seek an accommodation with the state had lessened. If the circumstances had been different, it is difficult to predict what the outcome would have been. While many heads and governors may have been prepared to settle for legislation along the lines of the Fleming Committee's recommendations, there were powerful political pressures, especially within the Labour Party, against an association on these terms, and it is unlikely that legislation could have cleared Parliament before the demise of the National government and the election of Attlee's administration. In effect the election of the Attlee government was the final blow to any remaining hopes of implementing Fleming's recommendations.

Since the Newsom Report was proposing that some 50 per cent, as opposed to Fleming's initial minimum of 25 per cent, of boarding school places should be filled at the expense of the Exchequer, it was critical that its case carried conviction. In fact it failed on at least three accounts. Even if it could be demonstrated that there was a large number of children whose social circumstances and personal problems seemed to suggest that they would benefit from a boarding education, there was no evidence that this was a particularly desirable strategy for dealing with such children. For example, rather than removing children from overcrowded homes to boarding schools, perhaps it would be preferable to improve the housing stock.

Secondly, and most importantly, because there may be a need for boarding education it does not follow that there is also an unfulfilled demand for it. On this point criticism, including criticism from within the commission itself, was especially scathing. In 'A Note of Reservation' to the Report, John Vaizey wrote: 'It is difficult to see how any valid measure of boarding demand could be devised: certainly the evidence on which the commission is relying is tenuous in the extreme' (1968, 221). If Vaizey's point was correct, then it was meaningless to make the predictions and costings that the commission had constructed; in effect it was a report based upon wishful thinking (perhaps that demand could be generated) rather than hard evidence.

Thirdly, even if pupils with a need for boarding education could be persuaded of its possible benefits, it seemed a very odd way to further the integration of maintained and private schooling. There are private boarding schools which provide excellent learning environments for children with a range of special educational needs, but it would be a peculiar form of integration if it were to depend primarily upon the transfer of children with exceptional qualities or problems, however defined, from maintained primary schools to independent secondary schools. Moreover, assuming that the recommendations of both the Fleming and Newsom Reports had been acted upon, there still remained the problem that most of the boarding places in the independent schools were for boys. Do boys have a need for boarding education, whereas girls do not? At best, pursuing the integrationist strategy along these lines addresses the alleged needs of only one half of the population.

The crucial problem, therefore, that has dogged all the schemes which seek a closer form of association between the maintained and fee-paying sectors (including the current assisted places scheme) is that they have been based upon the transfer of special categories of pupils from the former to the latter. This may result in a form of association between the two sectors, but it is a peculiar form of association and certainly falls far short of meriting the label of interpenetration.

Whereas the Commission's analysis of boarding need generated widespread scepticism and opposition, there were the expected attacks from the specific interests. One could not expect many elements on the political left to be happy with an understanding of integration which allowed boarding schools to retain a 50 per cent fee-paying entry and assumed that those in receipt of grants would not be drawn from the whole ability range. This smacked of partial association rather than integration. In complete contrast, powerful voices within the independent sector expressed their alarm at the proposed pace and scope of change. In his address to the AGM of the Headmasters' Conference, the incumbent chairman, D. D. Lindsay, reflected:

> I can only plead for mutual trust as we work this out together. There isn't a hope in hell of a 50 per cent start by a few schools, but there is every hope, even with a modest influx of Government money, that we could all make a start. So my plea is simply this: Don't fix an exact percentage to qualify for integration – all our schools are fully prepared to accept a substantial proportion of assisted pupils. Find out the exact nature of the need and how far it is accompanied by a demand for boarding. Then, with the minimum of administrative machinery and the maximum of goodwill, let us get down to working out a scheme capable of steady expansion (Chairman, 1968, 7).

These hurt tones implied that the schools were facing forced integration, whereas what was required were mutually acceptable schemes of association. Of course even if the sums involved were to be modest, there remained the critical question as to whether it would be money wisely spent. It has never proved difficult for the opponents of private schooling to suggest different targets for public expenditure, and in view of the contemporary drive towards comprehensive secondary schooling the need to establish expenditure priorities was indeed pressing. To many it must have appeared little short of criminal to spend public money on supporting pupils at the independent boarding schools while denying local education authorities the resources to complete an effective transition from selective to comprehensive secondary schooling.

CONCLUSION

The approach of the GBA and HMC to the National government to investigate the possibility of a closer association between the maintained schools and the independent boarding schools was a crucial stage in the institutionalisation of power within the private sector of schooling. Indeed, the Governing Bodies Association emerged out of 'the negotiations that led to the setting up of the Committee' (Le Quesne, 1970, 11). Although in the case of the Public Schools Commission the initiative for action came from the political arena, the response of the schools was again expressed in essentially institutional terms. During the course of the publication of the two reports of the Public Schools Commission, the institutional network of the world of public school education steadily assumed a mutually supportive stance. The consequence was that some of their traditional internal differences (for example, between boys' schools and girls' schools, and the independent boarding schools and direct grant schools) were at the very least papered over in public. It was as if government intervention was generating a united front. In a comparatively short time this convergence of thinking was converted into institutional convergence, as witnessed by the increasing use of the unifying label 'independent', and the creation of both a common publicity arm (the Independent Schools Information Service) and a central policy-making body (the Independent Schools Joint Council).

Integral to the negotiations was the question of the divisiveness – social and otherwise – of the private sector. The Fleming Committee concluded that the independent boarding schools reflected, rather than caused, the social divisions in society at large (1944, 23). Somewhat less charitably, the Newsom Commission stated that one of its goals was 'to create a socially mixed entry into the schools in order ... to reduce the divisive influence which they now exert (1968, vii). Interestingly, in spite of this tacit acceptance that the independent boarding schools were indeed socially divisive institutions, there was no in-depth reflection on the possible repercussions of placing a large number of pupils in an alien environment. Both Fleming (with its more modest target) and Newsom believed that, with a measure of circumspection in the selection process, such pupils would be capable of making smooth transitions between the two sectors of schooling. But would this actually reduce social divisiveness? Or would it resolve the financial crisis facing the schools, while extending to the selected individuals the advantages of a boarding education acquired in an independent school? If there was indeed a latent demand for boarding education, it may have been most pronounced among those parents who perceived its long-term advantages, especially to the future social status and job opportunities of their children.

In his 'note of reservation' to the Newsom Report, John Vaizey made the following witty observation:

> The main objection to private schools is that they are socially divisive. Some of them happen to have beds. It therefore seems less revolutionary to change the bodies in the beds than to eliminate the beds (1968, 221).

Vaizey's initial concern was the fate of the displaced middle-class pupils, with his expectation that either the private sector would expand to accommodate them, or the pupils selected to be publicly subsidised would be drawn from their very ranks. His second concern took the form of suggesting an entirely different approach to the problem: 'I do not think that the central question of the public schools is finding enough poor children to fill their beds; I believe, rather, it is what is the future of independent educational institutions drawing their pupils from a restricted social group, in contemporary England ...' (1968, 224). In other words, and drawing upon the conflict theory of social stratification outlined in the first chapter, the schools continue to prosper – at least in the long run – because it is believed they confer upon their pupils distinct advantages in the pursuit of scarce resources. Were this perceived link to be broken then the question of social divisiveness would evaporate, or at the very least would be recreated by different means and perhaps in a different form.

On the one hand, the institutional network of the private sector can be perceived as acting to defend class interests; on the other hand, the network itself rejects the claim by countering that its central concern is the welfare of its schools. Not surprisingly, the issues of independence, fee-paying and academic selection are always high on its agenda of concerns – but not class privilege. However, even if the change process is inextricably linked with the evolving character of social stratification, the pressures exerted by such forces are increasingly expressed through institutions. And undoubtedly the intervention of governments, the role of the state, and the making of public policy are all tied into a complex process of institutional politics. Today, in marked contrast to the nineteenth century, these broad forces for change can be accommodated by the schools without the pressure of the state. Hostile political forces undoubtedly made them think seriously about their future, for there is nothing like the threat of government intervention to concentrate the mind. However, the reforms proposed by both the Fleming Committee and the Newsom Commission were essentially, and expectedly, pragmatic in their nature. But they were incapable of bridging the enormous political divide generated by the independent boarding schools, and equally unable to satisfy more specific questions directed at boarding need and costs. Good intentions were all too easily frustrated.

6

From the Direct Grant Schools to the Assisted Places Scheme

The rewriting of founders' statutes in the nineteenth century led to the creation of a scholarship tradition whereby a limited number of talented pupils from humble social origins could aspire to enter the locally endowed secondary schools, and perhaps even continue their education at one of the ancient universities. This was a scholarship ladder sustained by endowment income. It was not until the passage of the 1902 Education Act that the state acquired the unequivocal right to provide secondary schooling. This task was undertaken by the local education authorities whose existence was ushered in by that Act. However, the LEAs frequently purchased places in the existing secondary schools, many of which were local grammar schools, sometimes old foundations which continued to exist precariously (in spite of the work of the Taunton Commission and the Charity Commissioners) on the basis of small endowments and fees provided by a none too exalted bourgeoisie.

The free-place system, that is the purchase of places in secondary schools by the LEAs, both created a scholarship ladder and linked the maintained elementary schools to the fee-paying secondary schools. In a well-worn metaphor, a bridge was built between the two sectors of schooling. From the beginning two key problems emerged. First, the provision of free places varied widely across the country. This was true even after the Board of Education attempted to regulate the pattern of access from elementary to secondary schools in measures such as the 1907 Regulations for Secondary Schools. In his introduction to Lindsay's seminal *Social Progress and Educational Waste*, Viscount Haldane noted that 'It is clear ... that the percentage of children obtaining a secondary education varies very greatly ... both from one area to another and, within the same area, from school to school' (1926, 2). As a consequence, in many parts of the country pupils who would benefit from a secondary education were being denied the opportunity.

Second, there was increasing criticism, not only of the overall narrownesss of the scholarship ladder, but also of the fact that its very existence implied that only a limited number of elementary school pupils could profit from a secondary education. Moreover, secondary schooling was accessible to pupils whose parents could afford the fees but inaccessible to possibly more talented children from poor families. It was partly in response to this state of affairs that the Labour Party, under the guidance of R. H. Tawney, had issued in 1922 its policy document, *Secondary Education for All*. There was growing official support for the creation of a universal system of secondary education, but one that was stratified to cater for pupils with different abilities and aptitudes (Banks, 1955, 119–22).

A more subtle problem associated with the scholarship ladder was the state's acceptance of a tradition of secondary education that had taken shape in the fee-paying schools. Could the local education authorities establish alternative forms of secondary schooling which would have equal status to, for example, the grammar school tradition or a public school education? From the beginning, the state and fee-paying sectors of secondary schooling were not seen as complementary parts of a unified whole but rather as competing definitions of education with unequal status. What was especially galling for those who believed that the traditions of schooling developed within the private sector were flawed was the willingness of the local education authorities to support the transfer of talented pupils from the elementary schools and educate them at public expense in schools that charged fees.

By the time of the 1944 Education Act the extension of the free-place system had widened the scholarship ladder, although this was constrained by the economic difficulties of the inter-war years. However, it had steadily become less of a bridge between the maintained and fee-paying sectors of schooling. The LEAs were constructing their own grammar schools which, with varying degrees of imitation, followed the established grammar school tradition. Furthermore, the number of free-place pupils was increasing inexorably in the endowed schools, and, in terms of their financial base, one tradition (rate support/central government grants) was gradually replacing another (endowment income/fee-paying). If Olive Banks was correct in pointing out that secondary education in England was built upon two fused traditions (see p.77), then the glue that held the traditions together was losing its strength well before the passage of the 1944 Education Act.

What the 1944 Education Act did for secondary education was to encourage thinking about alternative definitions of secondary schooling, while instigating a sharper divide between the maintained and private sectors. It also left in place a comparatively small bridge of direct grant schools. These schools had come into existence in 1926 as a result of Circular 1361, which required secondary schools taking free-place pupils to opt either for a direct grant from the Board of Education or for support from the local education authorities. This remnant was small (in 1945 the direct grant list was reopened and the number of schools reduced from 232 to 166) and – although most of the schools were academically prestigious – was of a varied character: schools with different denominational allegiances, single sex schools, some with a high boarding component, and large differences in the relative balance of fee-paying and free-place pupils (Edwards *et al.*, 1989, 19–20). How did this small fragment come to survive the gaze of the Fleming Committee and escape the grasp of the 1944 Education Act, only to succumb some thirty years later to the logic implicit in the idea of comprehensive secondary schooling?

THE FLEMING COMMITTEE AND THE DIRECT GRANT SCHOOLS

Along with the independent boarding schools, that other segment of the first-class carriage, that is the direct grant schools, had been shunted by Butler into the siding known as the Fleming Committee. In its 1944 Report the Committee argued that there were three weaknesses to the direct grant system:

1. The capitation grant which central government made to the schools reduced the fees of pupils whose parents could well afford the full cost.

2. It was a technically inefficient system inasmuch as central government subsidised the fees of those pupils supported by the local education authorities (through its capitation grant), and then assisted the local education authorities with the payment of those fees.

3. The number of free places needed to be renegotiated (1944, 62; and Glennerster and Wilson, 1970, 58).

In order to remedy these defects it recommended that the local authorities should be able to reserve a negotiated number of places (day or boarding) in the schools prepared to participate in the proposed new scheme. The tuition fees of these pupils would be paid in full by the local education authorities whereas parents would pay means-tested boarding fees with the local authorities making up the shortfalls. The Board of Education would make grants available to local authorities on their expenditure. Other places in the schools could be filled by the governors but it was required that fees should be means-tested (1944, 62–3).

Clearly the general loss of momentum in resolving the question of access to the independent boarding schools also weakened the force of the Fleming Committee's proposals to reform the direct grant system. Moreover, it is easy to appreciate why a Conservative President of the Board of Education (R. A. Butler) lacked the political will either to terminate the direct grant list or to prevent the schools – several of which were prominent members of HMC – from admitting fee-payers. However, the direct grant schools were heavily dependent upon public money, and there was no reason why the Attlee government could not have legislated to squeeze the fee-payers out of the direct grant schools just as they had been squeezed out of the locally supported endowed secondary schools by the 1944 Education Act. However, some local authorities lacked grammar school places and needed the direct grant schools to meet their commitments. They would be inconvenienced if the schools decided to take their chances in the marketplace rather than become fully paid-up members of the maintained sector. Futhermore, a change of government would not alter the Treasury's view. It is more than likely that the schools would have continued to admit much the same body of pupils, with all the fees paid by the Exchequer rather than a proportion of them by the pupils' families. While this may have satisfied some principled Labour Party politicians, it could scarcely be expected to appeal to the mandarins.

Although the Fleming Reports did not lead to a root-and-branch reform of the direct grant system, they did result in changes which were probably just enough to satisfy the broad spectrum of contemporary political opinion. To qualify for the grant all the schools had to offer a minimum of 25 per cent of their places to the local education authorities, and an additional 25 per cent could be reserved by local authorities (often, with the agreement of school governors, a higher percentage of places was reserved). The remaining places (residuary places) would be available to fee-payers although on a means-tested basis. Central government continued to make a capitation grant as well as an additional grant to the schools to cover the cost of remitted or reduced fees (Glennerster and Wilson, 1970, 58–9).

Consequently the local authorities could, obtain a high enough percentage of the places to meet their own needs, and no one was excluded because of family income. In fact, rather than excluding the poor, the system subsidised the well-to-do. The capitation grants kept the fees comparatively low, and the only condition for competing for a free place was two years' prior attendance at a maintained primary school.

FROM SELECTIVE TO COMPREHENSIVE SECONDARY SCHOOLING

From the beginning the system of secondary education that emerged after the 1944 Education Act, though based upon broad political support, was challenged by those who objected to its selective basis. In practice a bipartite model took root in much of the country. Although the official ideology may have suggested that children were selected according to their age, aptitude and ability, inevitably the different forms of secondary schooling were not of the same status. Moreover, the secondary modern schools, not surprisingly, failed to evolve a distinctive tradition which could allow them to accumulate merit on their own terms (Taylor, 1963). In the eyes of many parents they were the schools to be avoided.

The Achilles' heel of selective secondary education was the infamous 11+ examination, the means by which the sheep were separated from the goats. And, whereas the grammar school tradition may have been widely admired, the 11+ examination was almost universally disparaged. The pressure to modify the selective system emerged at the local level with experiments in multilateral models, the Leicestershire plan and alternative versions of comprehensive secondary schooling. These experiments quickly had an impact upon the direct grant schools. Long before the publication of Circular 10/65, which requested the local education authorities to submit proposals for the reorganisation of their secondary schools along comprehensive lines, the minutes of the Headmasters' Conference are peppered with anguished references to local education authorities reneging on agreements. As early as November 1962 HMC's Direct Grant Schools Committee met to discuss the results of a survey 'on the disengagement of local education authorities from direct grant schools and agreed that these should be made known to the Ministry of Education, and that a summary should be sent to all headmasters of HMC Schools' (HMC, *Bulletin*, No. 1, 1963). To some extent the disengagement was principled: that is, the local authority was committed to reorganising its secondary schools along comprehensive lines, but in other cases it was pragmatic. If the local education authorities were expanding their own grammar schools, they would have less reason to buy places in the direct grant schools. Moreover, as Saran has shown (see p.82), the disengagement was not one-sided, for some schools were disenchanted with the academic quality of the pupils sponsored by the LEAs, and withdrew into the fee-paying sector.

However, the consequences of local authority disengagement for most direct grant schools were very serious indeed. In order to retain their direct grant status, and thus their central grants, they had to admit a minimum 25 per cent of free-place pupils who had been educated for the previous two years at maintained primary schools. Of course schools could weary of the struggle and decide to phase themselves out of the direct grant system, but this was a risky strategy for they needed to attract a sufficient number of fee-payers to remain solvent. Could they survive in the marketplace?

The response to a local authority's withdrawal of support was either to seek redress in the courts (if it was felt that the LEA's action had been unduly precipitate), or – more likely – to look to other local education authorities to take up the slack. These worrying times generated ambivalent attitudes among the ranks of the direct grant schools towards the local education authorities. Many of their heads and governors saw the direct grant schools as serving the interests of the local community, and thus regretted the breaking of what were, in some cases, long-established ties. Moreover, there was a strong sentiment within the ranks of the private sector against centrally imposed directives and in favour of local deals between particular schools and the education authorities. Supposedly, each school had its own individual character to which centrally imposed legislation could not possibly be sensitive. However, because the direct grant schools felt themselves increasingly squeezed by what they saw as hostile local authority action, many were led to the conclusion that the LEAs had to be excluded from the assisted places scheme which was to emerge later.

The pressure that the movement towards comprehensive secondary education put upon the direct grant schools consisted, therefore, of both pragmatic considerations and issues of great principle. On the pragmatic front it was the straightforward question of whether the local authorities would continue to underwrite a sufficient volume of pupils to enable the schools to remain solvent. The principle at stake was that of selection: what should be its role in the pedagogical process? In theory the expansion of comprehensive secondary schooling threatened the interests of the private sector as a whole, given that it was selective both academically and/or by virtue of charging fees. The direct grant schools, however, were more vulnerable, for they combined both forms of selection while at the same time receiving most of their income from public funds: 66 per cent in 1965/66 according to the calculations of Glennerster and Wilson (1970, 30).

It was logically difficult to sustain an argument that would enable the direct grant schools, perhaps along with a number of the more prestigious grammar schools, to survive while all other maintained secondary schools were incorporated into a comprehensive system. Either one accepted the principle of comprehensive secondary schooling or one did not, and to advocate a halfway house was to support a different model of secondary schooling. In effect, however, it was this messy compromise position which many supporters of the grammar schools, including the direct grant schools themselves, advanced. In the meantime, the tenor of the debates at the Conservative Party conferences in the late 1960s reveals that the position of its shadow education minister (Edward Boyle) was coming under increasing threat from the rank-and-file members of the party. At the 1967 Conference there was the almost unprecedented spectacle of a formal vote on the anodyne motion supported by the platform. Although the motion was carried comfortably (1,302 to 816 votes), the radical elements within the party wanted a more distinctive educational policy: certainly one that would incorporate unequivocal support for the remaining grammar and direct grant schools.

Boyle's compromise position contained a number of different threads: to oppose early secondary school selection in the form of the 11+ examination, to support comprehensive secondary schools where 'they made sense' (which invariably meant when approved by Tory-controlled local education authorities), to support the retention of the direct grant schools, to oppose 'botched-up' schemes of reorganisation (where one school was located on widely dispersed sites), and to attack the policy of the complete comprehensivisation of maintained secondary schools in the large cities.

On the latter point he made a most revealing observation to the 1965 Conference which was to become a powerful theme in subsequent party thinking:

> Do not let us limit, by accident of neighbourhood, opportunities to those who, by their ability and character, manage to transcend the limitations of their background. I do not believe that it can be right in big cities to have nothing but neighbourhood comprehensive schools, with no other alternative at all (Conservative Party, 1965, 57).

The quintessential Tory moderate was, therefore, of the opinion that the cultural milieu of inner-city comprehensives would swamp the talent of their gifted working-class pupils. In parallel fashion, important elements within the direct grant system were advocating the possibility of retaining at least a few direct grant schools which, as super-selective grammar schools, would provide the necessary environment to stimulate the full potential of their highly intelligent clientele.

The key forum for the airing of these issues was to become the Public Schools Commission. The private sector interests wanted a public airing of the relevant arguments in order to prevent the quiet winding up of the direct grant schools, as the government was legally entitled to do, by administrative fiat. Thanks in part to their pressure the terms of the Public Schools Commission, now under the chairmanship of Professor Donnison, were extended:

> To advise on the most effective method or methods by which direct grant schools in England and Wales and the grant-aided schools in Scotland can participate in the movement towards comprehensive reorganisation, and to review the principle of central government grant to these schools (1970, viii).

In their submissions to the Commission, the direct grant interests, with the Direct Grant Joint Committee (DGJC) now in the van, kept to the line that the 'co-existence of selective direct grant schools and non-selective maintained schools was neither illogical nor impracticable' (DGJC, 1969), and it was possible that 'some direct grant schools might well be able to broaden their intake'. But was the committee really convinced by its own reasoning? Reverting to the practical arguments of size and finance, it claimed that the direct grant schools could not be expected to assume 'a fully comprehensive role'. And in any case: 'Some measure of selection was essential in direct grant schools for a long time to come and the future of a comprehensive system was still too uncertain to justify long term prognostication.' Such sentiments imply that there was little real conviction in the viability of a compromise position, and it is difficult to avoid the conclusion that it was floated because of the political circumstances.

Certainly the Donnison Commissioners were not persuaded, and expressed their unequivocal opposition to any compromise:

> It would be illogical and self-defeating if central and local government were to bend their efforts towards creating a comprehensive secondary system while simultaneously supporting schools outside that system which frustrate its development. We concluded that schools which intend to secure continuing support from public funds, for themselves or their pupils, must participate in the movement towards comprehensive education (1970, 4).

And, for all but two of the commissioners, it followed that:

> ... the aims of this movement cannot be attained if the selection of children for particular schools depends on their parents' willingness to pay fees. Thus places in day schools participating in comprehensive systems should be free (1970, 4).

The purpose of the Public Schools Commission was to recommend ways in which the public schools could be integrated with maintained schools, and its First Report (the Newsom Report) in effect advocated a form of association which it believed would result in a steady change in the character of the independent schools (see p.103). Clearly the Donnison Report operated with a different interpretation of integration: one dependent upon the immediate incorporation within the maintained sector of the direct grant schools as non-selective comprehensives. The result would be an overnight change in the direct grant schools rather than a gradual evolution of their characters.

The advantages of Donnison's approach were its clarity and rigour. It avoided debates on broadening or narrowing the academic range of the direct grant schools, changing selection techniques, raising the age of entry, or changing the curriculum that any attempt to formulate a compromise position would have generated. Comprehensive secondary schooling was to mean what the label clearly implied, and it could not be implemented in a watered-down form without its meaning being changed fundamentally. Politically Donnison's recommendations were likely to galvanise the support of like-minded zealots: that is, it would be intense if narrow. Historically the British educational system had changed incrementally, and to many the Donnison Report represented a negation of that tradition. To others, however, it was a manifestation of support for a long overdue reform.

Unlike the proposals of the Fleming and Newsom Reports, those of the Donnison Report were enacted, although the election of the Heath government in 1970, with Mrs Thatcher as Secretary of State for Education, not surprisingly delayed action in the short term. The Report found in the subsequent Wilson government a sufficiently large measure of sympathy to ensure action on its proposals. The direct grant system was phased out, and the purchase of places at independent schools was to be more closely monitored by the DES. There is some irony in the fact that the proposals of the Fleming and Newsom Reports, which attempted to establish a broad base of political support, should founder while those of the Donnison Report, which were more politically partisan, should succeed.

BACK TO THE FUTURE WITH THE ASSISTED PLACES SCHEME

There were those who felt that, although the direct grant schools should be defended, it was equally vital to make positive proposals for reforming the system. The hope, probably no more than wishful thinking, was that such an initiative might receive a wide measure of political support, and so help to place the direct grant system on a more stable foundation (see the editorial in *Conference*, June 1982, for a reflection on those misplaced hopes). The key element in the reform package was that assisted places should replace free places; this in varying forms had been raised by both the Fleming Committee and Donnison Commission. Probably the most forceful advocate of an assisted places scheme was Peter Mason, former High Master of Manchester Grammar School. At a meeting in February 1970 of those direct grant heads who were members of HMC, he urged the need to offer counter-proposals to the likely recommendations of the Donnison Report, and, to this end, he argued that assisted places should replace free places, and unless LEAs were expressly forbidden to do so, the schools should work closely with those local authorities that were still prepared to co-operate (HMC, April 1970). Almost immediately thereafter a subcommittee of HMC was set up to draft a policy statement. This paralleled developments in the Direct Grant Joint Committee (which represented all the direct grant schools, rather than just those that were members of HMC), with Mason and James Cobban (former Head of Abingdon School) acting as the link between the two committees.

It was often asserted that the direct grant schools had a less socially exclusive pupil intake than the traditional public schools, and that for many of their pupils they acted as a ladder of opportunity. But it is a claim that needs to be treated with a measure of scepticism. Edwards and his colleagues have argued that, while the pupils at the direct grant schools were less likely to have parents who were professionals or managers than those attending public schools, 'it was also true that the proportion whose fathers were in semi-skilled and unskilled manual occupations (eight per cent) was almost as low as in the public schools'. Moreover, the social composition of the direct grant schools was 'almost identical with that of fully independent day schools like St Paul's' (1989, 19). Although these data may tell us that the direct grant schools were far from socially representative of the general population (would one have imagined otherwise?), they can also demonstrate the perhaps surprising social heterogeneity of the independent public day schools. This is yet another case in which the evidence can be used to show that the glass is half full and yet remains half empty.

Of more concern to the direct grant interests was that free places were not necessarily awarded to pupils from economically disadvantaged families. To qualify for a free place it was necessary for the candidate to have completed the prior two years of formal education at a maintained primary school. It made economic sense for well-heeled parents to see whether their child could win a free place, and failing that, to try to secure entry as a fee-payer. Furthermore, even the fee-payers were subsidised by the capitation grants awarded to the schools by central government. The advantage of an assisted places scheme was that it could be structured so that only children from genuinely needy families would have the full costs of their schooling met out of public funds. It was this particular change which its advocates hoped would make an assisted places scheme attractive to the political enemies of the direct grant system.

None the less, such a reform could not within itself counter the continuing fundamental objection that these would remain pupils selected on the basis of their academic ability. The comprehensive schools would still be deprived of talented pupils, which – allegedly – would lessen the chances of their demonstrating their worth. Ironically, an assisted places scheme specifically designed to pick up talented children from exclusively poorer homes could be seen as *more* harmful to the interests of comprehensive schools than the old direct grant system. If in the direct grant system public resources were being used to underwrite the fees of middle-class parents who had no intention of sending their children to maintained secondary schools, then the comprehensive schools were not being deprived of talented pupils –

the local authorities and the Treasury were simply wasting public resources.

The second, and critical, reading of the 1980 Education (No. 2) Bill, which placed the assisted places scheme on the statute book, occurred on 5 November 1979 and in September 1981 close to 4,000 pupils secured an assisted place at an independent school. The general political background of this extraordinary coup for the private sector been dealt with fully elsewhere (Salter and Tapper, 1985, 185–209; Edwards *et al.*, 1989, 29–32). Of particular interest is the close political parallel between the passage of the assisted places scheme and the abolition of the direct grant schools: in both cases important changes to the educational system were carried through on a comparatively narrow political base in the teeth of bitter opposition. On the question of access to secondary schooling the key problems posed by the assisted places scheme are the differences between presumed and actual beneficiaries of the awards, and the implications for the relationship between the maintained and private sectors.

In formal terms the beneficiaries of the assisted places scheme, as originally enacted, were easy to describe: they had to satisfy the admission requirements of at least one of the schools participating in the scheme, at least 60 per cent of those awarded assisted places by a school were required to have spent the prior two years of their schooling in the maintained sector, and, as the size of the award was dependent upon parental income, the lower the family income the larger the award. Initially it was proposed that when the scheme was fully operational there would be 25,000 pupils with assisted places; subsequently this figure has been raised so that in 1996 there were close to 30,000 beneficiaries (although this is still less than a full take-up). Currently plans are afoot to double the number of assisted places but this will only be achieved by extending the scheme to embrace the preparatory schools.

Beneath this simple facade of who formally benefits lies a world of treacherous quicksand. In view of the fact that the major drive for an assisted places scheme originated within the former direct grant schools, it is not surprising that it was designed particularly for pupils with high academic potential. However, given the determination that the scheme should embrace the fee-paying secondary sector as a whole (as long as the schools were conducted exclusively for charitable purposes), there have been repeated attempts to incorporate an element of 'boarding need' into its terms. While schools are able to negotiate agreements with the DES (now the DFEE) which permit them to admit assisted place pupils as boarders, there has been a persistent official refusal to underwrite boarding costs. Inasmuch as some schools have been prepared to meet these costs themselves, and many public schools which were once exclusively boarding institutions now admit day pupils, this has resulted in a wider participation in the scheme than just the former direct grant schools.

However, the resistance of government to paying boarding fees has rankled. If a school is prepared to use the scheme to admit boarders, it has to take into account a wider range of considerations than the straightforward academic potential of the candidates. Most importantly it has to make a judgement on whether the individual is likely to fit into, and benefit from, a boarding environment. The contrast with schools offering a large number of day places is stark, for the latter will invariably rely upon how the individual has performed in an examination taken on one particular day. What the boarding provision enables the school to do is to take into account the possible social needs of the candidate. Thus it may be a means of assisting the pupil with broader concerns than simply his or her academic development. It could also be argued that this is a worthwhile goal in its own right, and thus one that governments should be prepared to recognise by meeting its costs. But it also has wider ramifications. If the assisted places scheme met boarding fees, it would be easier to sustain the argument that it was designed to complement provision in the maintained schools. Moreover, the demand from British families for boarding provision appears to be in terminal decline, and for some schools an infusion of public support for this purpose would prove very beneficial. Indeed, with respect to the assisted places scheme in general, what benefits a selected number of pupils is also beneficial to a selected number of schools (Walford, 1987).

In the course of the parliamentary debate on the Second Reading of the Education (No. 2) Bill, Rhodes Boyson, in typically robust fashion, claimed that the government was providing assisted places because it wanted to rebuild the ladder of opportunity for bright working-class children which the Labour Party had removed:

> But the ladder of mobility was knocked down by the Labour Party to permit Socialist feudalism and Socialist rotten boroughs in the middle of cities. We want to rebuild the ladders for those children. If the move is divisive it is divisive on the side of those for whom it should be divisive – not for the rich but for those who cannot afford to go (*Hansard* [Commons], 5 November 1979, Col. 158).

Although this may have been *one* of the purposes of the Bill, certain clauses showed quite clearly that it was not the sole purpose. In the negotiation of draft versions of the scheme, the independent sector was determined not to exclude needy parents whose children were already being educated in fee-paying schools. So it was possible that parents already committed to paying school fees could have their financial obligations lightened by the passage of the scheme. Furthermore, recent plans to broaden the scheme propose extending assistance to those who have yet to complete their preparatory school education, as long as the school is the junior department of an independent secondary school. The evidence also shows that schools offering assisted places to 16-year-olds (that is, for the purpose of a sixth-form education) have experienced particular difficulties in attracting a sufficient number of applicants. Most of those receiving awards at this age are already in the independent sector. The suspicion is either that they are pupils seeking schools with better resourced sixth forms (mainly girls moving to co-educational schools) or that the assisted place makes the difference between staying at the school or pursuing a sixth-form education in the maintained sector.

It is perfectly correct to claim that the primary purpose of the scheme was to underwrite the fees of talented children from less well-off families. In this sense it would be hard to dispute that the scheme has achieved its main goal with a large percentage of pupils entitled to a full remission of fees. But it has not been demonstrated that the schooling of these children would have been severely impaired if their education had continued in the maintained sector. Equally, while the recipients of assisted places may be members of low-income families, they do not represent a substantially different kind of clientele for the private sector. The low income of their families is often a consequence of unemployment, of a single-parent family structure or of breadwinners being in poorly paid lower-middle-class occupations (vergers appear frequently). Conspicuously under-represented are children from families in which the major wage-earner pursues a manual occupation. In other words, few of Boyle's mythical, gifted working-class children who may sink into the abyss of the inner-city comprehensive will be rescued by the assisted places scheme.

There is, therefore, some ambivalence concerning the social targets of the scheme, combined with differing interpretations as to what constitutes underprivilege. Inevitably evaluations of the scheme (invariably made on the basis of very limited evidence, or even none) have been coloured by political predispositions. As educational policy serves political ends this was to be expected, but rarely can the point have been illustrated so vividly. This is only a problem in the sense that it generates heat rather than light. In fact it is difficult to imagine any other outcome. The private sector negotiators could scarcely have failed to take into account the representations made on behalf of their poorer parents, particularly by the heads of the preparatory schools. Furthermore, it seems scarcely equitable to award assisted places on any other basis than family income.

The evidence suggesting that the take-up of assisted places by working-class children is disproportionately low implies that perhaps some measure of cultural deprivation should have been taken into consideration. But this merely opens up a can of worms: definitions of cultural deprivation, its measurement, and whether the state should be so intrusive. Perhaps the social pattern associated with the awards reflects the considered self-exclusion of some social groups rather than purposeful institutional bias. Like the abolition of the direct grant schools, the assisted places scheme has failed to restructure the relationship between the maintained and private sectors of schooling. The bulk of the direct grant schools were not integrated into the comprehensive system of secondary schooling, and the assisted places scheme – at least to date – has presented the fee-paying sector with a clientele to which it is all too accustomed: that is, the more impoverished ranks of the bourgeoisie.

The 1979 AGM of the Headmasters' Conference, meeting at Trinity College, Cambridge, held a special session on the assisted places scheme. John Rae, then Headmaster of Westminster School, expressed his strong opposition to the scheme. Inevitably there will always be tensions and splits within such organisations, but this was one of the few occasions when a split within HMC was revealed publicly. The Headmaster of Bolton School (David Baggley) put the following resolution to the session:

> That HMC is committed to the principle of Assisted Places and strongly believes that any such scheme should have two aims:
>
> 1. It should be so constructed that its prime purpose is to benefit children who have some form of need, especially that for an academic education;
> 2. It should operate in such a way that it is clearly complementary to the provision in the maintained school system (HMC, *Bulletin*, No. 6, December 1979).

Although the resolution was carried very comfortably (136 votes to 15 with 19 abstentions), it was very unusual for HMC to put formal motions and record votes. Rae, albeit very belatedly, had stirred up strong passions.

If the private sector interests were serious about constructing a scheme that operated so as to complement provision in the maintained sector, then one would have expected them to have incorporated representatives of the maintained sector in the negotiations leading to the construction of the scheme. In fact, they were conspicuous by their absence. Although both HMC and the Direct Grant Joint Committee had expressed occasional concern at how the maintained sector would react to an assisted places scheme, there was no apparent attempt to explore this in depth in the only viable manner - through face-to-face contacts. One is left with the feeling that clause 2 of Baggley's Trinity College resolution is more an expression of collective guilt than a serious statement of intent. Besides Rae's opposition, the scheme was not receiving the best of presses, greatly aided by the fact that the government was pruning educational expenditure, although this allowed HMC to attempt some fence-mending by expressing its own concern with these cuts.

It was easy to pronounce that the assisted places scheme would operate in a manner that complemented provision in the maintained sector but much more difficult to demonstrate it. The private sector's negotiating team should have made this one of its priorities, although the government's refusal to recognise and pay for boarding need made it a difficult task. The schools have been left to pick up boarding costs with the inevitable consequence that there have been comparatively few assisted place pupils who have also been boarders. It is possible that a few pupils have been persuaded to transfer into the sixth form of an independent school because of the availability of particular A-level options. However, this potential widening of choice has to be weighed against the possibility that A-level courses in some maintained schools have become unviable because students are opting out. Again, a few parents could be attracted by an independent school's denominational character, or by the fact that it was a boys' only or girls' only school. But there are such schools in the maintained sector, and, on their own, these seem rather fragile grounds to attempt a transfer.

The only substantial grounds for suggesting that the assisted places scheme was part of a complementary relationship was to claim that the independent schools offered a high-quality academic education, or excellent facilities for those offered awards on the basis of their talent in one of the performing arts, which was unavailable in the maintained secondary schools. In other words, the pupils who succeeded in obtaining assisted places would have the quality of their educational experiences substantially enhanced by attending an independent school, and the outcome would be improved individual performances. Given that the heads and governors of independent schools had no wish to offend their colleagues in the maintained sector (note that the heads of both maintained and independent schools belong to the Secondary Heads Association which roundly condemned the assisted places scheme), it was impossible for them to argue such a case - at least in public. Conceivably particular targets could have been specified – we are back to the inner-city comprehensives – but blanket negative statements would have been politically unwise and, moreover, unwelcome to dominant opinion within the independent sector itself.

An alternative line was to maintain that, far from having an impact upon the maintained sector, the assisted places scheme was of such limited scope that its repercussions would be negligible. Mark Carlisle, who as Secretary of State for Education in Mrs Thatcher's first government was responsible for piloting the scheme through Parliament, made the point: 'I don't believe that a provision which will be no higher than the Direct Grant intake used to be when fully operational will harm anyone' (*Times Educational Supplement*, 15 February 1980, as quoted in Edwards *et al.*, 1989, 66). In strictly numerical terms such an observation may have been justified, although Pring has argued to the contrary with respect to sixth-form entrants (1983), but the debate was not about numbers alone.

Carlisle seems to have forgotten that the assisted places scheme has operated within a different educational environment from that experienced by the direct grant schools. In the context of selective secondary schooling it was more difficult to argue *in principle* against the direct grant schools, although the interests of the maintained grammar schools were undoubtedly harmed by their continuing presence. What the assisted places scheme seems to be saying is that many comprehensive schools are incapable of catering to the interests of gifted pupils.

The independent sector, through the auspices of the assisted places scheme, therefore provides a complementary experience of schooling by making available academic opportunities which can no longer be found in many maintained secondary schools. Even if this argument is true, it is not likely to find wide favour. The selective removal of gifted pupils from the maintained schools may merely create a self-fulfilling prophecy and delay what to many would be a more acceptable approach to the problem, that is to devise strategies that would require the comprehensive schools to fulfil their obligations to their academically talented pupils. To remove such pupils obviates the need to take direct action.

In key respects the assisted places scheme is a return, not so much to the direct grant system, but rather to the free-place tradition. A limited number of scholarships are made available to academically gifted children from poor families who, allegedly, would not otherwise be able to fulfil their full potential within the maintained sector. Private schooling is often regarded by government ministers as the last remaining bastion of high educational standards in secondary schooling. Furthermore, while the assisted places scheme may enhance the educational opportunities of selected individuals (whether it actually does so remains unproven), it also benefits the schools which participate in the scheme. It provides them with income, and some appear as dependent financially upon the scheme as many of the endowed secondary schools were upon their free-place pupils before the 1944 Education Act required them to make a choice as to their future destinies. It widens socially, while raising academically, the range of their pupils. Finally, it gives the schools an official seal of approval: they provide the most desired form of secondary schooling just as the endowed grammar and public schools did before the arrival of a maintained secondary sector.

Therefore, like the free-place tradition before it, the assisted places scheme has established a form of association between the maintained and private sectors of schooling. But it has generated the same resentments by recreating equally unfair terms of exchange. While the 1944 Education Act resolved the problem by separating the maintained from the fee-paying sector more sharply, the way forward now is to ensure their greater interpenetration but in ways which are mutually supportive rather than demeaning to one and threatening to the other.

CONCLUSION

For families with solid bourgeois aspirations, who none the less lack large economic resources, it is vitally important to ensure the access of their children to prestigious secondary schooling. Moreover, the political advantage of helping to sponsor such access should not be overlooked. Of course what is good for the individual may also be good for the school, and in this respect the financial advantage of an assisted places scheme to newly independent schools has been important. Although the assisted places scheme may be phased out by a future Labour government, it has already eased the passage to full independence of many former direct grant schools. Of course there may be a danger to the schools in being financially dependent upon the state (Walford, 1990, 69), but adroit management should prevent most schools from sliding into severe economic crisis. A Labour government is more likely to phase out assisted places than terminate them abruptly.

In terms of the institutional well-being of the private sector the assisted places scheme has the distinct advantage of allowing schools to tailor their commitments to suit their circumstances, and thus has embraced a wider segment of the private sector than the former direct grant schools. It has helped, therefore, to smooth over a long-standing breach within the private sector. In the context of possible future political threats to private schooling this is an important development for it means that there is broad and directly interested support for existing public policy. Inasmuch as the phasing out of the direct grant was closely tied up with the push to end selection in the maintained secondary schools, those independent schools wholly dependent upon fee income were somewhat removed from the sharp edge of that debate. That will be less true should the assisted places scheme be terminated, although the impact of such a move will have varying financial repercussions for the participating schools.

Although it may be possible to understand the varying bridges that the state has constructed between the maintained and private sectors of schooling in terms of both class reproduction and institutional survival, not unexpectedly, the proponents of such schemes have preferred alternative interpretations. Invariably the argument is that a valued form of schooling should be accessible to a wider range of individuals. From this perspective, the bridges have been constructed to assist deserving pupils, and the institutional and social consequences are incidental. Even if one accepts at face value this argument, the fact that there are social and institutional repercussions cannot be denied. Inevitably, these will generate responses, and so schooling becomes entangled in the ongoing battles of the political parties.

Supporters of the assisted places scheme have argued that its long-term survival is best assured by constructing a broad basis of political support. The problem of building such a support base is that it cannot be achieved without establishing the principles which should determine the relationship between the maintained and private sectors of schooling. Clearly within the ranks of the Conservative Party there was widespread unease at the movement towards comprehensive secondary schooling. It was believed that many comprehensive schools failed to develop the full academic potential of many – especially the brightest – of their pupils. The assisted places scheme was intended to provide a narrow escape route into the apparently greener pastures of fee-paying schools. In effect the two sectors of schooling are competing for official approval of what constitutes good practice, with talented pupils as the reward.

It seems very unlikely that the idea of linking maintained and private schooling by means of a narrow scholarship ladder will gain wide political support. The terms of the exchange are so one-sided that many interests – educational and political – are deeply offended. The alternatives are straightforward: either to reconstruct different patterns of state-sponsored access or to withdraw all public funding from such endeavours. In the latter situation the fee-paying sector would be left to sustain its presence through its success in the market. The opposition to such a strategy stems from the widely shared belief that access to such resources should not be rationed by the ability of families to pay fees, coupled with the contention that, although private institutions, fee-paying schools have such critical social repercussions that they cannot – and should not – be left to their own devices. As long as these remain powerful sentiments the question of access to private schooling will not disappear from the political agenda. Thus the question of how the state should intervene remains. In the final analysis, all that the current assisted places scheme can look to for political support is the continuation of Tory governments. Sooner or later a new accommodation must be sought for no government can last for ever.

7

Principles and Politics in the Process of Educational Change

The central issue to be addressed is why the various reports of the Fleming Committee and the Public Schools Commission were either not acted upon, or acted upon in ways that generated intense political hostility rather than a reconciliation of two contrasting educational traditions. Although the differing historical circumstances contain their own particular nuances, this chapter – drawing upon the theory of educational change presented in Chapter 1 – will present more general lines of argument. The proposition is that reconciliation in the past has been impossible because of key differences of principle between the major political parties. Moreover, these principles are central, not only to the educational debate, but also to other areas of social policy. Attempting to restructure the relationship between the maintained and fee-paying sectors of schooling has been only one manifestation of a much wider political struggle. Until the terms of that wider struggle were redefined then the preconditions for building meaningful bridges in the educational arena were missing. The building of those bridges remains the task for the final chapter.

Although in the years immediately before the Fleming Committee the financial basis of the fee-paying schools was parlous, this did not last. Thus, although there may have been considerable goodwill within the fee-paying sector for a closer liaison with the maintained schools, the prolonged financial pressure to reinforce this sentiment was lacking. In other words, one of the key pressures for change was absent. At the same time there were powerful political forces for a sharper separation of the maintained and fee-paying sectors of secondary schooling. These were successfully realised, albeit not in full, in the 1944 Education Act. The idea of free secondary education for all was accomplished in the form of creating a maintained sector of secondary schooling which excluded fee-payers but embraced an accommodation with the churches most of whose schools acquired the voluntary-aided or voluntary-controlled status.

The judgement of the Board of Education's President, R. A. Butler, to place the question of the independent schools to one side in the negotiations preceding the 1944 Education Act was therefore fully justified. To have put the issue on the agenda would have merely generated a great deal of hostility, and even jeopardised the Bill's chances of success. To many the compromise on the direct grant schools, which left the old system substantially intact, may have been unsatisfactory, but at least it was possible. If the direct grant issue was so divisive, it does not take much imagination to surmise that negotiations for putting the whole relationship between the maintained and fee-paying sectors on a different basis would have been swiftly deadlocked. The chasm between the respective interests was too great to bridge.

In effect, regardless of what many reasonable persons may have hoped, there was no sustained economic or political pressure in 1944 for creating a new association between the two sectors of schooling. The fortunes of the independent schools were on the mend, it had proved possible to stitch together a deal on the direct grant schools, and political sentiment was predominantly against using public money to construct new bridges. Indeed, given the widespread political influence of the post-war Labour Party, it was expedient for those in favour of change to let the matter lie fallow. Forces hostile to the interests of the fee-paying schools had a large parliamentary majority in the immediate post-war years, and to have kept the issue on the agenda could have stimulated them to push the Attlee government into taking more radical action. The desire for closer association can, as the Report of the Donnison Commission all too vividly illustrates, readily be turned into pressures for integration in a form which threatens the established identity of the fee-paying sector.

The creation of the Public Schools Commission was more politically driven. Its task was to devise means by which the independent boarding schools could be accommodated within the movement towards comprehensive secondary schooling. One suspects that if the commission's terms of reference had not been widened to incorporate the direct grant and independent day schools, then the direct grant system would have been swiftly terminated by administrative fiat. It was, therefore, in the fee-paying sector's interest to ensure that this did not happen, and its lobbying was successful. As was discussed in Chapter 5, the recommendations of the Newsom

Commission satisfied no one and were quickly buried. The Donnison Report, however, strongly appealed to those who had long sought the ending of the direct grant system, and action was merely forestalled by the election of a Conservative government under the leadership of Edward Heath.

While economic factors played an important part in the emergence of the Fleming Committee, the Public Schools Commission was first and foremost a product of political considerations. Although the evidence suggests that the fortunes of the fee-paying schools were in decline at this time, there was no rush to seek public assistance. The schools were in the process of finding out more about themselves and steadily changing their ways. In effect they were responding to market pressures, and Rae's Public School Revolution was under way. Furthermore, they probably felt that they could expect little from a Labour government, and certainly not on terms that many of them would find acceptable. Until the balance of national political forces had changed, the best way forward was internal regeneration. It could even be argued that, given the strong political pressure in favour of the reorganisation of secondary schooling along comprehensive lines, there was even less chance of building a political consensus in favour of a closer, and mutually acceptable, association between the two sectors of schooling than there had been in the mid-1940s. The policy gap on educational issues was growing wider, in spite of some attempts within the major political parties to maintain a semblance of consensus.

It is important to remember that while these macro-political struggles were taking place, the fee-paying schools were steadily responding to their apparently declining position within the marketplace. Institutional self-preservation demanded change, and change was forthcoming. Alongside this internal impetus for change occurred the more public political struggles which attempted to preserve or enhance the educational advantages of particular social groups. For example, the defence of the direct grant schools and the enactment of the assisted places scheme had broad social consequences as well as life-and-death significance for the fee-paying sector. Educational conflict was driven by contrasting interpretations of the purposes of schooling. For many schooling was as much about changing society as about encouraging individuals to fulfil their potential. Before the political debate on the relationship between the maintained and fee-paying sectors could bear fruit, a deeply entrenched value schism had to be bridged, and only then was the political system likely to produce a mutually acceptable inter-penetration of the two sectors of schooling.

Although there was little explicit in-depth discussion of values within either the Fleming Committee or the Public Schools Commission, both are implicitly infused with value conflicts which they struggled valiantly to reconcile. In the sense that they made recommendations that were almost unanimously agreed, they could be said to have bridged the unbridgeable. However, it is one thing to strike a bargain within the context of a commission of inquiry, and quite another for it to stick in the more robust world of party politics. The political struggles generated in recent years by the presence of the fee-paying sector are centred, therefore, upon attempts to restrict or secure access to a form of schooling that is considered to be an important resource in determining the individual's position in the structure of social stratification. Integral to the political struggles enveloping the process of educational change are underlying value conflicts. Either these are reconciled and change progresses consensually or they are not. In the latter circumstances the course of change will be determined by those who have the preponderance of political and/or economic resources, coupled with the ability to use them effectively.

CONFLICTING PRINCIPLES

Three key value conflicts have underwritten the relationship between the maintained and fee-paying sectors of schooling:

1. The schools provide an education to those who can afford to pay their fees, and parents have the right to purchase that education. None the less the state retains the authority, usually in defence of community interests, to restrict the activities of both producers and consumers.

2. The schools perceive themselves as independent corporate bodies, which have the right in law to control their own affairs. However, because schooling has important social consequences, there are demands that all schools should be democratically accountable.

3. A central component of the independence of the schools is their right to select their pupils on the basis of whatever criteria they determine. Inevitably this runs up against the insistence that each school should be a neighbourhood school with a pupil intake as

comprehensive in character as possible, although in reality the social composition of many neighbourhoods will make such a goal unrealistic.

What is at stake here is a more general conflict between those who believe that there is a range of social services that can be provided more equitably, and perhaps even more effectively, by the state rather than by the marketplace. Intrusion upon the right of parents to purchase an education in schools that charge fees is based upon the principle that education is a scarce resource which should be distributed by publicly determined criteria. If it is provided by schools that charge fees then it is the purchasing power of the parents, rather than the publicly determined criteria, that shapes the patterns of access to schooling. Whether the parents are actually purchasing a higher-quality education, which presumably many of them feel they are, is beside the point. It is their purchase of the resource, based upon inequalities in the distribution of wealth and income, that constitutes the privilege, rather than the quality of the educational experiences they are buying.

Those who oppose restrictions upon the right of parents to purchase schooling do so on both principled and pragmatic grounds. While it may be accepted that the state has a duty to provide a range of social services, including schooling, this does not negate parental rights. Most parents feel obliged to do their best by their own children, and if they believe that by paying school fees they are fulfilling that obligation, the state has no right to deny them. The pragmatic objections would focus on the alleged ability of the fee-paying schools to enhance both the quality and variety of the nation's schooling, while questioning whether universal state provision really does enhance equality of educational opportunity. Moreover, the state could experience great difficulties were it to establish, and attempt to enforce, very severe prohibitions. For example, what kind of machinery would be needed to enforce a prohibition on private tutoring? Or what other goods and services are parents to be forbidden to buy because they apparently enhance unfairly (because other parents lack the economic resources to purchase them) the educational opportunities of their children?

Fee-paying has been a long-standing sensitive issue in the history of British education. Initially the direct provision of elementary schooling by the state, although compulsory, was not free of charge. However, to increase the provision of free schooling was one of the central objectives of the progressive forces within the educational policy-making process. There was the attraction of establishing a sector of schooling that was not tied to sectional interests (most notably the churches); moreover, free schooling allegedly enhanced educational opportunities because it made schooling available on the basis of individual merit and needs rather than the ability of parents to pay fees. However, while the expansion of free schooling would extend educational opportunities it would not within itself equalise those opportunities. The next vital measure was to establish, at all levels, a system of free schooling for all. And for others the aim was to follow this by prohibiting schools from charging fees, so making it impossible for parents to purchase private schooling. All these varying sentiments received a public hearing both in evidence to the Fleming Committee and during the passage of the 1944 Education Act.

The most explicit recognition of the tension between the right of parents to purchase schooling and the interests of the community was expressed by the Trades Union Congress in its evidence to the Fleming Committee: '... the history of liberty was the history of encroachment on private rights in the interests of the freedom of the community' (as quoted in Gosden, 1976, 349). In fact none of the Reports analysed in the previous two chapters made a serious attempt to undertake any in-depth exploration of the tension between community interests and individual rights. Either these were not conducive arenas for the discussion of fundamental points of principle or there was a general awareness that to have done so would only open up ideological wounds, so making it more difficult to reach pragmatic compromises. However, given that such confrontations were bound to emerge within the political arena – indeed were raging while the commissions were in progress – perhaps it would have been wiser to have explored some possible lines of reconciliation, or at least the strengths of the respective positions.

Suffice it to say that to date those who have been opposed to the right of parents to purchase schooling have lacked sufficient political muscle to enact the necessary legislation. Indeed, as was noted in Chapter 4 (see p.85), the 1944 Education Act (Chapter 31, Section 76) actually required the local education authorities to educate children in accordance with the wishes of their parents. Furthermore, this requirement was used by parents to press the LEAs into paying school fees. Even the very politically divisive 1976 Education Act did not remove this right. It reintroduced a closer monitoring of these local deals by the DES (reverting to the 1944 legislation) while – and this was the contentious point – preventing the LEAs from purchasing places in the fee-paying sector for children on the grounds of their academic ability and/or special talents. Furthermore, although the Donnison Report called for the ending of the direct grant system, and urged the schools to join the movement towards comprehensive secondary education, it recognised their right to ignore its advice and take their chances in the marketplace. In other words, it accepted the right of schools to charge fees and of parents to pay them.

In spite of considerable hostility towards the fee-paying schools on the part of some elements in past Labour governments, it is widely recognised that to prohibit the charging, and thus the paying, of fees would be such a significant political step that it is better contemplated than actually taken. In such circumstances by far the wisest political course is a long process of attrition rather than an attack upon principles that are widely and deeply held. Essentially, this has been the strategy adopted in the past by the Labour Party.

The tension between institutional independence and democratic accountability has never been as sharp as the conflicts generated by fee-paying, although it has been an equally persistent issue. The 1944 Education Act allowed schools to negotiate entry into the maintained sector with either voluntary-aided or voluntary-controlled status. With either status, however, they were ultimately the responsibility of a local education authority which would have its representatives on the governing bodies. How heavy-handed local authorities exercised their rights was a matter of judgement, and, in any case, would vary from local authority to local authority. The Fleming Committee recommended that schools participating in its Scheme A (which was to replace the direct grant system) should have at least one-third of their governors nominated by the LEAs sending pupils to the schools (1944, 65), whereas the schools participating in Scheme B (designed to encourage pupils from the maintained primary schools to enter independent boarding schools) would have up to one-third of their governors nominated by the Board of Education, although if there were direct agreements between schools and individual local authorities then governors should be nominated by those authorities (1944, 67).

The question of local authority input into the government of schools loomed less large in the Newsom Report, not surprisingly given its proposition that assisted places should be distributed nationally by a Boarding Schools Corporation, but it was a key issue for the Donnison Report. While recommending that the direct grant system should be ended, Donnison argued that:

> Governors, heads and staff at direct grant schools which choose
> to become full grant or locally maintained schools should retain
> the essential freedoms they already have... (1970, 13).

In an effort to reinforce the strength of this argument, the Report went on to say that 'maintained secondary schools should have the same essential freedoms as former direct grant schools', and to this end, the Secretary of State should issue the LEAs with a memorandum of guidance on the government of schools (1970, 13). Though apparently arguing for a greater measure of freedom of action for all schools, Donnison added that in exercising their 'essential freedoms' those direct grant schools incorporated within the maintained sector would be 'subject to prior agreement about the role of the school within the comprehensive system and about the arrangements for the admission of pupils' (1970, 13). In view of the Report's support for the reorganisation of secondary schooling along comprehensive lines, this was an inevitable qualifying statement. However, it could be of little comfort to schools which in the past had controlled their own admissions process, and saw such control as one of the hallmarks of their independence. Institutional independence, as circumscribed by Donnison's terms, would have a hollow ring.

Many of the direct grant schools felt that to receive financial support from central government, rather than the local education authorities, gave them a distinctive status. Not surprisingly, they were loath to lose it. Moreover, their dealings with local education authorities had not always been harmonious. Some authorities were more obdurate than others, as Donnison's recommendation that the Secretary of State should issue a memorandum of guidance implied. In fact, the tension between local authorities and the direct grant schools mounted as the comprehensive reorganisation of secondary schooling progressed. The local authorities were pulling out of arrangements to fill places in direct grant schools as they moved towards comprehensive secondary education (see p.115). Although this was an inevitable development, it was none the less crucial in persuading the private sector interests that the local authorities should be excluded from any future assisted places scheme.

While it is difficult to contemplate any easy bridging of the ideological gap on the fee-paying issue (its possible resolution, as will be argued in the final chapter, has been brought about by long-term political and economic developments), the question of a school's authority to control its own affairs has always been more amenable to compromise. For example, it is interesting to note that, while the

Donnison Report was urging the direct grant schools to become part of the general movement towards comprehensive secondary schooling, it was prepared to recommend compromises on the question of school management. Partly because of its traditional principles, and partly because of the need to sustain internal cohesion, the Labour Party remains committed to the idea that the best means of ensuring the democratic accountability of schools is by retaining the local education authorities as the bodies ultimately responsible for their management. However, it has accepted the loss of local authority control over governing bodies, and will not rescind the 'local management of schools' clauses in the 1988 Education Reform Act which give enhanced financial powers to those governing bodies.

The question, therefore, of who formally controls the schools, and determines school policy, is open to considerable political manoeuvring. The idea of local democratic accountability can be interpreted in a number of different ways, and the current Labour Party position is to stress the need for partnership between schools and their local authorities with the possibility that alternative models of co-operation can be established (Labour Party, 1995). However, at its 1996 Conference the party turned its attention away from the divisive question of control to those of selection and standards around which it can construct a more united front (*Times Educational Supplement*, 4 October 1956, 4). Nevertheless, as the fine print of the Donnison Report illustrates, the superficially attractive can be less appealing on further inspection. Institutions that are independent corporate bodies in law and do not have either to follow the national curriculum or to submit to key-stage testing, and – subject to market pressures – can admit whom they like, might take some persuading that to embrace the state is indeed in their best interests.

While the private sector is selective in that it makes schooling available to parents who can afford to pay fees, many schools also adopt – with varying degrees of rigour – a policy of academic selection (see p.153). Although a few famous public schools, most notably Winchester College, have imposed demanding entrance standards, the direct grant grammar schools had the reputation of being the most academically selective institutions, and some – perhaps most notably Manchester Grammar School – have been perceived as highly successful examination factories. Although obviously aware of this situation, the Fleming Committee was sensitive to the danger of selecting pupils for its proposed independent boarding school bursaries on the basis of competitive examinations. The commissioners argued that to do so would offend the maintained sector and work against the idea that the boarding school needed to be 'a true community' composed of children with varying intellectual abilities 'as well as those of different temperaments and interests' (1944, 71).

But in the context of a maintained sector of secondary schooling which at the time, with a few local experiments to the contrary, followed an academically selective bi- or tri-partite model, there was limited *principled* objection to academic selection, and certainly an accusatory finger could not be pointed at the private sector alone. Moreover, the majority of independent day and boarding schools undoubtedly contained a wider range of academic ability among their pupils than most schools in the selective system of state secondary schooling. Winchester College and Manchester Grammar School were the exceptions rather than the rule.

None the less, as the movement towards comprehensive secondary schooling gained momentum, so academically selective admissions policies became an increasing focus of attention, and the direct grant schools in particular were to feel the heat. We have already considered how the movement towards comprehensive secondary schooling led the bulk of the Donnison Commissioners to believe that the incorporation of the direct grant schools was a logical conclusion. While the Newsom Report proposed the retention of a measure of academic selection in the awarding of its assisted places, like Fleming, it flatly rejected the idea of competitive examinations. The drift, implicitly accepted by Newsom, was to accept the movement towards a common model of secondary schooling with each individual school as comprehensive in character as local circumstances permitted.

However, as if in a grudging willingness to accommodate the critics of the common school model, the Newsom Report contemplated the possibility that 'one or two schools might become "academies" catering for children with special aptitudes in music or ballet' (1968, 8). And even more niggardly: 'Proposals to cater entirely for gifted children from an early age should be viewed with considerable caution, but are not excluded by our recommendations' (1968, 8). There were parallel debates in the Donnison Report, which accepted the principle of separate schools for children with special aptitudes but was not prepared to endorse, even in the very guarded terms of the Newsom Report, the proposition that perhaps academically gifted children were better catered for in their own schools, although this did not prevent a few commissioners making positive claims for super-selective grammar schools.

In 'A Note of Reservation' to the Newsom Report, two of its commissioners, Kathleen Bliss and John Dancy, contended that a very few highly selective schools would have little general impact, and, in a more critically important argument, insisted that such advocacy was consistent with the Commission's own terms of reference which were directed – as they saw it – at the overall character of the public school sector rather than at individual schools. In effect they were placing under scrutiny the very idea of what is meant by a comprehensive system of secondary schooling. If every school should approximate to a common model, then the scope for institutional diversity was negligible. In the common school model if individuals were to follow different educational paths, this was a choice to be exercised within schools rather than between them. Of greater immediate political significance was the fact that the advocacy of such a model made it impossible to achieve compromises for it ruled out the flexibility that a focus upon the general character of the private sector would have provided. Compromise was possible only if provision was made for internal diversity; some schools had distinctive characters which they had no intention of willingly compromising.

The Fleming Committee firmly believed that, although it was advocating a form of association between maintained and private schooling, its proposals would result in the creation of a coherent whole:

> But it is vital to our conception that the system, should from now onwards, be regarded as a single whole, with schools of different types (1944, 63).

However, both the Newsom and Donnison Reports believed that the educational system could not form a single whole unless the two sectors were integrated. And, in spite of their radically different interpretations of integration, both reports saw the individual maintained and private schools as moving steadily towards a common model. In other words, the single whole was not constructed from mutually reinforcing different parts but rather the parts were replicas, or in time would become replicas, of one another.

In my judgement, the possibility of bridging the ideological divide on the issues of fee-paying, independence and academic selection is dependent today upon an acceptance of the Fleming Committee's understanding of unity: that is, the association of schools with differing characters. But it does raise a very pertinent question: if there are to be different types of schools, how can the system at large be regarded as a single whole? Except for arguing that those receiving assisted places in the independent boarding schools should not be selected by competitive examination, the Fleming Committee conspicuously failed to explore this question, assuming, rather, that its reform proposals would have the desired effect. This was little more than wishful thinking, although the failure to implement the Report's recommendations meant that this was not subsequently demonstrated. While other matters have come to dominate the educational agenda, there can be no long-term reconciliation of the maintained/private sector divide without resolving the question of pupil selection. It is the central problem that the state needs to address, and it will form the core of the analysis in the final chapter.

INTEGRATION WITHOUT INTERPENETRATION

Unlike the recommendations of the Fleming and Newsom Reports, those of the Donnison Report were enacted, although not before the interlude of the Heath government with Mrs Thatcher as Secretary of State for Education. In the subsequent Wilson government the Report found a sufficiently large measure of sympathy to ensure action on its proposals. Probably the most obvious lesson for those intent on pursuing educational change through the political process is the need to ensure that proposals for reform, sooner or later, have the sympathy of a government with a comfortable parliamentary majority. The direct grant system was phased out by administrative fiat, and the 1976 Education Act empowered the Department of Education and Science to monitor more closely the purchase of places in fee-paying schools by the local educational authorities.

There may be some irony in the fact that the Donnison Report's more politically partisan recommendations should be enacted while the Newsom and Fleming Reports were left to moulder. There is a double irony inasmuch as the most pertinent reason for Donnison's success is, in fact, a consequence of its weakness rather than its strength. The Donnison Report sought to reshape the educational system in only a negative sense: there was no attempt to establish a new relationship between the direct grant schools and the maintained comprehensive secondary schools – the former were to lose their distinctive identities by integrating them with the latter. For all their wishful thinking, the Fleming and Newsom Reports were trying to suggest ways in which the relationship between the maintained and fee-paying sectors could be positively restructured by the state. The dominant sentiment within the Donnison Commission was that the schism could not be breached, which may have been both logical and politically realistic but, in the sense that it followed an undemanding path, was also both cautious and conventional.

Moreover, although it is impossible to reach a conclusive judgement, the Report's recommendations may well have been self-defeating. The move towards comprehensive secondary schooling probably persuaded a wider range of middle-class parents to consider seriously the possibility of sending their children to fee-paying schools. After a long period of decline the private sector stabilised in the 1970s and expanded slowly in the 1980s. Using DES statistics, Walford has calculated that by 1976 only 5.8 per cent of pupils in English primary and secondary schools were in fee-paying schools. Thereafter it expanded slowly, and by 1987 had risen to 7 per cent (Walford, 1990, 17). Perhaps it is simply a coincidence, but 1976 is the very year in which the phasing out of the direct grant began.

More significant is the fact that approximately two-thirds of the schools (some 118 out of 171) survived the phasing out of the direct grant to take their chances in the marketplace. Of those schools that joined the maintained sector, forty-eight were Catholic schools, the bulk of which had accepted a much larger quota of free-place pupils than the statutory minimum of 25 per cent. At a stroke, therefore, the fee-paying sector had received a massive boost, for this was the most rapid expansion in the whole of its history. Although it would be unfair to credit the Donnison Commission with sole responsibility for this calamity (from its self-confessed perspective), none the less, its terms of reference were to suggest effective means by which the direct grant schools could join in the reorganisation of secondary schooling along comprehensive lines. Most decidedly, the goal was *not* to encourage the growth of the independent sector.

The Donnison Commission's recommendations, while logical in principle and technically feasible, were self-defeating in practice. Although politically successful, inasmuch as its Report helped to shape subsequent government action, it was unable to persuade those who should have counted most in its thinking – the direct grant schools themselves. One suspects that the commissioners failed to anticipate the eventual outcome, and, in any case, there was overwhelming evidence that the schools would not willingly participate in any schemes of comprehensive reorganisation on the terms of the Donnison Report, regardless of the arguments. In effect the outcome was virtually predetermined, and all that remained to be decided was

143

how many of the direct grant schools were prepared to forfeit the state's financial support and trust to their market appeal.

CONCLUSION

From 1944 to 1976, the period under observation in this and the two previous chapters, the political left intensified its opposition to the independence of the fee-paying schools, the right of parents to purchase education, and selective secondary schooling. It succeeded in capturing the high ground of educational thinking, which enabled it to shape both how people thought about the key issues and to determine the direction of the policy debates. For a number of years it carried along in its wake large elements from all the major political parties in Britain. Indeed, the tradition of state control was deeply embedded in the Conservative Party, especially within the local authorities. For example, it was usually Conservative MPs who defended the direct grant schools in 1944 rather than Conservative local councillors who often believed they knew more about the efficient management of schools than governors. Moreover, while Conservative-controlled local authorities tended to resist the movement towards comprehensive secondary schooling, their opposition was restricted.

The years from 1976 to 1979 were the high watermark of statism. However, during those years it was driven forward by a government with a small and shrinking parliamentary majority, which seemed bent more on maintaining the unity of its party base than on offering leadership to the nation and, most significantly of all, started to express its own doubts about the very values which had guided its educational policy in the recent past. Of course during these years the direct grant schools were phased out, the purchase of places in the fee-paying sector by the LEAs was restricted, and there was a concerted attempt to require local authorities to reorganise their secondary schools according to comprehensive principles. However, these were relatively soft targets, although those who like to engage in wishful thinking might perceive them as preludes to legislation that would prohibit schools from charging fees. Furthermore, they were pushed through in a context which was no longer dominated by the political left's educational agenda, which is vividly illustrated by the length of parliamentary time it took to pass the comparatively short 1976 Education Act. It was obvious that none of these measures would be accepted by a subsequent Conservative government should one be elected.

There had always been elements within the Labour Party who

believed that if the maintained schools offered an improving standard of education then the fee-paying schools would wither as they were steadily deserted by their middle-class clientele. With the abolition of the direct grant schools, and the relentless squeeze upon the local authority-controlled grammar schools, this became an increasingly unviable strategy. There is a range of empirical evidence to suggest (see p.191) that middle-class parents are more likely to remain within the state sector of schooling if it is organised along selective lines. Once the grammar and direct grant schools started to disappear, it could be expected that middle-class parents would gravitate towards the fee-paying sector in increasing numbers. In effect, the strategy of undermining the fee-paying sector by improving the maintained schools became untenable. It was logical, therefore, for the Labour Party to embrace the idea of prohibiting schools from charging fees; it was now the only way forward for those who believed that this fundamental divide within the educational system had to be closed.

In the meantime the Conservative Party, under the leadership of Mrs Thatcher, was starting to challenge the dominant values which had directed the educational debate since 1944, and by 1979 what remained of the fragile vestiges of consensus had all but evaporated. The opportunity for creative thinking about the relationship between the maintained and fee-paying sectors of schooling is a consequence of the new inter-party consensus which has slowly, and with considerable difficulty, emerged over the past decade.

The argument, therefore, is that the objective conditions required by the state or the market to bridge the maintained/private sector divide did not exist at the time of either the Fleming Committee or the Public Schools Commission. Several critical developments, within both the political parties and the fee-paying sector, had to occur to make this a possibility. Unlike the recommendations of Fleming and Newsom, those of the Donnison Report were implemented, but it is a perverse view of the change process that would count Donnison as a success for, far from integrating the direct grant schools into the maintained sector, it helped to reinforce the strength of the private sector. The Donnison Report was a monument to past thinking, but something different was needed to bridge the divided system. The new consensus, like the old moderate position within the Labour Party, is built upon the need to change the maintained sector of schooling. As this has occurred, so the private sector has been reshaped by the pressures of the marketplace. Do the preconditions for a constructive association now exist?

8

Making the Product More Widely Available

In this century, the various bodies that represent independent schooling have periodically called for a closer relationship between the fee-paying and maintained sectors. Invariably the appeal has been for the state to underwrite the fees of those who desire, and would benefit from, independent schooling but whose parents cannot afford the costs. The argument is that fee-paying schools have a quality product, which should be made more widely available. Whereas cynics might wonder why such siren voices seem to be heard most often when demand for places in fee-paying schools is in decline, the more reflective response is to ponder the implications of such action for the vaunted idea of independence. In a very sophisticated political interpretation of a possible future relationship between independent schooling and a Labour government, the 1996 chairman of the Headmasters' and Headmistresses' Conference (Tony Evans, Headmaster of Portsmouth Grammar School) broached this very issue (*The Times*, 9 February 1996, 33).

After making the usual point that the fee-paying sector can cater to the needs of certain children more effectively than maintained schools (referring specifically to that hoary old chestnut, boarding education), Evans went on to argue that the schools have to be careful not to 'compromise their academic values and freedom', and 'they would be unwise to barter such freedom against even assisted places ...'. But he expressed his hope that:

> ... a Labour government would seek to draw strength from independent schools and devise an alternative scheme in partnership which reconciles their independence with a range of admissions across the social spectrum on the basis of need.

In partnership or not, if the parties are serious about arriving at a mutually agreeable consensus, there will have to be give-and-take in the negotiating process. Clearly a Labour government would want to know precisely what are these 'academic values and freedom' which cannot be compromised, and whether it would not be better to respond to the actual demand for, rather than the alleged need of, schooling in the fee-paying sector.

One suspects that if political pressure, or sheer economic necessity, are great enough, then the schools will always find that they have acted in ways that are indeed consistent with their core values. In other words, the independence of the fee-paying schools is inevitably threatened by their interaction with both the marketplace and the state, and is always a matter for negotiation. This is not to suggest either that the fee-paying schools take the defence of their independence lightly or that they will always act pragmatically to further their own interests. But it does mean institutional self-preservation is their ultimate concern, and this struggle for survival occurs within the framework of a value system which is problematic with respect to its meaning, the relative weight of its component parts, and how it should be implemented. Over time all these factors can change.

In recent years the balance between day and boarding pupils in many schools has swung markedly in favour of the former, while some schools have decided to admit day pupils for the first time. Many schools are now fully co-educational, and others have actively sought out overseas markets. While there may be a range of motivations for such innovations, they are also clear responses to marketplace pressures. Although such changes may not threaten 'academic values and freedom' as such, they must clearly modify the character of a school which had been proud of its Christian ethos, and had been educating only boys and only boarders. How much change must occur before a school's basic values are threatened? What are the core values that must be defended at all costs?

The chapter on the assisted places scheme reflected with some interest upon the fact that the schools were determined to control the admissions process: setting their own entrance examinations, keeping the local education authorities at bay, and accepting numbers that matched their circumstances. Their only serious setback was the failure to persuade the government to underwrite the fees of those who would benefit from a boarding education. But this emerged as an issue only after the scheme had been tainted by the serious charge of poaching academically gifted pupils from the maintained sector. The partnership which constructed the scheme therefore reached a compromise which suited the interests of the fee-paying sector. The state, thanks to the sentiments of the Conservative government, had proved most amenable. If the respective interests decide to act on Evans's proposal, it will be instructive to see whether the negotiating partners – influenced this time by a Labour government – will be equally successful.

Regardless of the broader pressures for change and the threat they pose to independence, the admissions process – especially to the fee-paying secondary schools – has inevitably become more institutionalised over time. Formally schools may control whom they admit, but they do so through procedures which have not necessarily been determined by themselves as individual parties; that is, the schools exercise their own institutional controls within a widely agreed admissions process. First, there is the division of the fee-paying sector into its two main, or at least best-known, sectors: the preparatory schools and the independent secondary schools with pupils passing from one to the other usually at the age of 13+. This divide was established by the much repeated interaction in the nineteenth century of the reforms instigated by the headmasters and the pressures exerted by the great Royal Commissions. In the late 1830s, Thomas Arnold decided to abolish the first two forms at Rugby School, thereby ensuring 'thereafter that no boy under twelve could enter Rugby' (Leinster-Mackay, 1984, 109). But apparently other leading public schools were slow to follow Arnold's initiative, and there was not a general shift in the same direction until the Clarendon Commissioners had urged similar action.

Leinster-Mackay argues that the reason for separating the younger boys from the older ones was 'for the sake of moral protection and shelter from predatory bullies' (1984, 110). And with particular reference to Eton College (which among the leading public schools was most inclined to admit younger boys), the Clarendon Commissioners expressed their enthusiasm for such a division: 'We shall propose that every boy in the Lower School be required, unless he lives at home, to board in the house of the Lower Master, or in one of the houses kept by the Assistant Lower Masters, and that neither the Lower Master nor the Assistant Lower Masters be allowed to receive any but Lower School boys, or to keep them after they have risen into the Upper School' (1864, 110). The natural consequence was the emergence of preparatory schools, either as junior schools within the public schools or as separate foundations.

Once the preparatory schools had started to flourish, there was the inevitable question of how they would relate to the public schools: more particularly what procedures would determine how pupils passed from one level of schooling to the next. As Leinster-Mackay has shown (1984, 110–13), strong links were often forged between preparatory and public schools when the former had been established by an assistant master from the public school. This may have been a question of obliging personal favours, but was also likely to reflect the preparatory school's success in turning out pupils who could cope with the demands of public school life; that is, the public schools knew the product and were prepared to trust it. Presumably experience would either confirm or deny the judgements, and previous decisions could be adjusted accordingly.

Not surprisingly, the nineteenth-century commissioners were unlikely to trust decisions made on the basis of either conventions emerging from personal ties or the experience of trial and error. Like the good rational human beings they were, they turned to examinations to form the link between the two levels of schooling. The Clarendon Commission asserted:

> We have recommended that at every school there shall be an entrance examination, which shall not be merely nominal, and the standard of which shall be graduated according to the age of the candidate. We are well aware that some difficulty may be found in maintaining such a test with the strictness which we deem necessary; that plausible excuses may be constantly urged for relaxing it; and that the interests of the schools themselves, superficially regarded, may seem to militate against it ... . When it is known that the test is established, and known that it will be adhered to, parents will have themselves only to blame if their sons are deprived of the advantage of a public-school education for want of qualifications which might have been secured by proper and timely care (1864, 40).

That proper and timely care increasingly meant sending the boy to a good preparatory school, and, if the parents had a particular public school in mind, even the right preparatory school.

We have discussed how, following yet again the interaction of reforming headmasters and commissioners, public school scholarships were increasingly awarded on the basis of competitive examinations as founders' restrictions were swept away (see p.42). The Clarendon Commissioners, therefore, also urged that all entry to the schools should be partly determined by examination. The outcome was that the schools, including the newly founded public schools, conducted their own scholarship examinations while entrance for other pupils was dependent upon a far less demanding qualifying test. Since 1903 this qualifying test has been known as the Common Entrance Examination (CEE), when it was placed under the auspices of a committee composed of members of HMC and the then AHPS, the Association of Headmasters of Preparatory Schools (Leinster-Mackay, 1984, 173–4). Currently the CEE falls under the jurisdiction of a Joint Standing Committee of GSA, HMC and IAPS (which, significantly, 'provides a forum for the discussion of matters of common interest to the three Associations') and is administered by an Independent Schools Examinations Board (Harries, 1995/96, p. xxxii).

In a very real sense the introduction of the Common Entrance Examination represented a major step in the integration of the fee-paying sector of schooling. Thanks to the joint control of the examination process, the links between the preparatory and public school sectors were institutionalised. Henceforth their respective representatives had to meet on a scheduled basis to oversee a matter of common importance. In effect they could no longer conduct all of their affairs independently of one another. Inevitably the examination has shaped the curriculum of the preparatory schools, and, as their label implies, they can be perceived, albeit perhaps unfairly, in the narrow terms of grooming pupils for a public school education. In the latter half of the nineteenth century the preparatory and the public schools came to form two complementary parts of a common purpose: the making of the English gentleman.

As far as the wider world is concerned, it is the lubrication of the entry process by money which represents the most critical form of institutional control. Although the demands of the Common Entrance Examination could suggest that examination success is the motor that drives the fee-paying schools, the popular image of the private schools is that they are sustained by well-to-do people. In spite of all the attempts in recent years to scotch the traditional myths associated with the fee-paying sector, the idea that it is essentially reserved for privileged children is difficult to shake. The fact that the independent sector's publicity (note, for example, the ISIS *Newsletter*) so often extols the virtues of thrifty widows merely serves to confirm the point. The need of the schools to cover their costs means that the fee barrier is a double-edged form of institutional control. On the one hand pupils may be excluded (invariably it is also a process of self-exclusion) whom it would be rewarding to teach, while, on the other hand, pupils may be admitted whom the schools would prefer not to educate. Regardless, the fee barrier makes it impossible for the schools to claim that they are educating only those who will make the best use of their educational resources. Among the self-excluded, or those who simply cannot afford the fees, there may be many who are more worthy. To evaluate more fully the limits these financial and academic constraints place upon individual opportunity and institutional independence, we must first consider some of the actual data patterns that emerge from the admissions process.

CLEARING THE ADMISSIONS HURDLES

In the preceding discussion of the relationship between admissions and independence, it was suggested that three variables determined the individual's ability to move smoothly from a preparatory school to a public school: age, academic ability and sufficient financial resources to pay the fees. But the fee-paying sector is wider than these particular models of private schooling, and, moreover, generalisations have been made which fail to convey the subtlety in the relationship between preparatory and public schools. For example, some of the members of HMC have always been predominantly day schools with a tradition of accepting boys at the age of 11+. Such schools have invariably been very academically selective and their choice of pupils has not usually depended upon the Common Entrance Examination which, although it can be sat at either 11+ or 12+, was initially designed for those aged 13+. Furthermore, most fee-paying schools, especially the prestigious boarding schools, provided an education for boys only, which inevitably meant that the range of choices for girls was more restricted. However, with the widespread movement towards co-education this bias has been steadily eroded.

It is reasonable to make the generalisation that over time entry to the fee-paying sector has become less restrictive in the sense that there is more choice for all pupils of a decent academic standard whose families can afford to pay the fees. Even Eton College, which remains a boarding school catering exclusively for boys, has a junior scholarship scheme designed to recruit boys from the maintained sector at about the age of 11. Those who are successful hold their scholarship at a preparatory school until they are 13+ and ready to enter Eton either as Oppidans (with the fees met, at least in part, by the College) or as successful candidates in the Scholarship Examination. In effect, this novel mode of entry bypasses, to some extent, both the Common Entrance Examination and admission at the age of 13. Not surprisingly, Eton College feels that the main cause for celebration is that the scheme enables a number of boys (initially there were to be six awards each year) to come to the College who otherwise would not have had the opportunity.

Table 8.1 gives some idea of this internal social diversity. Although the figures in Table 8.1 cover only those schools which are members of ISIS, they represent the broad base of the fee-paying sector; undoubtedly they include almost all the reputable institutions that provide an education for pupils in the age range 7 to 18+. Moreover, thanks in part to the work of ISIS, they are the schools for which the most reliable statistics are available, and, with the help of the ISIS Annual Census, it is possible to make comparisons over much of the past twenty years. If it is accepted that the only restriction exerted by the individual's age is upon the level of schooling desired (that is, transfer to secondary schooling occurs between the ages of 11+ and 13+), and that gender has all but disappeared as a social barrier to access, then the two variables which need to be considered further are the financial and academic hurdles.

TABLE 8.1
PUPIL NUMBERS BY ASSOCIATION, 1995

	HMC	SHMIS	GBA	GSA	GBGSA	IAPS	ISAI	TOTAL
No. of schools	237	51	13	238	7	516	285	1,347
Full Boarders								
Boys	30,081	4,383	675	74		9,374	1,826	46,413
Girls	8,399	1,679	293	14,000	46	2,904	1,076	28,397
Weekly Boarders								
Boys	1,343	409	22	4		1,941	411	4,130
Girls	363	131	9	2,521	58	975	277	4,334
Day Pupils								
Boys	95,050	6,688	3,493	2,309	523	63,379	26,328	197,770
Girls	25,268	3,898	1,352	92,550	1,975	33,106	26,289	184,438
TOTALS								
Boys	126,474	11,480	4,190	2,387	523	74,694	28,565	248,313
Girls	34,030	5,708	1,654	109,071	2,079	36,985	27,642	217,169
TOTAL	160,504	17,188	5,844	111,458	2,602	111,679	56,207	465,482

Source: ISIS, *Census*, April 1995, Table 1, p. 8.

Note: Some schools belong to more than one association but have not been recorded twice. For the full titles of the associations listed in this chapter's tables see p. ix.

The Common Entrance Examination

The Common Entrance Examination represents a convenient starting-point for evaluating in more detail the academic entrance hurdle. First, it remains the guide that many of the most prestigious secondary fee-paying schools employ to test the basic competence of their applicants; that is those who achieve the school's standard are deemed to be capable of coping with its academic programme. The 1995/96 edition of *The Independent Schools Yearbook* lists 161 members of HMC, 45 members of GSA, 30 members of SHMIS and 19 other schools (several of which are located overseas), which use the Common Entrance Examination to assist them in the selection of candidates (Harries, 1995/96, xxxiii–xxxv). With one exception (Winchester College), all the nine schools investigated by the Clarendon Commission require their candidates to sit this examination. Second, because it is a widely used examination, there is more publicly available information about it, although it remains a much under-researched topic.

The first point to note is that the CEE does not provide a universal academic link between the differing levels of the fee-paying sector. This is partly explained by the fact that many of the independent secondary day schools were for so long firmly tied into the grammar school tradition with an entry that was to a considerable extent underwritten by support from both central government and the local authorities. Many of their pupils came to them via the old 11+ examination route, which was controlled by the LEAs. Furthermore, many of these day schools still retain a more narrowly defined academic ethos than most of those independent schools that historically have been centred on a boarding tradition, and they would probably find an entrance examination modelled on the CEE less suitable for their purposes.

It is significant that only Winchester College of the Clarendon Nine Schools retains its own entrance examination, although for a long time this had also been true of Westminster School. Winchester is well-known for priding itself on very high academic standards: in somewhat Olympian tones, a former head, John Thorn, described the College's examination as a 'sharper instrument' than the CEE (Wilby, 22 November 1981, 41), by which, presumably, he meant that the school needed a more rigorous mechanism than the CEE for excluding all but those few candidates deemed capable of profiting from a Winchester College education, which gives a clear insight into the College's official ethos.

The CEE, as John Thorn's observation implies, is a qualifying test, rather than a demanding examination barrier. Or, in the words of John Dancy, 'The Common Entrance examination itself is intended rather as a qualifying test of attainment than as a competitive test of intelligence' (1963, 40). By way of contrast, scholarship examinations are highly competitive. While papers for the CEE are set by examiners appointed by the Independent Schools Examinations Board, they are marked 'by the senior school for which a candidate is entered' (Harries, 1995/96, xxxii). The continuing use of the examination as a convenient backstop for the senior schools is suggested by the fact that most candidates sit the CEE in order to secure the confirmation of a conditional offer. Other candidates are likely to be either those who are using it as a prelude to a scholarship examination or those who have been entered by their junior schools for a trial run. Dancy, in an admittedly dated guess, conjectured that approximately 80 to 85 per cent of candidates pass the examination at their first attempt and enter senior schools of their first choice (1963, 39). Those who fail to meet the standard of the school for which they have applied (probably a percentage that has declined since Dancy's guess) have either to resit the examination or to find a school with less demanding academic standards, and to this end the Independent Schools Examination Board operates a clearing-house system. The impression is that candidates who struggle with the entrance examination are retained within the fee-paying sector but need to move to a school with less demanding academic standards if they wish to secure a place.

There are, therefore, several features about the CEE that make it an interesting compromise between the desire to sustain the right of the individual schools to determine whom they admit as pupils, and the wish to establish a more centrally co-ordinated pattern of admissions control. The centralising features are self-evident: policy-making is in the hands of a joint standing committee of three associations (GSA, HMC and IAPS); there is a central administrative body (the Independent Schools Examinations Board); the papers are set by the Board and sat by the candidates on dates the Board fixes; the examinations form a schedule whereby candidates for groups of schools take the examination on different dates which rotate from year to year; and the Board operates a clearing-house system to assist those who have not been accepted by their first choice school. Thus a measure of order is brought to a potentially chaotic and highly charged process.

None the less, within these broadly agreed parameters the individual schools can exercise considerable discretion as to whom they admit. As the senior schools are responsible for marking the papers of their own candidates, and setting their own pass mark, they can determine how a rigorous a test they wish it to be – it could not have escaped Dancy's notice that some qualifying tests are more demanding than others. Moreover, and perhaps more significantly, candidates usually sit the examination after '... they have been offered a place at a senior school, subject to their passing the examination' (Harries, 1995/96, xxxii). In other words, a school has already reached the conclusion that the candidate should be capable of meeting its demands. The purpose of requiring the candidate to sit the CEE is to confirm this preliminary judgement; in this sense the examination acts as a fail-safe mechanism for the schools.

What predisposes a school to make a preliminary offer of a place? And what discretion, if any, can the school subsequently exercise should the candidate not perform up to expectations in the CEE? Obviously the answers will vary from school to school, and from one candidate to the next. Most schools, however, do feel an obligation to accept the children of their former pupils as well as the brothers/sisters of present pupils, and in some cases it must help to have social ties to governors, and, perhaps, even teachers. Furthermore, putting a child's name down for a school when he or she is of tender years should also help to impress the school of parental resolution. In effect, what is under consideration is the influence of social capital in securing a school place. When the various forms of capital – social, economic and cultural – reinforce one another, the decision should be a foregone conclusion. The more interesting cases emerge when this fortunate overlapping of resources fails to occur. In recent years some schools, in an attempt to enhance their academic reputations, have required a somewhat higher pass mark in the CEE. Occasionally this will have made it more difficult for former pupils to find a place for their offspring. What do the schools do in such circumstances? Either the new standard can be rigidly enforced, or the school might decide to make a trade-off in terms of the would-be pupil's resources. As one former headmaster once put the question to me: 'Can a headmaster say no to a duke?'

We are told that the nation's future king succeeded in meeting Eton College's standard in the Common Entrance Examination, and thus the school was happy (one assumes more than happy) to accept him as a pupil. What would the school have done if he had failed to reach the required marks? In what circumstances, if any, can one conceive of a school refusing to educate the nation's future head of state? Given the attendant publicity that would have followed from such circumstances, undoubtedly there was very strong evidence that in this particular case the individual would meet Eton's requirements. In the event everything turned out as expected, and all concerned were rewarded with very favourable media attention. While this is an extreme example, it does illustrate perfectly the potential dilemmas that can emerge. Although it would be improper to suggest any duplicity on the part of the schools, the fact that they mark the papers and set the standard means that they are well-placed to exercise their discretion at the margins should they choose to do so. And it could be argued that this is not to act improperly, but represents the exercise of institutional independence.

More significant than these exceptional *individual* cases is the fact that the schools can tailor their CEE requirements to meet the circumstances of the day. If demand for places is deflated by socio-economic conditions – for example, the economy is in recession or the demand for boarding education is in decline because of changing social mores – then the schools are likely to lower their pass marks and exercise their discretion in favour of, rather than against, candidates. Immediately after the First World War a high demand for places was relieved only by a combination of the founding of new schools and subsequent economic stagnation. Again, this time thanks to the age bulge, demand was high in 1950s, and more rigorous entry standards for the public schools apparently caused consternation among some IAPS heads (Leinster-Mackay, 1984, 279–80). Recently we have had sharp fluctuations in the fortunes of the independent schools over a comparatively short period of time: decline in the early 1980s, boom years in the mid-1980s, and back to decline in the very late 1980s/early 1990s. Coupled with these sharp oscillations has been the consistent pressure to raise academic standards across the board. What emerges is a more unstable picture.

The CEE was created in part to bring about a greater measure of co-ordination between the different levels of the fee-paying sectors: that is, to make the transition from junior to senior schools more efficient and equitable. But working constantly against the drive for institutional rationalisation have been the pressures of market forces and the desire of the schools to retain some independent control over their own admissions process. Inevitably, therefore, the interaction between the differing levels within the fee-paying sector generates a number of tensions which have to be reconciled, and from which there is no easy escape. While these tensions have generally been contained within the world of the fee-paying schools, the restriction of entry to those who can afford to pay the fees has stimulated broad political discussion. Much of this is because the schools have sought assistance from the state in order to secure their futures, and perhaps in the process to broaden their social base. But what have the schools themselves done to increase their accessibility to those for whom the fees are forbidding?

Scholarships and Bursaries

The significance of the scholarships and bursaries that are awarded by the schools is only apparent in relation to the fees that they charge. Again the ISIS Census provides the most comprehensive figures (see Table 8.2). ISIS also provides some very interesting data on the range of school fees by Association. While the average fees confirm the conventional wisdom that the schools offer an education which is out of the price range of most British families, the variation in fees suggests a more equivocal evaluation. Moreover, one would hope that, given these fee ranges, the schools are indeed providing services of a different quality. If they are not, it is difficult to see how such large differences can be justified.

Not surprisingly the differences between day and boarding fees are substantial, but of greater interest are the fee differentials between Associations, and even more significantly, within Associations. Some of the fees for the day schools are modest, and, depending upon individual family circumstances, are within the range of average income families. But for such families to take advantage of low fees,

TABLE 8.2
AVERAGE TERMLY FEES BY ASSOCIATION, 1995

	Boarding Fee £	Fee for Weekly Boarders £	Day Fee £
HMC	3,718	3,211	1,540
SHMIS	3,330	3,181	1,563
GBA	2,496	3,083	1,347
GSA	3,418	2,942	1,445
GBGSA	2,500	2,552	1,348
IAPS	2,697	2,463	1,517
ISAI	2,779	2,835	1,215

Source: ISIS, *Census*, 1995, Tables: 14B, 15B, 16B, 17B, 18B and 19B.
Note: The termly average fees suggest that for some Associations those who board weekly pay a higher fee than those who board termly. This is a result of calculating averages for Associations and would not be true for any individual school.

there needs to be a relatively low-cost day school in the neighbour-hood, and the family has to be from a socio-cultural milieu that supports the idea of sending its children to fee-paying schools.

TABLE 8.3
TERMLY FEE VARIATIONS BY ASSOCIATION, 1995

	HMC £	SHMIS £	GBA £	GSA £	GBGSA £	IAPS £	ISAI £
Day Fees							
Highest	3,920	3,520	2,160	2,960	1,600	2,480	4,160
Lowest	400	880	560	800	120	560	480
Average	1,540	1,563	1,347	1,445	1,348	1,517	1,215
Boarding Fees							
Highest	4,320	4,320	3,680	4,240	2,480*	3,360	4,240
Lowest	1,200	1,920	1,440	1,280	2,480*	800	1,440
Average	3,718	3,330	2,496	3,418	2,500*	2697	2,779

* *Note:* There is only one school in this category. The scale used by ISIS to construct its fee variations table accounts for the slight discrepancy in figures.
Source: ISIS, *Census*, 1995, Table 5. See also the source for Table 8.2 above.

The problem is that the number of comparatively low-cost day schools is small, as is illustrated by the distribution of schools across the fee bands (see Table 8.4). Again, the extent to which such fee levels

TABLE 8.4
TERMLY FEE BANDS AND NUMBER OF DAY SCHOOLS BY
ASSOCIATION, 1995*

	HMC	SHMIS	GBA	GSA	GBGSA	IAPS	ISAI	TOTAL
Under £1000	4	1	2	3	0	41	103	154
£1000–£2000	130	37	10	192	7	428	169	973
£2000–£3000	86	9	1	39	0	40	11	186
£3000–£4000	8	1	0	0	0	16	1	26
Over £4000	0	0	0	0	0	0	2	2
Total	228	48	13	234	7	525	286	1,341

* *Note:* Many of these schools will also have boarders.
Source: See the source for Table 8.3 above.

exclude working- and lower-middle-class families depends on individual circumstances: how many income earners there are in the household, the financial support other relatives (especially grand-parents) may be prepared to offer, the number of dependants in the family, and personal lifestyle patterns. However, the general magnitude of these fees is such as to put the fee-paying sector as a whole beyond the reach of the overwhelming majority of British families. This would be even more apparent if the distribution of boarding – as opposed to day – fees had been analysed. How then have the schools, and their Associations, acted to make their educational product more widely accessible?

The process by which schools founded for poor and needy scholars came to serve the interests of, first, the landed gentry and, increasingly from the nineteenth century onwards, the bourgeoisie has already been discussed in some detail (see Chapter 2). A critical part of this transformation was that scholarships meant for needy scholars came to be awarded by competitive examination, rather than through the systems of patronage that had grown out of their founders' statutes. In effect, scholarships were no longer meant to support the schooling of those in financial need; they became a reward for those who could demonstrate their academic competence in competitive examinations. Consequently, from the latter half of the nineteenth century onwards, it was almost impossible to obtain a scholarship unless one had first attended a good preparatory school. Scholarship success was not only a reward for the individual but also helped to establish the credentials of the preparatory schools. In a similar fashion, a public school's reputation could be made or broken by the number of Oxbridge scholarships and exhibitions won by its boys.

There seemed to be a gentlemen's agreement that the financial rewards of a scholarship would not be accepted unless the money was needed. However, success in the first place was dependent upon the ability to meet the fees of a prep school – scarcely a sign of poverty. Moreover, regardless of financial circumstances, there was no formal bar upon the acceptance of a scholarship, and it is difficult to find any reference to the monitoring of the scholarships awarded by the fee-paying schools. Quite recently HMC established guidelines as if in recognition of this possible 'abuse'. Its current listing of the scholarships available in its members' schools is preceded by the following cryptic note: 'The policy of the Headmasters' Conference is that Scholarships should not exceed 50 per cent of the fees. Any award of more than that should be subject to parental need identified by means testing' (HMC, 1996).

The architect of the new policy was Martin Marriot, the former head of Canford School, and it was piloted through HMC in 1991 by David Jewell when he was the Conference's chairman. Both Marriot and Jewell were evidently aware that scholarships rarely went to those in financial straits, and that to limit their value would release resources to aid the more needy, and, coincidentally, also help the schools to enhance their reputations as charitable institutions. In the reported words of Marriot:

> Most of the schools have pretty limited resources to put into scholarships and bursaries. Often the scholarships go to boys whose parents are already paying the full fees. I felt I would rather give a limited sum to reward a pupil academically, but save some of the money to give to other boys and girls as bursaries. This ties in happily with the fact that we are all charitable institutions (O'Leary, 4 February 1991, 27).

As reported in the same article, the final sentiment was strongly supported by Jewell: 'I would like to see the limit set at 30 per cent but it was important to make a start. One of the things I feel strongly about is that if we are charitable institutions, we should act charitably', a point he was to reinforce strongly at a later date (Jewell, 20 January 1992, 32).

While such a move is to be welcomed, inasmuch as it releases moneys which the schools can then use to assist pupils in greater financial need, it is far more doubtful that it will also achieve another of Marriot's reported goals: 'I think it is appropriate that we should be giving away more of our money to enable children to come to our schools who otherwise could not do so' (O'Leary, 4 February 1991, 27). It is likely that the provision of additional income-related bursaries will ease the financial pressure upon those families who are experiencing difficulties in paying school fees. Moreover, it is possible that in the economic crisis of the early 1990s some children were kept within the system thanks to a bursary award. But this is not the same as saying further bursaries will necessarily encourage an inward movement from families who would otherwise rule out private schooling. This is a possibility only if there are families who are minded to use the independent sector, are aware of the availability of bursaries, and can obtain an award which is sufficiently large to bridge the gap between the resources they can afford and the school's fees. In other words, a number of factors have to come together to fulfil Marriot's expectations. An alternative outcome is that additional bursaries hold in those who are already part of the fee-paying sector, rather than increase the social range of its appeal.

An interesting feature of many bursary schemes is not so much that they are designed to aid those with financial needs, but that assistance is often directed at very specific occupational groups. The scholarships for the senior schools tend to fall into one of three categories: academic, music and art. While such resources may not be directed at the most needy, their distribution has a rational basis: those who have demonstrated the greatest talent will be duly rewarded. By way of contrast, many bursaries have a quaint feel about them, presumably reflecting the wishes of those who gave the endowments that sustain them, and/or the fact that the school has established a reputation for educating children from particular social backgrounds. In his 1984 analysis of the data, Griggs showed that bursaries, and occasionally some scholarships, were restricted, or preference was given, to the offspring of the clergy, officers in the armed services, servicemen in general, and former pupils. Among the further restrictions could be found residential requirements: 'for boys who live outside the Sevenoaks catchment area'/'boys resident in Sutton Valence or neighbouring villages' (1985, Appendix 11).

The 1996 lists continue to show similar prescriptions: 'Closed awards are available for children of Clergy of the Church of England; serving, retired or deceased members of HM Armed Forces and Old Ardinians ...' (Ardingly College), and 'Those applying must have been resident in Norfolk for the past five years' (Gresham's School). While Griggs has correctly made the point that the specifications rarely seem to favour children from especially needy backgrounds, or for that matter from solid working-class families, what has to be kept in mind is that the scholarships and bursaries, like the schools themselves, are the product of historical circumstances. Minor genuflections to past traditions seem harmless enough as long as the bulk of the resources are directed at those who genuinely need them. That is the issue that needs to be addressed.

The resources that have underwritten the schools' scholarships and bursaries have invariably been made available by founders or subsequent benefactors. Such resources are currently administered by trusts and may serve the interests of one school or a number of schools usually founded within one locality (for example, the Bedford (Harpur Trust) Charity, or Alleyn's College of God's Gift from which Dulwich College, Alleyn's School and the James Allen's Girls' School all draw support). Some trustees, while sympathising with the spirit of HMC's reforms, have had to be mindful of the statutory conditions that govern their awards. Consequently, it has not always been possible for them to restrict the size of their scholarships and bursaries.

However, while historical restrictions do not inhibit the recent extension of scholarships (such as Eton College's junior scholarships), it is unwise to assume that these newer schemes are motivated by unalloyed eleemosynary sentiments. One innovation has been the introduction of sixth-form scholarships, for which at some schools those already in attendance can compete. The suspicion is that financial inducements are being offered to pupils in order to persuade them to complete their sixth-form education at their current school. In the hard times of the early 1990s, especially with the additional tension between the girls' schools that had decided to retain their single-sex identity and the boys' schools that had decided to go co-educational, an apparent extension of charity could generate barely disguised bitterness (O'Leary, 6 December 1993, 3).

In spite of the mixed motivations, the fee-paying sector has extended its bursaries over the past decade. Moreover, besides the awards which are formally listed (for example: Senior Independent (HMC/SHMIS) Schools Scholarships or GSA Senior School Scholarships), schools have undoubtedly been making concessions on an ad hoc basis to many of those families which have faced mounting financial difficulties as a consequence of the severe recession of the early 1990s. Obviously schools have had to make difficult pragmatic decisions: on the one hand, it may make financial sense for the school to tide a family over a short period of crisis, but on the other hand it could endanger the future of the school if it were to help out too many families for inordinate lengths of time – open-ended commitments are the road to institutional ruin. In parallel vein, some charitable trusts must occasionally wonder, notwithstanding their statutory obligations, whether it makes good long-term sense to spread their largess thinly among several schools.

As the work of Marriot and Jewell within the HMC implies, the broad institutional motivation for increasing expenditure upon bursaries was to defend the schools' charitable status, which even many of those sympathetic to the idea of fee-paying education are inclined to regard with some suspicion. The extent to which the official ground on educational trusts has shifted is illustrated by the decision of the Charity Commission to remove from its register those educational trusts designed to assist parents with the payment of school fees. While this is a long way from saying that fee-paying schools should not have charitable status, the apparent reasoning behind the decision of the Charity Commission is revealing. A spokesman for the commissioners is reported to have remarked that these educational trusts did not fit in with 'today's idea of what is charitable. The benefit from them flows not to the public but to private individuals' (O'Leary, 11 April 1996,

4) If this is indeed the line of argument which the Commission intends to pursue in the future, then the schools may have to demonstrate that they continue to serve a public purpose. The danger, from their perspective, is that the provision of schooling may not within itself be judged sufficient to fulfil this end unless it is also accessible to the community at large. And so the pressure to provide ever more bursaries intensifies.

In 1992 Jewell claimed that 'the schools benefited by almost £41.4 million from charitable status but gave away more than £55.3 million in scholarships and bursaries' (20 January 1992, 32). However, the amount received by any one individual is comparatively small, and HMC's move to limit scholarships to 50 per cent of fees has reinforced this tendency. For example, the HMC/SHMIS Schools Scholarship list for 1996 provides the following fairly typical examples: 'Major Exhibitions worth 20 per cent of fees' (Bedstone College whose termly fees are £1,907 for day pupils and £3,060 for boarders); 'Lloyd Cuthbert Heath Memorial Bursary' worth up to £1,000 per annum (Brighton College which charges its boarders £11,940 per annum and its day pupils £7,854); and 'In addition one Scholarship of up to £500 and Exhibitions of up to £250 are offered annually' (Stamford School with boarding fees of £7,782 per annum and day fees of £3,891). To spread the jam thinly may be the most equitable way of distributing the resources, but it does mean that all, except those comparatively few receiving the major scholarships, still have to find sizeable sums to cover their fees.

The ISIS *Census*, while not listing the sums of money, does record the number of pupils receiving contributions to fees. If the contributions from public funds – the assisted places scheme, help given to those serving in the armed services, diplomatic allowances, and the purchase of places by the LEAs – are also included, then a sizeable minority of families (approximately a third) are receiving some assistance with the payment of school fees. Moreover, the ISIS

TABLE 5
NUMBER AND PERCENTAGE OF PUPILS IN RECEIPT OF FINANCIAL
ASSISTANCE FROM THE SCHOOLS, BY ASSOCIATION, 1995

	HMC	SHMIS	GBA	GSA	GBGSA	IAPS	ISAI	TOTAL
Numbers	32,650	4,920	972	17,393	493	18,369	9,039	83,836
Percentage	20.3	28.6	16.6	15.6	18.9	16.4	16.1	18.0

Source: ISIS, *Census*, 1995, Tables 1 and 7.

Censuses show that over time that there has been a relative increase in the input of the schools compared with the direct support provided by the state.

However, in their preparation of statistics for the Public Schools Commission, Glennerster and Wilson claimed that as long ago as 1965/66 approximately the same proportion of pupils were in receipt of fee reductions: 'About one in five of all pupils received some reductions in fees. The total amount of money involved was, however, very small, under five per cent of all income' (Public Schools Commission, 1968a, 292). Their breakdowns were as follows: out of a total of 108,460 day and boarding pupils, 12,270 (11.3 per cent) were in receipt of allowances, 6,020 (5.6 per cent) held scholarships and 4,150 (3.8 per cent) bursaries. The allowances to which Glennerster and Wilson refer are comparatively small reductions given by many schools to pupils such as the children of staff, or those who already have brothers or sisters in the school. In the ISIS *Census* these would fall into the bursary category. Moreover, the figures presented by Glennerster and Wilson are roughly comparable with those to be found in Kalton's contemporary survey of the HMC schools: over 20 per cent of boarders received assistance from the schools, and while a higher percentage of the day pupils received help with the payment of fees this came mainly from the LEAs (Kalton, 1966, 37).

Obviously the data base of the ISIS *Census* is broader than the research of both Glennerster and Wilson and Kalton, and it includes associations such as the IAPS whose schools in the past did not have many scholarships or bursaries. However, it does cast doubt upon the claim that there has been a steadily increasing percentage of pupils in receipt of help with the payment of their fees. Clearly we have entered a minefield in which the politics of charitable giving is perhaps as important as, if not more important than, the giving itself – and will continue to be so.

THE EROSION OF SELF-CONTAINMENT

The reform of the endowed schools in the nineteenth century led to an increasingly self-contained fee-paying sector, especially at its more elevated levels. A number of variables combined to create this separate world of schools: the erosion of local ties, the recruitment of pupils nationally, the award of scholarships on the grounds of competitive examination with the virtual removal of all preconditions for entrants, the instigation by the senior schools of first their own qualifying examinations and then the CEE for all candidates, the standardisation of the age of entry into the public schools, the growth of the preparatory schools and the recognition of their critical role in preparing candidates for initially the scholarship examinations and then the CEE. These developments were reinforced by the institutionalisation of the fee-paying sector seen, for example, in the creation of HMC and the Association of Headmasters of Preparatory Schools (AHPS, now replaced by IAPS) with widening co-operation across these institutional boundaries.

Inevitably, as the fee-paying sector became more internally coherent, in both institutional and pedagogical terms, so it also became more differentiated from the maintained sector of schooling. Although the grammar school tradition formed a bridge between the two sectors, for much of the twentieth century powerful political pressures have favoured its removal, inevitably leading to even sharper sectoral differentiation. In this context it is scarcely surprising to find that the two sectors have contrasting social bases which have been reinforced by differing admissions procedures. Indeed, even those variables which one would have expected to establish a measure of interchange – scholarships (rewarding the most competent), bursaries (rewarding the most needy) and a qualifying test in the form of the CEE (suggesting a general level of competence, rather than the possession of special qualities) – have merely reinforced the barriers.

Given this legacy, it is difficult to contemplate that in the short run a greater interpenetration of the two sectors would result from an internal reform of the fee-paying schools' admissions procedures, including changes to the CEE. However, this is not to deny that there have been some, and can be further, supportive changes at the margins. There is no reason why, instead of simply restricting the value of scholarships to a percentage of fees, they should not be purely honorific awards with all the released resources channelled into means-tested bursaries. Certainly it makes little sense to use endowment income to restrict fee levels across the board so that all families benefit regardless of their financial circumstances. Again, if the best gloss is put on the data, the expanding commitment of the schools to providing bursaries can be maintained. While it may be true that in the past it has been easier to persuade benefactors to underwrite capital projects (with the buildings duly named after them!) rather than endow scholarships, there is no reason to assume that this must always be the case. Furthermore, a school's endowment can be augmented for bursary provision by imposing a surcharge on existing fee-payers.

Indeed, the threat of the Labour Party to phase out the assisted places scheme gives many schools a high incentive to increase their support for bursaries.

In spite of such measures, it is difficult to imagine that they will have anything other than a marginal effect upon the necessity for most schools to attract a healthy supply of pupils who can afford to pay full fees. Given the costs involved in providing high-quality schooling, especially a boarding education, enormous endowments have to be sustained in order to generate sufficient income to cover the costs of a relatively small number of pupils. Few schools are so wealthily endowed, and few are ever likely to be. The obvious exception is Christ's Hospital, which is so richly endowed that its average fee is remarkably low and which has many free places. It is the exception that proves the rule. In such circumstances it is not surprising that the schools spread their largess thinly, and consequently, they have looked to the state to underwrite any significant broadening of their social base.

To spread out bursary resources inevitably means supporting families who, although possibly not particularly well-to-do, are none the less in a position to make some contribution to the payment of school fees. Moreover, these are also likely to be families that are already attuned to sending their children to fee-paying schools. The evidence seems to suggest that, in class terms, school bursaries are moving in the same direction as the assisted places scheme: they are both directed at less financially secure middle-class families (see p.124). Either personal circumstances (for example, divorce, bereavement or unemployment) and/or comparatively low incomes (the clergy, teachers, shop assistants or clerical workers) make the payment of full school fees very difficult. Bursaries, of varying degrees of generosity, are the means of bridging the gap.

Of course, the vital step to broadening the recruitment base of the fee-paying sector is to widen its social appeal. Although help with the payment of fees may assist this development, it is impossible to say whether it would be sufficient to engender widespread changes in attitudes towards private schooling. However, the omens appear to be favourable, if double-edged. The work of Bridgeman and Fox (1978) and Fox (1984, 1984a) demonstrates that the majority of parents who choose fee-paying schools do so for pragmatic reasons: they believe their children receive a better education and enhanced opportunities. If the schools can reinforce such an appeal there is no reason to predict anything other than a long-term increase in demand. However, genuinely pragmatic parents might start to wonder whether grant-maintained schools and city technology colleges are offering a comparable educational experience at a fraction of the cost.

Furthermore, there has been an increasing number of parents who, although themselves educated in the maintained sector, are prepared to send their children to fee-paying schools (Halsey *et al.*, 1980, 76). This can be coupled with evidence of many educational careers embracing both the fee-paying and maintained sectors. For those who can afford the fees it is possible to think in terms of an educational market which embraces segments of both the private and the maintained systems. If bursaries and scholarships widen participation in that market then, perhaps at least as far as middle-class – or even middle-income – parents are concerned there are few socio-cultural barriers to participation. Moreover, the changing character of the fee-paying sector – in particular the growing preponderance of day-school pupils – needs to be built into the equation. Finally, for those who have children with special gifts, for example with musical or artistic talent, there may simply be no choice but to seek a place in a fee-paying school, for few maintained schools have the resources to develop such talents.

Both state pressure (the need to demonstrate a charitable purpose) and market pressure (the need to retain and expand the recruitment base) are pushing the schools' bursary and scholarships systems in the same direction. Individual financial need is increasingly the basis on which awards are made, and in the process it appears to be the less elevated segment of the bourgeoisie which is the main beneficiary. Although this is the general direction of change, present arrangements reflect an interesting and curious mix of past and contemporary values. Plenty of genuflections to original statutory prescriptions are to be found in the residential qualifications as well as in the restriction of awards to children from particular social backgrounds, in which the clergy figure prominently. And yet, while schools vary enormously in character, there is still widespread commitment to the idea that even fee-payers have to demonstrate a measure of academic competence. In effect, scholarships and bursaries developed as an integral part of a relatively self-contained system of independent schooling. Now they form one of the important channels through which both state and market pressure can be exerted upon that system. Consequently, the system is less self-contained, and certainly less independent.

CONCLUSION

If the private schools were asked to define in precise terms what independence meant to them, undoubtedly many would stress their ability to control the admissions process: to select the pupils they wished to teach. The purpose of this chapter has been not to deny that they have this authority, but rather to show that it is circumscribed in very important ways. In the nineteenth century the state reshaped access to the public schools by encouraging them to admit only older boys, to award their scholarships on the basis of rigorously competitive examinations, and to set a qualifying test for all entrants. This external pressure for change interacted with internal pressures, and these reforms were set in motion. The consequence has been a considerable increase in the institutionalisation of the admissions process, at least to the leading independent schools, as is most clearly seen in the control and operation of the qualifying entrance examination, the Common Entrance Examination.

Few schools have large endowment incomes, and they cannot survive for long without attracting enough pupils who can pay their fees and thus underwrite the schools' costs. The schools, therefore, can be flexible as to the academic standards they demand of their would-be pupils, raising them when demand is high and lowering them when it declines. Moreover, in order to survive, the schools have been very adept at adjusting the character of their intake to meet their changing circumstances as seen in: the incorporation of younger pupils in feeder schools, the willingness of the single-sex schools to admit both boys and girls, the big shift in the relative balance of day to boarding pupils, and the recruitment of overseas pupils. While it is debatable whether the schools have changed their fundamental values (whatever is meant by these), many have changed both their social and pedagogical characters over time.

It is the fact that these schools charge fees, and often very exorbitant fees in relation to average incomes, which has aroused the most controversy in recent years; especially as the schools have looked to the state for a financial input, ostensibly in part to enable them to widen their social base. In effect, the scholarships and bursaries offered by the schools have become a means of responding positively to both state and market pressures for change. In order to assist a wider range of pupils the schools have moved towards offering less generous scholarships (partly because they recognised that these did not always go to those in the greatest financial need), and directing the released resources to increasing the amount spent on bursaries. Furthermore, the total amount of assistance given by schools towards the payment of fees has also increased but whether a higher percentage of pupils is now receiving some form of assistance is less certain. Bursaries are now one of the cards used to justify the charitable status of the private sector; that is – so it is alleged – resources are directed at families who otherwise would not be in a position to send their children to schools that charge fees. While it is difficult to substantiate this claim, it is almost certainly true that bursaries help some families who are experiencing difficulties in paying school fees, and thus are a means of keeping pupils in the private sector. Undoubtedly a few schools have also offered sixth-form scholarships in the hope of retaining the wavering loyalties of some parents. Such possibilities are probably very important for a widening range of parents should there be a general downturn in the economy. Thus bursaries can serve to assuage market forces as well as negative political pressure.

However, although it is important not to disparage these internal attempts to place more financial resources into broadening the social base of the fee-paying schools, it is equally important to stress that the schools simply lack the resources to encourage substantial change. The divide between the maintained and private sectors is being breached by the fact that many parents who were educated in maintained schools are prepared to educate their children privately, and that there appears to be an increasing trend to make use of both sectors – with the consequence that fee-paying schools face real challenges from sixth-form colleges, the grant-maintained schools, and CTCs. Of course these are developments, reinforced by the assisted places scheme, that are confined essentially to the middle class, although this would also incorporate many lower-middle-class families. For a swifter narrowing of the divide much more purposeful state action is needed, not to encourage pupils out of maintained schools and into the private sector but to change the character of maintained schooling.

9

In Pursuit of Policy Consensus

The dominant policy thrust of the sociology of education in Britain since the 1944 Education Act has been that selection in education is undesirable. Thus this branch of the social sciences has been pitted against the interests of the grammar schools – selection by individual merit – and the private sector – selection by the family's ability to pay school fees. Not surprisingly there were close links between the Labour Party and important figures in the sub-discipline's academic ranks. Interestingly, although the individuals have changed and the research strategy has become more eclectic, the bond continues, and several contemporary educational sociologists look to the Labour Party to redirect the current course of educational policy. However, to draw the ties in such a straightforward manner is to misinterpret academe's input into the policy-making process. The consensus against selection was so pervasive as to be central to the logic of social democracy, regardless of its party colours. To use the striking metaphor of Sir Keith Joseph: the ratchet was set to turn inexorably in one direction (1976).

As the reorganisation of secondary schooling along comprehensive lines gathered momentum in the 1960s and 1970s, so the fee-paying sector's share of the educational market declined, reaching its nadir in 1976. On the face of it the private schools were retreating steadily into a narrow and isolated heartland, sustained by those parents who had been educated privately themselves and who had never contemplated any other fate for their children – the 'traditionalists', as Bridgeman and Fox have called them (1978). Underneath this image of decline and stagnation, however, important changes were taking place. The process of reversing the ratchet had started within the schools long before it was reinforced by a shift in the climate of political opinion. So great has been the transition that it is the future of the maintained sector of schooling that is now in question.

Inevitably the internal regeneration of the fee-paying sector evolved over a protracted period of time, but it was highlighted by specific initiatives: HMC's sponsorship of a factual survey designed to scotch ten prevalent myths (Kalton, 1966), the creation of the publicity arm ISIS (1972) and the evolution of the umbrella policy body ISJC (1974). The pressures for change emerged out of the interaction of a seemingly irreversible decline in parental demand for private schooling, and the changing requirements of the institutional network to which the fee-paying schools belonged, in particular the intensification of the competition for places in elite institutions such as Oxbridge. Several of the alleged myths that HMC wanted to counter questioned the relevance and quality of education in the fee-paying sector: the stress upon the classics, the traditional pedagogical style, the absurdity of some of the rituals, the prevalence of bullying and homosexuality, and the unnaturalness of a boarding education. While the charge of perpetuating individual privilege, along with the maintenance of an ossified class structure, is still levelled at the schools, there are far fewer attacks upon the educational experiences which they offer. Indeed, quite the contrary, for they are all too readily perceived as conferring educational advantages: that it is possible to purchase a privileged form of schooling.

The nineteenth century witnessed a revitalisation, through the intervention of Parliament, of both the great public schools and the endowed schools. This was accompanied by the foundation of new, more socially relevant, public schools as an expanding bourgeoisie sought to transmit its class privileges to its offspring. In effect, the middle classes, excluded from the traditional public schools and disenchanted with the endowed grammar schools, used their wealth to create schools that were more in tune with their interests, until, by the end of the century, they had penetrated the ancient institutions and reformed the endowed grammar schools. In contrast, since the Second World War, the process of change has occurred within the existing schools as they have vied with one another to ensure the steady flow of their middle-class clientele. The ethos, therefore, has been remoulded within the prevailing network, rather than transformed as a consequence of direct external intervention, although the independent boarding and day schools did respond to competition from the grammar schools, and the fee-paying sector as a whole felt the need to react positively to the intensified political pressure.

How far this internal regeneration would have succeeded without a concomitant change in the political environment is impossible to ascertain. While the interests of the private sector were undoubtedly threatened by the exclusion of fee-payers from the grammar schools, maintained or aided by the local authorities (accomplished by the 1944

Education Act), and the phasing out of state support for the direct grant schools (from 1976 onwards), there has been a marked reluctance to legislate more punitive measures. While Labour governments to date have lacked the political will to prohibit schools from charging fees, so successive Conservative governments have, at least since 1979, offered the private schools various forms of comfort. There has been general encouragement of the idea that individuals have a personal responsibility for their own social welfare. Thus private or fee-paying schools become independent schools catering to individuals who are standing on their own two feet. Given that the intention has been to encourage independence, it could scarcely be expected that the financial succour which many schools receive from their charitable status would be remotely threatened. Moreover, the maintenance of such indirect support has been enhanced by the direct input, recently extended, of the assisted places scheme. It is not uncommon to see the fee-paying sector portrayed as a beacon of academic excellence whose practices need to be grafted on to the maintained schools if allegedly declining educational standards are to be reversed.

This resuscitation of private schooling has occurred alongside the expression of some extreme misgivings about the direction of maintained schooling, and in recent years a considerable restructuring of its character. The various charges levelled at maintained schools may have been neither justified nor widely supported, but that they generated considerable publicity and attracted crucial support in key policy-making circles is beyond dispute. And this concern has not been confined to the Conservative Party. Significantly, Morris and Griggs begin their edited volume *Education: The Wasted Years?* (1988) in 1973, and no self-respecting narrative of the recent evolution of educational policy could possibly omit James Callaghan's speech at Ruskin College, Oxford, in October 1976. Callaghan questioned the extent to which the nation had received a fair return on the increased resources devoted to education in the post-war years. In the mid-1970s the crises triggered off by the large increases in oil prices merely exacerbated Britain's long-term economic decline. To many, the United Kingdom was indeed 'the sick man of Europe'. More specifically, Callaghan's speech brought into sharp focus the relationship between schooling and the quality of the nation's labour force. Henceforth, the drive for educational change would be spearheaded by many who were not part of the traditional educational policy-making network (for example, David Young, former Minister of Employment and close political ally of Mrs Thatcher), and occasionally it was implied that their involvement verged on being illegitimate (Simon, 1988, 13).

With the important exception of the controversy initiated in 1980 by the enactment of the assisted places scheme, the fee-paying schools have *not* been in the political limelight for the past seventeen years. They have been free to focus their attention upon educational issues and to devote their energies to, for example, countering the effects of the recession in the late 1980s, and the repercussions upon their student numbers of a slimming down of the armed services. The contrast with the maintained sector could not be more stark. As the changes have already been covered adequately elsewhere, albeit with the inevitable manifestation of sharply contrasting political biases, there is little point in adding further to the voluminous narrative. What is of importance, and will be analysed shortly, is the extent to which the recent changes have resulted in a convergence of the maintained and fee-paying sectors. The point at issue is that successive Conservative governments have felt it incumbent upon them to restructure the educational system, almost root and branch.

INPUTS INTO THE CHANGE PROCESS

The simple answer, therefore, to understanding this sharp reversal in recent years of the respective fortunes of maintained and fee-paying schools is to point to the record of four successive Conservative governments. Inasmuch as the Thatcher and Major governments have sought to diversify the institutional character of education, to locate schools in a more competitive environment, and both to localise and centralise the educational decision-making process, then the simple answer is correct. However, it is crucial to remember that educational policy is merely part of the broad canvas of social policy, and, as such, is deeply influenced by wider considerations. In recent years there has been a rethinking across the political spectrum of the social obligations of the state: the extent of those obligations, whether the state should both provide and finance the services or merely underwrite private provision, and on what terms public resources should be made available.

Political and economic considerations have interacted to bring about a fundamental rethinking of the state's priorities. Pressures, both social (for example, an ageing population) and technological (for example, increasingly sophisticated medical technology), fuel an inevitable expansion of state expenditure upon social welfare. And yet there is the political reality that the high levels of direct taxation needed to pay for such services are unpopular with the electorate at large. Various ideas have been floated: targeted state services (all the major political parties), earmarked taxation (a favourite with the Liberal Democrats), and the expansion of services 'as and when resources allow' (the Labour Party assumes that in government it would generate the economic growth which would allow the expansion of expenditure upon social services without necessitating increases in direct taxation – a delusion common to political parties in opposition).

The more narrowly defined economic arguments centre on what percentage of Gross Domestic Product (GDP) should be spent upon public services. If this were to expand indefinitely, there is the question of what remains for private consumption, and, critically, for investment in the economic infrastructure. Of course, there is no reason why there should not be considerable public investment in capital projects, programmes designed to retrain the work-force, and the purchase of plant and machinery. However, there is always considerable pressure upon public expenditure to direct it towards the resolution of short-term problems and the politically sensitive social concerns such as housing, education, health and social security. Given the cross-party concern with the relative decline of the British economy (and Callaghan's linking in 1976 of the nation's economic performance and the quality of its educational system is critical in this context), the apparently inexorable demands of this pressure had to be resisted. The most obvious way to accomplish this was simply to limit in the first place the percentage of GDP devoted to the public purse.

There is now a broad political consensus that the state's share of GDP should be limited (certainly no higher than 45 per cent), and the Conservative government has signalled its intention to lower this over time. Naturally there is no guarantee that such a strategy will generate long-term benefits for Britain's economy. At present all that can be safely concluded is that the dominant political mood is against raising taxation levels, placing an ever-increasing percentage of the nation's wealth in the public domain, and allowing the public sector borrowing requirement to expand indefinitely. Prudent housekeeping is a widely shared contemporary soundbite.

Given the macro-political and economic developments sketched out above, it was inevitable that the state's expenditure upon education would come into sharp focus. While some issues continue to be politically sensitive (for example, the provision of nursery education

174

and teacher-pupil ratios) both the government and opposition parties have been prepared to challenge entrenched educational interests. For the Labour Party this has caused considerable tension with one of its traditional bastions of support, the National Union of Teachers.

If it was seemingly part of the logic of the politics of social democracy that the fee-paying sector of schooling would inevitably be absorbed into the state system of education, it follows that if this was not to take place, then the continuing well-being of the private sector had also to be seen as consistent with the values of a social democratic polity. On a narrow political front this was accomplished by the wide appeal of Thatcherism, including its advocacy of the virtues of private enterprise (fee-paying schools as businesses in the marketplace) and personal self-reliance (parents purchase schooling on behalf of their dependants – not the state's dependants). Of broader appeal was the comparative evidence, coming both from those to whom private schooling is attractive (Mason, 1989) and from those to whom it is anathema (Walford, 1991, 1994), that private schooling flourishes in a large number of countries with impeccable social democratic credentials. The parental purchase of schooling is widely perceived as a basic right which governments curtail at their peril.

More interestingly, there has been a serious attempt to reinterpret the history of the British educational system. For all his concern with the grassroots development of what he has termed the common school and popular education, Brian Simon – the long-established doyen of British educational historians – has been an ardent advocate of the expansion of state schooling. A constant theme in his criticisms, reiterated by Griggs (1988, 197) and Chitty (1995, 234), is that government policy represents 'a turning back of the clock' (Simon, 1988, 1992, 1994). However, over time his influence has waned and alternative interpretations have taken root. For example, E. G. West (1970, 1975) has argued that major educational advances were achieved long before the state made any direct provision for schooling; progress in, for example, improving literacy rates was startling in the nineteenth century and had little to do with the state and much to do with the input of voluntary associations (especially the churches), frequently supported by financial contributions from the poorest of families. This suggests that the lessons of history, like those of the social sciences, can serve different political interests.

These broad parameters, within which social policy will be constructed, are unlikely to change substantially in the near future. If anything, they are likely to be further reinforced in Britain by the drift to the right of the Labour Party under the leadership of Tony Blair. Moreover, other social democracies are not offering alternative models. But policy parameters are far from a straitjacket and there is enormous scope in the field of educational policy for reconstructing the role of the state and, in particular, for determining how the relationship between the public and private provision of the educational service should evolve. Whether one likes the outcomes or not, this process has already been set in train by a succession of Conservative governments. The challenge for a future government, with perhaps different priorities, is how to take this task forward while trying also to be true to its political traditions.

TOWARDS CONVERGENCE

Two different kinds of developments have occurred over the past twenty years which have brought the fee-paying and maintained sectors of schooling closer together. On the one hand there has been the restructuring of the state schools by successive Tory governments, and on the other hand the character of the fee-paying sector has evolved in ways that both reflect and enhance its regeneration. As a consequence, there is now a better than ever chance to bridge the divide between the two sectors of schooling. What is required is the recognition that this is a goal worth achieving (many would prefer to maintain the status quo or to return to those days when the imperative was to abolish the fee-paying sector as we know it by integrating it into the state system), and the political will to invest the necessary resources to fulfil that goal.

Richard Pring raised an early and disapproving voice against what has been widely referred to as 'the privatisation' of maintained schooling (Pring, 1983, 1986 and 1988). It is worth considering Pring's arguments in some detail as he makes important points of principle. He has distinguished between two main forms of privatisation:

> ... (a) privatisation in the sense of purchasing at *private* expense educational services within the *public system* and (b) privatisation in the sense of purchasing at *public* expense educational services from private means to enhance the public sector (1988, 92; stress in original text).

Somewhat reluctantly, Pring has come to accept the first form: 'Pragmatically, I can see good reasons for supporting limited privatisation in the first sense. Indeed, unless one does so there is a danger of exposing the public sector to yet further impoverishment with the consequent flight to the private sector of those with resources to do so' (1988, 96). Thus, while maintained schooling may still be a public service to which access at the point of entry is free (Pring, 1986, 67), an increasing range of its services are underwritten by parental contributions, private benefactors and school appeals.

Although Pring may continue to object to the second form of privatisation, it has long been an established part of the British educational system: the purchase of boarding places for children whose parents serve in the armed services or diplomatic corps, and for those who have special educational needs (see p.86). Pring's objection is against the extension of such schemes because: 'Some people will have the insight and access to make wise and well-informed choices. But the majority will not, thereby losing out on what could easily become a surreptitious form of selection – certainly a form of reinforcing advantage amongst those already advantaged' (1986, 95). Notwithstanding Pring's objections, if the maintained and private sectors of schooling are to be integrated, then part of the process will be to embrace this second form of privatisation. The premises upon which Pring bases his case need to be questioned: even if most people at present 'lack the insight and access to make wise and well-informed choices', they certainly do not lack the capacity to be so informed. The assumption is that empowering people enhances their potential to make informed judgements. Moreover, it is incumbent upon the state to ensure that as much information as can be reasonably expected is placed at the disposal of parents. One of the good things about the educational changes of the past twenty years is that schools are now much more open institutions.

Pring has also claimed that 'accountable rather than independent and private institutions (are required) to deliver essential public services' (1986, 96). The upshot of the state's increasing purchase of places in the fee-paying schools could be that 'before long those in receipt of public money will be asked to take on board public responsibility – to make their contribution to the educational needs of all as they have been determined by those who provide the financial support' (1986, 96). However, the whole point about Pring's second form of privatisation is that it allows agreements to be struck between the state and fee-paying schools that will inevitably impose obligations on both parties. It is, therefore, a deliberate means of limiting independence. How conscious the schools were aware of this when, for example, the assisted places scheme was taking shape is another matter. Moreover, one may object strongly to the present assisted places scheme, but still approve of the principle that the provision of schooling requires a mix of private and state resources; that is mixing is desirable but regrettably the current assisted places scheme is the wrong mixture.

Within the context of these broad privatisation pressures, a number of critical structural and organisational changes have reshaped the maintained schools in a manner that supports the idea of converging sectors. The key structural change is the emergence of the city technology colleges (CTCs), the grant-maintained schools (GMS), and now the specialist technology colleges. Although their admissions policies are regulated (the constraints have become less restrictive over time), and they are required to follow the national curriculum with its associated key-stage testing, these centrally funded schools have a legal status akin to many fee-paying schools: they have charitable status, they control their own budgets including the terms of employment of their staff, and their governing bodies are formally accountable for how they function. In fact, the 1988 Education Reform Act delegated responsibility for the management of budgets to all secondary schools, and this has now been extended. Moreover, the individual budgets of the schools are based upon the per capita funding of pupils which, in effect, should mean resources follow the individual pupil through the system. Per capita funding can be seen as a standardised fee, agreed by the local education authorities and central government, in contrast to the private sector in which fees are determined by the schools. Of course in both systems the fee can and will be varied to meet particular individual circumstances.

The reports of the Public Schools Commission (1968) and the Fleming Committee (1944) based their hopes for a closer association between fee-paying and maintained schooling on the belief that there was a significant latent demand for boarding education. Rightly, in my opinion, Vaizey – himself a commissioner – derided such aspirations. Vaizey's objections were based partly upon his dislike of boarding education, and partly upon an analysis which suggested that the claim was grounded more in wishful thinking than supportive statistical evidence (see p.106). The related major problem with any integrationist strategy was the tendency to focus almost exclusively upon the upper echelons of the fee-paying schools – those boarding schools belonging to the Headmasters' Conference (as it then was) – rather than the private sector as a whole.

But the traditional fee-paying sector has changed in ways which render redundant artificial attempts at integration. The big growth area is in day, not boarding, pupils. As a consequence, many schools which once catered only, or predominantly, for boarders have added or expanded their day provision. Since Dancy's initiative in accepting girls at Marlborough College many of the leading public schools have become heavily dependent upon the enrolment of girls to the point where they can be considered as fully co-educational schools, in contrast to accepting a few girls in their sixth forms. HMC is now an acronym for the Headmasters' and Headmistresses' Conference, entirely appropriate in view of the fact that women are now heads of schools which were members of the Headmasters' Conference. These two developments resolve a critical problem which faced both the Fleming Committee and the Public Schools Commission, namely that there was little boarding provision in the girls' fee-paying schools, and thus a limitation in pursuing an integrationist strategy designed to ensure that the beds were filled by different persons (to parody Vaizey, see p.109).

Undoubtedly the key charge against private schools in Britain has been their exclusivity in social class terms. This issue has bedevilled private schooling in Britain to an extent which is untrue of other countries where the private sectors are much more likely to be defined socially in religious terms. In Britain the charge is that the private sector has engaged in selective social class recruitment, and then socialised its pupils into a cultural mould which reinforces their sense of uniqueness, so perpetuating a rigid class structure. It is hard to imagine that such a potent legacy can ever be fully buried, but there are a number of important mitigating variables which have been reinforced by recent trends. After decades of political conflict, exacerbated by religious jealousies, most of the schools in Britain with religious affiliations were accommodated within the maintained sector. After the 1944 Education Act, most church schools – while retaining some doctrinal genuflections – were to all intents and purposes part of the state system of education. This greatly reinforced the image of the remaining fee-paying schools, even those with very close church affiliations, as catering to class, rather than religious, interests – an image strongly sustained, of course, by their actual patterns of class recruitment.

In the past two decades social variables other than class have assumed a more prominent profile in the evaluation of schooling. Feminists, some of whom would identify themselves as being part of the political left, have advocated the cause of girls-only schools, labelling co-educational schools – which expanded steadily in the maintained sector under the auspices of the movement towards comprehensive secondary education – as boys' schools in which girls happen to be present. Various 'league tables' of examination results reveal that standards in girls' schools are comparatively high, and it is widely believed this owes much to the success of the schools in creating a powerful academic ethos, facilitated by the absence of boys. Whether or not such claims would stand up to careful analysis is another matter, but there is no doubting that at least a substantial minority of parents are in favour of single-sex schools. While in the private sector many of the boys' schools have embraced co-education, equally many of the girls' schools continue to pride themselves upon the retention of their traditional status along with the special educational environment it allegedly helps to sustain.

Since the passage of the 1944 Education Act, Britain has received many immigrants from religious backgrounds whose needs were not explicitly catered for in the intricate negotiations that created the consensus upon which that legislation was based. The relevant legislative clauses could possibly embrace those interests, but without being a party to the original negotiations, the political pressure for incorporation has not been as strong. For example, although some communities want fee-paying schools for Muslims to be admitted into the maintained sector as either voluntary-aided or voluntary-controlled schools (the status acquired by most Anglican and Roman Catholic schools after the 1944 Act), not one such change of status has yet occurred. Now, however, such schools may acquire grant-maintained status, for the 1993 Education Act created the Funding Agency for Schools (FAS) which has the authority to initiate just this kind of inward movement.

While the number of schools wishing to change their status may be small (Walford has claimed there are about 15 Muslim schools and '… some 60 small Christian schools which range in size from less than 10 primary age children to over 300 children of all ages' (1994, 31)), they have widened the terms of the debate. For example, fee-paying schools may be better defenders of community values than those schools maintained by the local authorities. Athough Dooley is perhaps overstating the case, her pointed observation, 'for some Muslims who wish to have their beliefs taught in an ethos free from prejudiced harassment, private schools will be seen as the only alternative' (1991, 113), is telling.

Inevitably, the social profiles of fee-paying pupils will still show the expected class biases. However, given the relative expansion of day pupils over boarding pupils, the implementation and the enlargement of the assisted places scheme, and the emergence in Britain of schools whose purpose is not to perpetuate cultural traditions centred essentially upon social class, then one would expect a fee-paying sector whose social balance is shifting increasingly towards the lower ranks of the bourgeoisie. These may be socially ambitious families but with incomes which are little more than modest. Moreover, it is critical to remember that the changing technical relations of production have steadily eroded the working class as it was traditionally understood. While one may castigate educational innovations which are supposedly 'turning back the clock', it is important to ensure one's spleen is not being vented on behalf of a working class that has long since passed away.

Although the major structural changes within the maintained sector, coupled with the evolving character of the fee-paying schools, might in general terms suggest overall sectoral convergence, it is important to be sensitive to the development of an alternative scenario. The evidence can be interpreted to suggest that there is a growing diversity of school profiles *within* both the private and maintained sectors. The decline in the absolute and relative size of private schooling throughout most of the twentieth century was almost certainly accompanied by an increasing standardisation of its character; if you like, it was retreating steadily into its heartland. In similar fashion, it could be argued that the rapid spread of comprehensive schools led to a parallel standardisation within the maintained secondary system. The years of Tory governments have stimulated a return to diversification (admittedly more often honoured in theory than in practice), and with still more to come should the thrust of the 1993 Education Act be fulfilled. If such a situation is indeed emerging, then we will find shared interests developing between schools on differing sides of the maintained/private divide, and these schools could have more in common with each other than they do with other schools that are nominally in their own sector. In such circumstances, the question of whether school entry is secured by the payment of fees or not assumes far less relevance than it did in the past.

While the internal bifurcation of sectors, or even their disintegration into multiple alternative models of schooling, conjures up a more complicated picture than that suggested by simple convergence, the key point to remember is the increasing unreality of thinking in terms of bipolar structures which are differentiated neatly and simply by the faultline of fee-paying. Whether that world has disappeared for ever depends upon the range and depth of the political consensus in support of the new order, which can be expected to expand or contract as the objections of its many critics are either countered or sustained. How fragile is that consensus?

LOOKING BACKWARDS TO THE FUTURE

In 1980, Ron Hayward, then General Secretary of the Labour Party, in a foreword to the party's discussion document on private schools, wrote:

> Socialists have long understood that the existence of private schooling fragments society, enshrines privilege for the few at the expense of the majority and seriously impedes the establishment of a national system of education which is genuinely fair to the talents, aspirations and needs of every child (Labour Party, 1980, 3).

According to Hayward, the problems arising from a divided education system were exacerbated by the 'well-entrenched class interests' embedded within it. Consequently: 'Labour's longer term policy is the elimination of the private sector...'. In the meantime, a range of short-term measures would be pursued: the termination of the assisted places scheme, restrictions upon the right of local authorities to buy places in private schools, and the withdrawal of charitable status from all but a selected number of fee-paying schools (to name the most important options). In its subsequent general election manifestos the Labour Party committed itself to implementing such measures, along with the promise that the ultimate goal of elimination would be achieved by preventing schools from charging fees. This just goes to show that opinion in the party at large was broadly sympathetic to the general thrust of what was after all meant to be a discussion document.

Whereas, post-1945, the Conservative Party may have been ensnared in a ratchet which moved steadily leftwards, after 1979 it could be argued that the Labour Party has been increasingly required to work within policy parameters established by successive Conservative governments. Although these policy boundaries are a response to the wider political and economic pressures that have been discussed earlier (see p.172), the impression is created of a Labour Party dancing ever more willingly to a Conservative Party tune. It is inconceivable that in the contemporary political climate the Labour

Party could produce a discussion document that bore the remotest resemblance to its 1980 publication. While Ron Hayward, and presumably the fellow socialists from whom he implicitly drew support, were very clear about the ramifications of private schooling, today's new model Labour Party is far more equivocal.

Understandably, in view of the approaching general election, the Labour Party's educational policies are in a state of flux. Until its election manifesto actually appears, different options will emerge, and priorities will be restructured. However, while it can be expected that the present commitment to phasing out – not terminating – the assisted places scheme will be retained, it seems very unlikely that there will be promises to legislate on either charitable status or the purchase by both local and central government of places in the fee-paying schools. Even assisted places for children with special aptitudes in the arts would be continued by a Labour government. Finally, the long-term goal of preventing schools from charging fees has been well and truly buried.

In its *Opening Doors to a Learning Society: A Policy Statement on Education*, the party has given a glimmer of hope that it is contemplating an interesting policy initiative:

> We will take a fresh look at the scope for working with educational trusts such as the Steiner Foundation and the Human Scale Group with a view to encouraging research which could have benefit for the whole of our education system (Labour Party, 1994, 28).

The outcome could be innovative proposals for the further interpenetration of the private and public domains. However, it is difficult to believe that, in the short run, even so-called New Labour can proceed too rapidly down this path. There is vocal (and perhaps even broad) support within the party for the principle of comprehensive secondary schooling, and a· strong belief in certain quarters that it would be sacrilegious to suggest that educational services might be provided both more efficiently, and more in tune with community values, by the private sector. These would be matters to be considered only after an election victory. In effect the Labour Party can be expected to adopt a quiet line on private schooling.

Perhaps even more dramatic than the Labour Party's *volte-face* over private schooling has been its willingness to embrace the restructuring of the maintained sector by the Thatcher and Major governments. Following the government's acceptance of Sir Ron Dearing's recommendations for reforming the national curriculum and the associated key-stage testing, the party has come to terms with these massive innovations. Of greater pertinence to this book is the party's acceptance, albeit with some modifications which are no more than minor concessions to internal party critics, of the grant-maintained schools, the CTCs, formula funding (although the party is pledged to abolish the FAS), the local management of schools, the enhanced powers of governors, and the right of parents to exercise choice (or should it be to express a preference?). Even the once maligned remaining grammar schools, some 160, may be spared the legislative axe, as local parents are drawn into a consultative process that would determine their future. The result is that a Labour government would retain nearly all those changes which have brought at least segments of the maintained and fee-paying sectors much closer together. Moreover, it could even bring other interests, for example those representing either Muslim parents or the smaller Christian groups, into a closer relationship with the state. Inevitably the party will make its ritualistic commitments to the restoration of democratic local controls (the euphemism for restoring the local education authorities to their former glory), and its acceptance, at least in principle, of a universal system of comprehensive secondary schooling – although, as Hargreaves has suggested, it is possible to interpret the meaning of comprehensive secondary schooling in different ways (*Times Educational Supplement*, 29 March 1996, 24). Furthermore, it is important to look beyond the slogans to the specific policy proposals, or lack of them, and to draw the logical conclusions.

It is perhaps dangerous to suggest that there is an emerging political consensus in favour of the greater interpenetration of public and private inputs into the educational service, on the basis of a brief overview of the Labour Party's evolving policy position. However, there is no reason to suspect that the Conservative Party is about to undergo a fundamental conversion and pledge itself 'to turning the clock back' to pre-1979. If anything, it is more likely to speed up the process of change. At best, the Liberal Democrats can expect to be minority partners in government should the next general election result in a hung Parliament. In such circumstances it is impossible to predict what their impact upon the policy-making process would be. Interestingly, their educational policies seem to be stuck in more of a timewarp than those of the Labour Party. While there is no suggestion that, in the unlikely event of the Liberal Democrats forming the government, it would legislate against the interests of private schooling (except to end the assisted places scheme), but neither is there much support for bridging the divide between the two sectors. The Liberal Democrats are committed to retaining comprehensive schools, with the focus upon raising educational standards which it believes is most likely to be achieved through enhanced resourcing: hence its support for earmarked taxes.

The most trenchant criticisms of government policy have been voiced in academic circles and the policy think-tanks – critics to both the right and the left. The neo-liberal strand within the contemporary Conservative Party, chafing at what it considers to be the relatively slow pace of change, has repeatedly advocated a rapid move towards creating an educational market through the use of vouchers (see, for example, Seldon, 1986). This faction was deeply disappointed when Sir Keith Joseph decided not to follow the voucher route, in spite of its intellectual appeal to him. Since Sir Keith's refined slap in the face, there have been voucher experiments in both nursery and further education, but the compulsory school years, the five to 16 age-range, remain forbidden territory – for the time being.

It has been argued that, with the implementation of per capita funding and open enrolment, a voucher scheme is, to all intents and purposes, already in operation. While the present arrangements may indeed place market pressures upon the schools, it does not empower the consumers of educational services in quite the same direct manner. And it was that explicit enhancement of consumer power that made the educational voucher so appealing to its advocates: parents (presumably) would hold the vouchers, they (within some schemes) would decide whether or not to enhance their value, and schools would be explicitly aware of the fact that parents (presumably in conjunction with their children) were making decisions as to where they should spend their vouchers. The message for schools would be clear: their survival depended upon their ability to attract a sufficient number of customers to cover their costs. The affinity with fee-paying schools could scarcely be more evident.

Much of the analysis of the government's educational policy since 1979 has commented upon the tension between its neo-liberal and neo-conservative strands. The moves to increase parental choice and diversity of schooling, accompanied by a narrowing of the local education authorities' role, are seen as products of neo-liberal thinking; with the national curriculum, key-stage testing and the enhancement of the powers of central government as responses to the neo-conservative input. However, some very significant contributors to the on-going educational debate have embraced both trends (The Hillgate Group 1986 and 1987, Flew 1987), although not necessarily supporting all the various themes.

It is an integral part of the British political tradition that those receiving public resources must be held accountable for their use. In most cases this takes the obvious form of submitting standardised accounts which one hopes demonstrate financial probity. However, a wider understanding of the concept of accountability presents an opportunity to reconcile the neo-conservative and neo-liberal threads, supposedly embedded in contemporary Tory education policy. In return for receiving public moneys schools have to follow the national curriculum and their pupils have to participate in the key-stage tests. These measures can be viewed, not simply as mechanisms which will steadily enhance educational standards, as government ministers have repeatedly claimed, but also as a means of ensuring public money is directed at a desired objective (teaching the national curriculum) with efficacious results (which the testing will, or will not, reveal). Of course, following Pring's line of argument (see p.177), this inevitably curtails school autonomy. But public accountability is the price that has to be paid for the receipt of public resources, which demonstrates perfectly the tensions that institutions need to reconcile if they are located between the state and the marketplace.

Not surprisingly, whereas most critics of the right have been broadly sympathetic to the direction of the government's educational policies over the past seventeen years, critics of the left have been almost universally hostile. While it is widely conceded that it would be impossible to restore the *status quo ante* 1979, and there is some sympathy for innovations such as the national curriculum and the local management of schools, strong antipathy is directed at numerous targets: government support for private schooling in the shape of the assisted places scheme, the fragmentation of comprehensive secondary schooling through – most notably – the opting out clauses of the 1988 and 1993 Education Acts, the creeping reintroduction of selection in secondary education, and the erosion of the powers of local education authorities matched by an increase in central control often in the shape of quangos. In addressing these specific concerns the diverse left-wing critics, although paying lip-service to the fact that the world has changed since 1979, reveal the extent to which their own thinking remains trapped in the past.

There is a small group, with strong statist sympathies – especially towards the local education authorities – which believes that as much as possible of paradise lost should be reclaimed (Chitty, 1989; Lauder and Brown (eds), 1988, Introduction; Morris and Griggs (eds), 1988, Chapter 1; Simon, 1988, 1992). In proposing ways forward for the British educational system, Simon, who is the leading figure within this coterie, nicely illustrates the point:

> The first is simple and straight-forward. It is to encourage and strengthen the existing system of comprehensive education: to purge it of its current weaknesses, to allocate adequate resources to allow development, to encourage local and school-based initiatives, and, above all, to re-establish an effective partnership with the local authorities ... with the churches, and all other concerned voluntary bodies, with the teachers and their organisations, and with parents and theirs (1988, 43).

And to reinforce the message, in case there should be any remaining doubts, he goes on to write:

> The principle, as I see it, is acceptance of responsibility for the equal provision of a public good – education, health or whatever ... . The local education authority has a responsibility for the provision of education equally for all – and the emphasis is on the words *for all* (1988, 183).

The Hillcole Group, which has described itself as dedicated to 'changing the future', wants an Education Act which would put into effect most of the short-term measures against private schooling enumerated in the Labour Party's discussion document of 1980, incorporate CTCs, GMS and grammar schools within a comprehensive system of provision, restore – more or less intact – the powers of the LEAs including their right to control school numbers, re-establish the traditional partnership model of governance, and forbid schools from basing their admissions policies on individual attainment levels or special aptitudes. While parents would be permitted a choice of schools, it is scarcely meaningful given the wider context within which it would be exercised (The Hillcole Group, 1991, Chapter 8). It is difficult to take seriously the Group's claim (to use the title of one of its chapters) that it is establishing 'General Principles for a Socialist Agenda in Education for the 1990s and into the 21st Century'. In effect, the course of history has passed its members by, and the sooner they wake up to this, the sooner they can start making a serious contribution to the policy debate. This is no agenda for the future, but rather, notwithstanding bold pronouncements to the contrary, mere nostalgia for the past. Given Simon's well-known commitments this may be excusable, but the Hillcole Group combines delusions of grandeur with self-deception.

There are, however, some figures on the political left who do seem to grasp the fact that the world really has changed, and consequently put forward, or at least imply, policy options that embrace the possibility of the interpenetration of the public and private sectors. Walford, drawing in part upon cross-national comparisons, has made the point:

> In terms of equity and social mixing, the extent of the private sector, and the degree to which the state supports the private sector, are of only partial importance. A larger private sector could be more egalitarian than a smaller one (1989, 223).

To bring about the equity and social mixing that Walford considers desirable, increased government funding would have to be accompanied by regulations designed to achieve the favoured goals. In a not dissimilar vein, Lawton, as part of his own search for a new educational consensus, has suggested a possible modification of the assisted places scheme: 'so that it caters for various kinds of other needs (that is, other than the needs of academically gifted children) such as orphans, children from one-parent families, children whose mother is chronically ill or others who have a genuine need for the special provisions of a residential school' (1992, 104). But in both cases the embracing of radical proposals is exceedingly lukewarm, and it is evident that neither Walford nor Lawton is eager to break the statist mould. Lawton's timidity stems from his attempt to steer a course between differing principles while the whole corpus of his work has demonstrated his strong commitment to one of those traditions. Although his motives may be genuine, his words sound bogus, and consequently he is in danger of pleasing no one. Walford seems to have peered over the abyss, only to draw rapidly back, for by 1994 he is also entrapped essentially in the Hillcole mould: that is, the search for the future means embracing the past through the restoration of the powers of the local education authorities and a system of secondary schooling based essentially on the comprehensive model (1994, 164–9).

One of the most damning indictments of the British educational system in recent years emerged from the Education Group of the University of Birmingham's Centre for Contemporary Cultural Studies (1981). The central theme of their work was that the social-democratic reform of the educational system, strongly promoted by the LEAs and reflecting the professional interests of teachers and education officers, stimulated a populist backlash against what the Group referred to as 'unpopular education'. The outcome was a wide measure of sympathy for the Tory Party's claim that the educational system needed to be revamped. Given their left-leaning political credentials, it was impossible for the Group to support the Conservative government's educational policies, but they have offered few clear clues as to their own preferred alternative route. This is a pity, since they could scarcely advocate a return to the old statist mould that emerged from the social democratic politics of the past.

These confused libertarian elements of the British left seem to be more concerned with the organisation of knowledge within schools, rather than the structure of schooling and how it is governed. None the less, there remain the genuflections to local control (LEAs that are more democratic because they are more representative of popular opinion – hints of a call for elected school boards), and to 'common, non-segregated and publicly organised educational patterns and institutions (not necessarily as school-like as today)' (Johnson, 1989, 119–20), by which he presumably means 'genuinely comprehensive provision' – however that is to be understood.

For a small window of lateral thinking from the libertarian socialists we have to turn to Paul Hirst (1990), who has argued that the purpose of the state should be to stimulate the growth of a highly pluralistic society, as decentralised and as democratically organised as possible. The state should provide the regulatory framework and the financial means to achieve these ends, and then allow the associations to conduct their own affairs with as much popular participation as they can muster. In such circumstances schools would be publicly financed institutions but located firmly in society. Hirst's ideas, which need to be elaborated upon in an educational framework, demonstrate that there is an affinity of thinking between the libertarian left and right which would benefit politically from some constructive bridge-building.

LOOKING FORWARD TO THE FUTURE

In an interesting short article, published soon after the passage of the 1988 Education Reform Act, David Hargreaves claimed that complacent teachers and academics were more interested in resisting government reforms than in offering positive policy alternatives. Presumably, in an attempt to galvanise ideas, he exclaimed that:

189

'Controversies should be occasions for debating alternatives rather than mere opposition' (1989, 213). The academics have now had time to proffer their policy alternatives, and while judgements will obviously differ, the failure to break free of a self-imposed ideological straitjacket means that, by and large, their ideas are timid and conservative – anything but positive.

However, underlying the left critique of Tory educational policy is a vital concern: that over the past seventeen years the British educational system has become more academically and socially divisive; that, for all the talk about increasing parental choice and raising educational standards, this has been the major consequence of the legislative record of the recent Tory governments, if not its major purpose. In the pungent words of Stephen Ball:

> And I will finish with a stark conclusion. That is, the implementation of market reforms in education is essentially a class strategy which has as one of its major effects the reproduction of relative social class (and ethnic) advantages and disadvantages (1994, 103).

Anyone who knows the work of Ball will probably feel that his conclusion was pre-ordained rather than stark, although the point at issue still needs to be addressed.

Only the most naïve and committed supporters of 'the market reforms in education' could possibly believe that they would benefit all social groups equally. However, their more sophisticated advocates would claim that the benefits are not confined to just one narrowly defined social group. Indeed some zealots believe that vouchers, for example, would be of greatest assistance to the socially deprived, since, for the first time, they would possess the resources to make real educational choices. The crucial concern for the pro-market lobby is whether the outcome is a general rise in educational standards, as opposed to a narrowing of the relative class advantages/disadvantages of particular social groups, which Ball implicitly favours. Any evaluation, therefore, of educational reform has to be clear as to its purposes (reshaping class advantages/disadvantages or enhancing choice and educational standards), and how change is to be measured (the relative position of social groups versus changes over time within social groups).

While it may be an unfortunate trait of human nature, it is none the less true that many individuals are prepared to purchase services in the marketplace if they are dissatisfied with the public provision, and if they possess the necessary income. To use the powerful language of Hirschman: individuals are either locked into public services, or they are sufficiently loyal to them to exercise voice, as opposed to exit, should their satisfaction with the standard of service decline (1970). Notwithstanding the earlier blandishments of the Labour Party, it is difficult to imagine that within the context of a social-democratic polity a government would actually forbid schools to charge fees, so locking parents into the maintained schools. If such an option had been politically viable, then the Labour Party, following its 1980 discussion document, would have put it at the centre of its agenda as opposed to proposing an initial batch of measures designed to soften up the private sector first. The danger of allowing exit from public services is that, without any counter-proposals, the decline in the quality of those services is almost inevitable. In effect middle-class flight lessens the pressure of voice upon public services, and so hastens their deterioration.

Therefore, in relation to the provision of education, it is critical to know what will retain the loyalty of those parents who have opted for maintained schooling but who, none the less, could afford to pay the private sector's fees. Hirschman notes that some individuals have such a deeply ingrained sense of loyalty to public services that they can never fully leave them; even if they do so, the quality of those services continues to be of concern to them (1970, 100–2). Few, however, are likely to demonstrate that degree of loyalty, and most will take their custom elsewhere should they have the means, and should their voice have proved ineffective.

Evidence from the Netherlands leads Walford to the conclusion that:

> Affluent Dutch parents have no need to establish a separate elite private system of schools, since the selectivity which operates within the combined state-financed system has already ensured that their children are likely to have privileged access to higher education and the advantages which that bestows (1989, 21).

Walford's own research into the campaign which middle-class parents in Solihull conducted against the reintroduction of selective secondary schooling led him to conclude that as long as comprehensive schooling was serving their interests they were prepared to defend it. He found many parents who wanted to retain their leafy neighbourhood comprehensive school because it gave them ' ... some of the perceived benefits of independent schools without the necessary additional expense' (Walford and Jones 1986, 252). While this offended Walford's moral sensibilities, to many others – especially middle-class parents – it will make perfect sense. Generalising from the various case studies, Estelle James observes that the more selectivity – academically and socially – there is in the state sector, the less incentive middle-class parents will have to choose private schooling (1989, 228). Thus the Dutch case appears to be widely replicated. The evidence from England suggests that middle-class parents are prepared to use either voice (as in Solihull) or exit (as both Tony Blair and Harriet Harman have demonstrated) to preserve their privileges *within* the state sector. It is local circumstances that dictate parental decisions.

The obvious lesson would-be policy-makers have to learn is that they need to understand the world as it is. Although policy does not always have to be constructed in a fashion that will not offend the interests of those with privileges to defend, there is a need to understand those interests rather than adopt a morally superior stance in relation to them, and to appreciate the political costs and difficulties of challenging them. For example, it is hard not to reach the conclusion that those in favour of the movement from selective to comprehensive secondary schooling underestimated both the hold that the tradition of academic selection has on British education, and the ramifications of the fact that most schools in Britain are overwhelmingly neighbourhood schools. If the purpose of moving towards comprehensive secondary schooling was to promote equality of educational opportunity, then a further set of measures was needed to counter these 'unfortunate' facts. But how far is it possible to change the world within a social democracy before a backlash occurs? As if in recognition of the limits of social engineering, A. H. Halsey – the one-time father figure of those who sought social change through educational reform – has written: 'At some point equality of educational opportunity can only be obtained at the cost of freedom' (1985, 205). Halsey's bold statement needs to be refined, but it makes the powerful point that there are boundaries beyond which many of us are not prepared to go to fulfil someone else's interpretation of social justice.

Therefore, the first, and most important, lesson to be learnt from the educational policies of the long Tory years is that the place of selection within the educational system needs to be seriously evaluated. It is difficult to imagine an educational system in which, sooner or later, there is no selection. On the one hand, the Labour Party claims that it is against selective secondary schools, while, on the other hand, it suggests that academically gifted pupils should be allowed to complete their schooling at an accelerated pace within comprehensive secondary schools (Charter and Sherman, 28 February 1996). The Labour Party seems to be arguing that it is hostile to a selective process which segregates pupils into differing schools, but not to one which separates them within the same school. The wider debate should centre upon a number of key issues. In Britain selection has invariably depended upon the ability of parents to pay school fees and/or the academic ability of the individual pupil, while the CTCs and magnet schools select according to particular aptitudes and interests. At what age, or ages, should selection occur? Is it possible to construct flexible selection procedures so that mistakes can be retrieved? Most critically, can the social and educational effects of selection be controlled? It would be naïve to suggest that debate alone will lead to a consensus upon which agreed policies can be constructed, for, in the final analysis, educational policy reflects the values of those who control the political process. It is to be hoped, however, that some common ground can be established, the dividing lines – and why they persist – made clearer, the links between policy and its purposes clarified, and agreed lines for policy evaluation formulated.

Presumably if selection, whatever form it takes, keeps middle-class parents in the maintained sector then, at the very least, they can be expected to take a keen interest in the resourcing of that sector's schools. Moreover, if more middle-class parents have a reason for demonstrating loyalty to maintained schooling, then the debate about public policy is likely to be sharper. It is interesting to speculate on what direction the national curriculum and key-stage testing would have taken if the government's legislative proposals had incorporated the fee-paying schools. It is not just a question of securing a broader, and possibly more potent, parental input into the debate, for the private sector also has considerable institutional muscle at its disposal. The interpenetration of the sectors could result in the creation of a more formidable educational lobby.

According to its critics, questions of social equity have been scarce to the point of virtual absence in the educational policies of recent Tory governments (Walford, 1994, 142). If, as the trend of the Labour Party's policies suggest, the present system will not change substantially even with a government of a somewhat different political complexion, how can a greater concern with social equity be built into the model? Even more significantly, given the theme of this book, how can we best ensure that, in an educational system in which most schools are between the state and the marketplace, sharp academic and social selection is not associated with the two poles at either end of the state–market continuum? In the context, therefore, of the selection debate, the question of social equity has to be tackled pragmatically with the intention of constructing a wider cross-party consensus around the idea of interpenetration.

Before suggesting ways in which present policies may be enhanced, it is important to question whether the Tory record is quite as blemished as its critics argue. The national curriculum and the accompanying key-stage testing permit a close monitoring of the attainment levels achieved in individual schools, and indeed by individual pupils. With the further intrusion of the regular, if not sufficiently regular, inspection of schools, the state has no difficulty in identifying schools that are apparently failing their pupils, and individual pupils who require additional assistance. The 1993 Act empowers the Secretary of State to establish 'educational associations' (a peculiar label) to take over schools which are considered to be failing, and to close them if it is felt they are beyond redemption: procedures very much in line with the Labour Party's thinking. In effect the state is exercising a voice, in fact much more than a voice, on behalf of those who may be locked into the maintained sector. Within itself this may not be considered much of a strategy to enhance social equity, but it ensures some protection of the interests of those who cannot, or have no wish to, opt out of the maintained schools. Moreover, the information provided will enable those who wish to remain in the state sector to exercise a more effective choice of maintained schools. While this will favour some social groups over others, there is some interesting Scottish evidence which shows that those parents already expressing preferences are by no means drawn exclusively from the middle classes (Adler and Raab, 1988, 155–79).

The attempt to create a greater diversity of educational provision has the further merit that it could enable at least segments of a range of social groups to establish grant maintained schools which cater, within the context of the national curriculum, to their particular needs. Ball clearly implies (see p.190) that a market strategy is designed to reproduce class and ethnic disadvantage. What then is one to make of the growth within the private sector of all-black schools (often with a particular religious appeal) or Muslim schools? Are these schools manifestations of the reproduction of educational disadvantage? Or do they represent attempts to escape the cultural mores and low educational standards experienced in local authority-controlled comprehensive schools? One wonders, given the rich historical traditions of popular education, whether the English working class can reclaim its own heritage of schooling. And certainly, although most private and grant-maintained schools for girls are likely to cater to middle-class interests, this is no reason to assume that their class orientation is of any greater significance than the fact they are girls' schools. Although the faint-hearted may be worried, there is no reason why – given the national curriculum and key-stage testing – there should not be a greater measure of social diversity between schools.

A potentially powerful criticism of a market system which encourages competition in terms of the exceedingly narrow criteria of test scores and examination performance is that schools will come to value only those pupils who can enhance their performance in these terms. Considerable suspicion has already been aroused by the increase in expulsions, along with the fear that per capita funding may operate to the detriment of those children with special educational needs. But as Thomas and Bullock so pertinently observe:

> Formula funding rules can always be rewritten to lay down minimum rules about the allocation of funds to schools with levels of pupils with additional educational needs. We suggest that such an explicit approach to funding is to be preferred to the old system which relied upon various combinations of custom, practice, political and/or officer discretion and sheer ignorance (Thomas and Bullock, 1994, 50).

The manipulation of the formula-funding rules gives rise to all sorts of interesting possibilities. The rules could be structured to encourage schools to accept children not only with social and educational needs but also with behavioural problems such as truancy. One of the major objections to publishing the raw data of test scores and examination results has been that like is not being compared with like: that pupils vary in all sorts of ways from school to school. Consequently, it may be more meaningful to compare changes in results over time: that is, to build into the comparisons a value-added element. A formula-funding model could incorporate this dimension, rewarding those schools which show the greatest improvements over time. The intention would be to construct the formula in such a way that it offers positive incentives to schools to accept pupils who have traditionally not been highly regarded in our system, and, moreover, gives particularly generous rewards to those schools which can demonstrate a positive value-added input – and not only in terms of academic criteria. If it is felt desirable to aim for schools with particular mixes of pupils, then again the formula could be adjusted accordingly.

To date, Pring's second form of privatisation, that is the purchase of services from the private sector at public expense, has been directed at selected categories of pupils: the academically gifted who would be unlikely – so it is implied – to fulfil their promise in the state system (the assisted places scheme), those with special educational/social needs, and the children of parents who work for the state and are liable to overseas service. The latter two categories should cause – in spite of Pring's apparent objections – few qualms. However, the assisted places scheme, at least in its present form, is very difficult to justify. This is not because it assists the participating schools (this is part of the purpose of interchanging public resources and private provision), but because the terms of the private–public exchange are weighted too heavily in favour of the fee-paying schools. These are children who are likely to impose few unexpected demands, and equally, are likely to enhance the schools' academic reputations. The private sector itself wanted the government to build into the scheme a stronger social needs element along the lines suggested by Lawton. While this has been steadfastly resisted, some schools have assumed the commitment, and found ways to underwrite the boarding costs (see p.123). But this changes the scheme only at the margins, and, even in a new package, its central thrust is still likely to involve the transference of the academically gifted from the maintained to the fee-paying sector. The resources could be used to support more acceptable forms of interpenetration. At best a much slimmed-down assisted places scheme should be retained to aid only those with *both* academic potential and social/personal needs through a *boarding* education.

By creating a sector of schooling that is essentially publicly financed, but has many of the critical trappings of independence, the bridges between the public and private domains are much broader than the recruitment, at public expense, of special categories of pupils by the fee-paying schools. To maintain this wide base it is critical to ensure that the CTC, GMS and technology college stratum of schooling does *not* become socially and academically exclusive. Most decidedly, we do not want a general return to academically selective grammar schools. Moreover, although it may be desirable to attract fee-paying schools into the maintained sector (on this see the important contribution of George Walden, 1996, 74–102), it is vital that they should not all be schools with strong academic reputations, but represent a variety of pedagogical traditions (note the Labour

Party's reference to Steiner schools) with differing social characteristics, and even particular specialisations. It is to this end that formula funding needs to be manipulated.

When all is said and done, it must be remembered that schooling is part of the process of social selection in modern industrialised societies, and that inevitably many parents will attempt to use the educational system in ways they believe will enhance the opportunities of their own children. Without taking anything else into consideration beyond the differing ages, aptitudes and abilities of pupils, the pressures towards selection are immense. Ideally the educational system should value a number of qualities, and the move towards a more variegated provision could help to promote this possibility, for there is no reason why selection and differentiation should automatically mean hierarchy and inequality. However, schools are part of society and, inevitably, will reflect its dominant value system. What seems to bother the critics of Tory education policy is that it has worked with, rather than against, the grain of social stratification pressures. Critics of the right replace society with the individual (to quote Mrs Thatcher, 'there is no such thing as society'); critics of the left want to replace the present society with their own vague model, and see the educational system as a critical vehicle of change. But consensus politics means that in the near future we are likely to experience essentially minor policy shifts along the lines outlined above. Where does this leave the study of educational policy-making?

CONCLUSION

Over the past twenty years the character of the fee-paying sector of schooling in Britain has changed in all sorts of important ways. These changes were stimulated by one basic pressure: for some years the schools had been attracting a declining share of the school-aged population, and if this process were to continue many would be forced to close and the private sector of schooling would slowly melt away. Various economic, social and political forces have been put forward to explain this steady decline, and many sympathetic to the cause of the fee-paying schools wanted a response which would enable them to counteract these negative pressures and reverse their downward spiral. The consequence was not only a change in the character of individual schools but also in the institutional framework to which they belonged. The private schools became independent, setting up their publicity arm, ISIS, and establishing an over-arching policy-making body, ISJC.

Although the fee-paying schools found themselves on the political defensive from 1945 onwards, this did not exercise any discernible influence upon their ability to enrol pupils. However, by the mid-1970s a Labour government was starting to implement policies that would have a direct impact: the phasing-out of the direct grant schools, and a closer monitoring of the purchase of places in the private sector by the local education authorities. The obvious fear was that these represented tentative steps towards a full-frontal political assault upon the schools which would result in their immediate demise as opposed to the steady decline which market forces had apparently initiated. It was time, therefore, to take action or face the prospect of extinction.

Whether the changes that were introduced amount to a revolution or not is a matter of conjecture. But what is beyond dispute is that the fortunes of the independent schools have revived, and that this has been accompanied by a considerable amount of internal change, some of it generated by deliberate action and some of it as a seemingly natural response to social change (for example, the shifting balance between day and boarding pupils). Moreover, the political climate has become more favourable. This is partly a result of the election of four successive Conservative governments which have offered both tangible support by enacting the assisted places scheme and general ideological comfort. It could be argued, somewhat controversially, that the independent sector was also inadvertently aided by a Labour government which, to all intents and purposes, forced many of the prestigious direct grant schools to become independent, and a Labour Party which wanted to force the pace of change on the reorganisation of secondary schooling along comprehensive lines. However, although many elements within the Labour Party are still bitterly opposed to private schooling, it is now generally recognised that in formal educational terms the quality of such schooling is, by and large, very good. Now one is more likely to hear complaints that parents are purchasing educational privilege rather than that the schools are offering an outmoded form of schooling that is detrimental to the nation's interests.

The shift in opinion followed in part from the sustained attack upon the maintained sector of schooling. Whether all the threads of this attack were justified or not is beside the point: it was taken seriously in government circles and has been accompanied by concerted efforts to restructure state schooling. While the socio-cultural character of the fee-paying sector has become somewhat more diversified over time, so the maintained schools have come to resemble the independent schools more closely in terms of how they are governed, and both sectors – or at least elements within both sectors – have started to converge in terms of their educational values and practices. Admittedly there is criticism of the changes that have overtaken the maintained sector of schooling in recent years but this is confined more to academic, as opposed to party, circles. Although a Labour government would phase out the assisted places scheme (at least in part), and perhaps modify some of the constraints upon the local education authorities, the bulk of the reforms implemented since 1979 would remain in place. The prevailing educational order is underwritten by a greater measure of political consensus than has been true of much of the past decade or so. In part this reflects the determination of the Labour Party not to upset some of the key potential elements of its electoral support. But it should not be forgotten that it was a Labour Prime Minister, James Callaghan, who first raised serious doubts as to whether the nation at large had benefited fully from the enhanced post-1945 expenditure upon education and, more specifically, whether the educational system was serving the needs of the economy adequately. These developments have occurred within a political context that is generally hostile to raising taxation levels (or at least direct taxation), expanding the public sector borrowing requirement, or enlarging the percentage of the nation's wealth under the control of the state, and that – most impor-tantly within the educational debate – no longer believes that spending more money automatically brings about an improvement in the quality of the service. From this last point follows a broad commitment to making the provision of social services in general more the responsibility of society and less that of the state.

The thrust of this chapter has been to support these changes. The intention is not to encourage a decline in the state's financial input but to encourage an increasing input of societal resources. It is recognised, however, that to receive public moneys is to accept the requirement of public accountability, but it is hoped that this can be achieved within the context of parameters such as the national curriculum and key-stage testing rather than detailed procedures to ensure financial accountability (which would run counter to Skidelsky's recent proposal for a voucher system to enable private charitable educational trusts to take over 'the worst of our state schools … in inner-city areas' (20 September 1996, 18)). Clearly this constrains the general objective, which is to make schooling more part of society and less part of the state. Of course the other, and perhaps greater, problem is that such a shift may increase inequality within the educational system

– that is, there is more social divisiveness between schools, the funding differentials are increased, and the educational opportunities of particular social groups and individuals are further disadvantaged. This is the challenge to be met by those who desire the further interpenetration of the private and maintained sectors of schooling. Critical to this development has to be a serious discussion of the role of selection in the educational process, for to circumvent it appears to result in the flight of middle-class parents, while to accept it appears to increase social inequality. Equally clearly an integrated system of schooling cannot be achieved by denying an important part of our educational heritage; fee-paying schools cannot be wished out of existence, and to try to legislate the same end carries more political – and indeed moral – risks than it is worth. That has been tried and failed.

10

From the Politics of Education to the Economics of Education

All academic disciplines evolve over time as they embrace different issues and new theoretical positions. For over a decade now the sociology of education in Britain has placed policy-making at the centre of its agenda, and located that focus within contrasting interpretations of how power is organised in a social democratic polity bounded by a capitalist economy. Disappointingly, the overall thrust of the work has been descriptive and evaluative rather than theoretically based. In a review of some 'sociological perspectives' on contemporary educational reforms, Shilling wrote: 'This lack of theoretical development is the most striking and disappointing feature of *Voicing Concern*', and then uttered the despairing *cri de coeur*: 'But where is the theory in this analysis? In fact where is the sociology?' (1993, 111). Presumably, Shilling was not simply expressing his views, which were generally favourable, on one book, but making a statement which had wider ramifications, for he entitled his review 'The Demise of the Sociology of Education in Britain?'.

There are three reasons why we can anticipate not so much the demise of the sociology of education in Britain but rather the expectation that it will start to take up different concerns and draw upon alternative intellectual traditions. It is part of my argument that, unless this development occurs soon, then a decline can indeed be expected, for the sub-discipline is stuck in a narrow groove which generates increasingly sterile analysis. There are three forces which should bring about change.

The current policy focus was stimulated by the decline, from the mid-1960s onwards, in the political consensus established by the 1944 Education Act, and reinforced by the restructuring of the educational system by successive Conservative governments since 1979. It would have been somewhat surprising if this had not stimulated the interest of social scientists. However, it has been one of the sub-themes of this book that a political consensus on educational policy has re-emerged, or is in the process of emerging. The issues this will generate are of a different order: equally worthy of analysis, but centred on the need for long-term research, and less likely to call for an immediate policy perspective.

The long years of Conservative government have led to an extended period of politically driven educational change. It was to be expected that the intellectual inputs into the debates would, therefore, be drawn mainly from the fields of sociology (how to explain change) and politics (how to explain why some policy initiatives succeed and others fail). Obviously, educational change has not come to a standstill. For example, considerable developments in the financing of higher education can be expected after Sir Ron Dearing's recently appointed inquiry has reported, and the next general election is over; but the pace of change will be slower, and it will occur within a broad political consensus as to both the purposes of education and how they are to be achieved. This context is less supportive of policy analysis, and the concerns of the sociology of education will be more narrowly defined, even technical in nature. The issues that will dominate any serious analysis of the British educational system in the near future should focus upon the level of public resourcing, the relationship between the public and private financing of the educational system, how best to achieve value for money, and how to ensure that questions of social equity are built into the funding models.

If this prognosis is correct then the sociology of education will shift from what it has become in the past decade (the politics of education), to what it can expect to become (the economics of education). It will be driven by the concerns that underwrite any field of applied social policy: measuring the effectiveness of policy implementation in relation to resource inputs and prescribed policy goals. In the process of pursuing such ends it will draw, in particular, upon the research of the applied economists: Barr and his work on income-contingent loans (1993) Le Grand and his case for the development of quasi-markets in the provision of welfare (1990); Thomas (1994)/Thomas and Bullock (1994) and their suggestions for the manipulation of formula funding to achieve greater diversity in the provision of schooling, as well as enhanced public support for those with special educational needs; Glennerster and Wilson and their detailed analysis of levels of public support for private schooling (1970); and – of course – Hirschman's brilliant dissection of the relationship between loyalty, exit and voice in the promotion of institutional change (1970).

The policy analysis that has emerged within British educational sociology has been variously described as: education policy sociology, critical policy analysis (with education as part of a wider social policy brief), applied education politics, the political sociology of education, and the politics of education. The final and most important reason why the sociology of education in Britain should change direction is that, regardless of which particular label is applied, the policy analysis has, for the most part, been very disappointing. Whereas David Hargreaves was critical of academics for not offering alternative policy options (see p.189), a more serious shortcoming has has been their inability to develop convincing understandings of the direction of educational policy, a goal more integral to the academic enterprise.

As Shilling has noted, most of the research has a straightforward narrative quality. Within itself this is not a problem, but so frequently is the evidence turned into a rod with which to beat the government's educational policies that evaluation becomes everything and analysis is reduced to naught. After a while the well-trodden lines of condemnation can be readily anticipated by the least discerning of readers; they numb because they are expected and obvious. In effect, the bulk of the research represents a gross devaluation of the idea of critical analysis for it is unashamedly meant to serve partisan political purposes rather than aid the process of understanding. It is one thing to wonder imaginatively whether social science research can ever be value-free, but quite another to discover – remarkably! – that in some peculiar fashion the evidence is invariably consistent with one's own moral predispositions.

When we are fortunate enough to discover a genuine attempt at theorising, then we are as likely to find confusion as enlightenment. One of the leading figures in 'education policy sociology' (if it secures only the demise of such ugly phraseology, a new research direction would have proved its worth) has described his theoretical position thus:

> I am certainly not a pluralist, at least I do not think I am; I may be a Weberian neo-pluralist, to coin a phrase, but if I am I strongly hold to the tenet of a 'dual polity'. That is to say, the role of representative institutions in social democratic politics is constrained and distorted by the obvious inequalities of power inherent in capitalism (Ball, 1990, 2).

While Ball's attempt to fuse different theoretical traditions is to be applauded (he has drawn heavily upon the work of Althusser and

Foucault), the end product needs to be a coherent whole rather than the mish-mash that he himself implies is the consequence. If he wishes to stand foursquare in the Weberian tradition, along with Archer and Salter/Tapper, then there is no need to construct an artificial whole from incompatible parts. But he also has to accept the political constraints of that tradition, part of which would include a much wider understanding of the distribution of power in social democratic and capitalist societies than its 'obvious inequalities'.

In the best tradition of scholarship, Ball, as one of the editors of the *Journal of Education Policy*, has called for articles which will 'promote theoretical debate and development in relation to education policy analysis' (1992, 493). To date there have been two interesting, but highly predictable, responses. First, there has been Hatcher and Troyna's critique of Ball's work (1994) and Ball's inevitable response to that critique (1994a). This debate follows well-worn paths within the critical social policy field: schooling as cultural domination leading to the reproduction of the social relations of production appropriate to a capitalist economy versus schools as potential sites for resistance and struggle with teachers as interpreters, not merely transmitters, of socio-cultural values. While this may stimulate debate on policy analysis, with the journal as a convenient publishing forum for the inner circle, it is less certain that it will promote theoretical development.

Secondly, and more significantly, Ranson – in a sub-section of his article entitled '*Towards* a framework for educational policy analysis' – has called for yet another 'integrated approach to explanatory analysis':

> The fissiparous tendencies of theorists, striving to emphasise the virtues of a particular perspective, can fragment the task of explanation which requires some critical interrelating of those different perspectives. An adequate understanding of public policy demands a multi-theoretic and multi-disciplinary analysis (1995, 442).

Ranson continues by arguing that a theoretical analysis of public policy has to accommodate historical location and the inter-relationship between action and structure, and while providing a critical analysis of the values inherent in current policies should also 'theorise the conditions for a different form of polity and public policy' (1995, 443).

Ranson is in the company of Dale who, likewise, has made repeated calls for theory which links macro-social processes to education policy and practice (1994, 31-41). Dale has placed particular stress upon the need to analyse the role of the state in constructing this linkage (1989), but he would also retain the commitment 'to changing rather than merely analysing education' (1994, 31). But, like Ranson, Dale has made precious little effort to do more than present the briefest outline of his alternative approach. Evidently it is easier to reflect critically upon what we have, to point the way forward and then to wait. But the problem is that time and tide wait for no one. If my prognosis on future policy trends is correct, then the theoretical developments – especially if married to empirical work – along the lines suggested by both Dale and Ranson would be welcome, but equally they would have more relevance for the past than the current understanding of educational policy.

On the peripheries of the sub-discipline (that is, outside what we hope will be its new core, the economics of education), we can expect a return to the old concerns of access, curriculum content, and the role of the classroom teacher in the pedagogical process. The interest in access has already been restimulated by the assisted places scheme (who benefits), the enhancement of parental choice (who takes advantage), and the creation of the CTCs and grant-maintained schools (who is selected). Inevitably the emergence of a national curriculum has led to fierce debates as to how that curriculum is to be defined (the subject areas), and the precise content of those definitions (for example, whose English and whose History?). For some theorists (Ball, 1994, 177-8; Hargreaves, 1989, 215) the teacher remains a key figure in any understanding of schooling as a process of social reproduction and cultural transmission; it is the teacher who translates the meaning of the external messages in the micro-social setting of the classroom. It is fruitful to ask ourselves what the national curriculum actually means within the classroom context.

This book, drawing upon the work of Archer and Collins (see Chapter 1), has unashamedly adopted a macro-sociological approach in the Weberian tradition. Its empirical content represents a broad historical overview of the state's regulation of access to fee-paying schools. While the theoretical premises, and certainly the relationships drawn between theory and evidence, may be criticised, historically centred research has made the most fruitful contribution in recent years to educational sociology, and to British educational sociology in particular. The work of the school of critical social policy, at least as it applies to education, is, by comparison, second-rate. It has given us nothing to compare with the work of Archer (1979), Bowles and Gintis (1976), Clifford-Vaughan and Archer (1971), Green (1990), and Williamson (1979). I have tried to tie this book, despite its obvious policy implications, and the attempt in the previous chapter to make those implications more explicit, into what I consider to be the sociology of education's most fruitful, if not its most expansive, development in recent years.

However, there is no reason why this sociologically driven but historically centred work should not flourish in the future as a viable sub-section within the sociology of education. British educational sociology would then be comprised of:

1. An applied policy branch which is heavily reliant upon the economics of education.

2. A more narrowly defined sociological stream centred upon questions of access, curriculum and pedagogy.

3. A broad historical stream which draws upon macro-sociological theories.

Dale has made an interesting distinction between the politics of education and education politics. By the politics of education he understands 'the agenda for education and the processes and structures through which it is created', while education politics are 'the processes whereby this agenda is translated into problems and issues for schools, and schools' responses to those problems and issues' (1994, 35). His education politics would fall into either of the first two categories listed above. Inasmuch as his politics of education has a broad historical focus, it would fall into the third stream. However, if the intention – notwithstanding the new historical context – is to understand contemporary education policy, then it is a matter which would be best left to others, notably the political scientists. The educationists have offered us little more than narrative, theoretical confusion and a parading of their value preferences. The political scientists may not give us the links between social structure and policy that Dale craves, a link best established by macro-sociological theory in the context of broad historical sweeps, but they are more likely to give us medium-range theory that is soundly linked to empirical evidence and rounded off by sober evaluations. Moreover, they are also more likely to give us the comparative perspective, between nation states and across areas of public policy, which has been so sadly lacking. After all, education policy is merely a small area within public policy.

This book must stand or fall by evaluations of its contribution to the third stream within the sociology of education, that is the explanation of educational change in terms of macro-sociological theory. By relying on Collins's conflict theory of social stratification it has posited a more explicit dynamic to the process of educational change than is to be found in the seminal work of M. S. Archer. However, in line with Archer's work, it has supported the idea of two dominant lines of change: one economically driven in which schools are founded to fulfil private ends (the substitutive strategy), and the other politically driven, in which the state restricts the hold that established interests exercise over the existing educational system (the restrictive strategy), thereby opening up that system to alternative interests. Over time the restrictive strategy has grown in importance, while in contemporary Britain we have seen a merging of the two strategies in which those pursuing a substitutive strategy attempt to buy into – through political action – the maintained sector.

The move from substitution to restriction has brought about a critical development of great significance for all the themes within the sociology of education. This development is the central role played by the state in the process of educational change in modern, or even post-modern, industrialised societies. Large and prestigious segments of the so-called independent sector of schooling occupy an uneasy position between the state and society. In return for state largess it has been subjected to state interference and control, much of it unwelcome. Dale is right to stress the central role of the state in the process of educational change for it is the state that translates social change into new educational forms. While this may constitute a simple political response to class pressures (for example, Dale has argued that the assisted places scheme was Mrs Thatcher's reward to her lower-middle-class supporters), it is a response that emerges through the complex interaction of institutions. It was key elements within the fee-paying sector, interacting with various figures within the Conservative Party, which formulated the assisted places scheme. Mrs Thatcher's lower-middle-class battalions were conspicuous by their absence. If there is one central message of this book, it is that all the varying streams within the sociology of education have to centre their analysis of the British educational system upon the input of the state and its relationship to organised interests: a highly ironic development in view of the apparent promise of Thatcherism!

References

BOOKS AND JOURNAL ARTICLES

Adler, M., and C.M. Raab (1988) 'Exit, Choice and Loyalty: The Impact of Parental Choice on Admissions to Secondary Schools in Edinburgh and Dundee', *Journal of Education Policy*, Vol. 3, No. 2, 155–79.

Allsobrook, D. (1973) 'The Reform of the Endowed Schools: The Work of the Northamptonshire Education Society, 1854–1874', *The History of Education*, Vol. 2, 35–55.

Allsobrook, D. (1986) *Schools for the Shires, The Reform of Middle-Class Education in Mid-Victorian England*, Manchester University Press, Manchester.

Althusser, L. (1984) *Essays on Ideology*, Verso Editions, London.

Archer, M.S. (1979) *Social Origins of Educational Systems*, Sage Publications, London.

Arnold, M. (1864) *A French Eton*, reprinted in R.H. Super (ed.) (1962) *Democratic Education*, Michigan University Press, Ann Arbor, 262–325.

Ball, S. (1990) *Policy and Policy Making in Education: Explorations in Policy Sociology*, Routledge, London.

Ball, S. (1992) 'Theoretical Debates in Education Policy Analysis', *Journal of Education Policy*, Vol. 7, No. 5, 493.

Ball, S. (1994) *Education Reform: A Critical and Post-Structural Approach*, Open University Press, Buckingham.

Ball, S. (1994a) 'Some Reflections on Policy Theory: A Brief Response to Hatcher and Troyna', *Journal of Education Policy*, Vol. 9, No. 2, 171–82.

Balls, F.E. (1967) 'The Endowed Schools Act and the Development of the English Grammar Schools in the Nineteenth Century, Part One: The Origins of the Act', *The Durham Research Review, New Series*, Vol. 5, No. 19, 207–15.

Balls, F.E. (1968) 'The Endowed Schools Act and the Development of the English Grammar Schools in the Nineteenth Century, Part Two: The Operation of the Act', *The Durham Research Review, New Series*, Vol. 5, No. 20, 219–29.

Bamford, T. (1961) 'Public Schools and Social Class, 1801–1850', *British Journal of Sociology*, Vol. 12, 224–35.

Bamford, T. (1967) *The Rise of the Public Schools*, Nelson, London.

Banks, O. (1955) *Parity and Prestige in English Secondary Education*, Routledge & Kegan Paul, London.

Barker, R. (1972) *Education and Politics, 1900–1951*, Clarendon Press, Oxford.

Barnett, C. (1986) *The Audit of War*, Macmillan, London.

Barr, N. (1993) *The Economics of the Welfare State*, Weidenfeld & Nicolson, London.

Bowles, S., and H. Gintis (1976) *Schooling in Capitalist America*, Routledge & Kegan Paul, London.

Bridgeman, T. and I. Fox (29 June 1978), 'Why People Choose Private Schools', *New Society*, 702–5.

Butler, R.A. (1971) *The Art of the Possible*, Hamish Hamilton, London.

Cannell, G. (1981) 'Resistance to the Charity Commissioners: the Case of St. Paul's Schools, 1860–1904', *History of Education*, Vol. 10, No. 4, 245–62.

Carlisle, N. (1818) *Endowed Grammar Schools*, Baldwin, Craddock & Jay, London (reprinted in 1972 by the Richmond Publishing Company, Richmond).

Centre for Contemporary Cultural Studies (Education Group) (1981) *Unpopular Education*,

Hutchinson, London.

Chairman of HMC (1968) 'The Newsom Commission: The Chairman's Address to the AGM of the Headmasters' Conference', *Conference*, Vol. 5, No. 3, 3–8.

Chitty, C. (1989) *Towards a New Education System: The Victory of the New Right*, Falmer Press, Barcombe.

Chitty, C. (1995) 'Victory of the Minimalists and Privatisers?', *Oxford Review of Education*, Vol. 21, No. 2, 233–7.

Clifford-Vaughan, M., and M.S. Archer (1971) *Social Conflict and Educational Change in England and France, 1789–1848*, Cambridge University Press, Cambridge.

Coleman, D.C. (1973) 'Gentlemen and Players', *Economic History Review*, Second Series, Vol. 26, No. 1, 92–116.

Collins, R. (1971) 'Functional and Conflict Theories of Educational Stratification', *American Sociological Review*, Vol. 36, No. 1, 1002–18.

Cook, A.K. (1917) *About Winchester College*, Macmillan, London.

Dale, R. (1989) *The State and Education Policy*, Open University Press, Milton Keynes.

Dale, R. (1994) 'Applied Education Politics or Political Sociology of Education? Contrasting Approaching to Recent Education Reform in England and Wales', in B. Halpin and B.Troyna (eds), *Researching Education Policy; Ethical and Methodological Issues*, The Falmer Press, London, 31–41.

Dancy, J. (1963) *The Public Schools and the Future*, Faber & Faber, London.

Dooley, P. (1991) 'Muslim Private Schools', in G. Walford (ed.), *Private Schooling: Tradition, Change, and Diversity*, Paul Chapman, London.

Durkheim, E. (1956) *Education and Sociology*, The Free Press, Glencoe, Illinois.

Editor (1982) 'Editorial', *Conference*, Vol. 19, No. 2, 5–7.

Edwards, T., J. Fitz and G. Whitty (1989) *The State and Private Education: An Evaluation of the Assisted Places Scheme*, Falmer Press, Basingstoke.

Firth, J.D'E. (1936) *Winchester*, Blackie and Son, London.

Flew, A. (1987) *Power to the Parents: Reversing Educational Decline*, Sherwood Press, London.

Fox, I. (1984) 'The Demand for Public School Education: A Crisis of Confidence in Comprehensive Schooling?', in G.Walford (ed.), *British Public Schools: Policy and Practice*, Falmer Press, Barcombe, 45–63.

Fox, I. (1984a) *Private Schools and Public Issues*, Macmillan, London.

Gerth, H.H. and C. Wright Mills (1958) *From Max Weber: Essays in Sociology*, Oxford University Press, New York.

Giddens, A. (ed.) (1972) *Emile Durkheim: Selected Writings*, Cambridge University Press, Cambridge.

Gladstone, F. (1982) *Charity Law and Social Justice*, Bedford Square Press/NCVO, London.

Glennerster, H., and G.Wilson (1970) *Paying for Private Schools*, Allen Lane, London.

Gordon, P. (1980) *Selection for Secondary Education*, The Woburn Press, London.

Gosden, P. (1976) *Education in the Second World War: A Study in Policy and Administration*, Methuen, London.

Green, A. (1990) *Education and State Formation: The Rise of Education Systems in England, France and the USA*, Macmillan, London.

Griggs, C. (1985) *Private Schools in Britain*, Falmer Press, Barcombe.

Griggs, C. (1988) 'Fee-paying Education: The Favoured Sector', in M. Morris and C. Griggs (eds), *Education: The Wasted Years? 1973–1986*, Falmer Press, Barcombe, 181–202.

Hailsham, Lord (Editor in Chief) (1993) *Halsbury's Laws of England*, Vol. 5 (2), Butterworths, London.

Halsey, A.H. (1985) 'Schools for Democracy', in J. Ahier and M. Flude (eds), *Contemporary Education Policy*, Croom Helm, London, 191–210.

Halsey, A.H., A.F. Heath and J.M. Ridge (1980) *Origins and Destinations: Family, Class and Education in Modern Britain*, Clarendon Press, Oxford.

Hargreaves, D. (1989) 'Educational Policy and Educational Change: A Local Perspective', in A. Hargreaves and D. Reynolds (eds), *Educational Policies: Controversies and Critiques*, Falmer Press, Barcombe, 213–17.

Hatcher, S. and B.Troyna (1994) 'The "Policy Cycle": A Ball by Ball Account', *Journal of Education Policy*, Vol. 9, No. 2, 155–70.

REFERENCES

Heeney, B. (1969) *Mission to the Middle Classes*, SPCK, London.
Heward, C. (1988) *Making a Man of Him*, Routledge, London.
The Hillcole Group (1991) *Changing the Future*, The Tufnell Press, London.
The Hillgate Group (1986) *Whose Schools? A Radical Manifesto*, Hillgate Group, London.
The Hillgate Group (1987) *The Reform of British Education: From Principles to Practice*, The Claridge Press, London.
Hirschman, A.O. (1970) *Exit, Voice and Loyalty*, Harvard University Press, Cambridge, Massachusetts.
Hirst, P. (1990) 'From Statism to Pluralism', in B. Pimlott *et al.* (eds), *The Alternative*, W. Allen, London, 19–29.
Hollis, C. (1960) *Eton: A History*, Hollis & Carter, London.
Honey, J.R. De S. (1977) *Tom Brown's Universe*, Millington, London.
James, E. (1989) 'Public and Private Education in International Perspective', in W.L. Boyd and J.G. Cibulka (eds), *Private Schools and Public Policy*, The Falmer Press, Barcombe, 213–35.
Jeffreys, K. (1987) 'British Politics and Social Policy since the Second World War', *The Historical Journal*, Vol. 30, No. 1, 123–44.
Johnson, R. (1989) 'Thatcherism and English Education: Breaking the Mould or Confirming the Pattern?', *History of Education*, Vol. 18, No. 2, 91–121.
Jones, G. (1969) *History of the Law of Charity, 1532–1827*, Cambridge University Press, Cambridge.
Jones, M.D.W. (1983) 'Brighton College v. Marriott: Schools, Charity Law and Taxation', *History of Education*, Vol. 12, No. 2, 121–32.
Joseph, K. (1976) *Stranded in the Middle Ground, Centre for Policy Studies*, London.
Kalton, G. (1966) *The Public Schools: A Factual Survey*, Longmans, London.
Kirby, T.K. (1892) *Annals of Winchester College*, Henry Frowde, London.
Lambert, R. (1966) *The State and Boarding Education: A Factual Report*, Methuen, London.
Lambert, R., and R. Woolfe (1968) 'Need and Demand for Boarding Education', in Public Schools Commission, *Report, Vol. 11: Appendices*, HMSO, London, 241–79.
Lauder, H., and P. Brown (eds) (1988) *Education in Search of a Future*, Falmer Press, Barcombe.
Lawton, D. (1992) *Education and Politics in the 1990s: Conflict or Consensus?*, Falmer Press, London.
Leach, A.F. (1899) *A History of Winchester College*, Charles Scribner's Sons, New York.
Le Grand, J. (1990) 'Rethinking Welfare: A Case for Quasi-Markets', in B.Pimlott *et al.* (eds), *The Alternative*, W. Allen, London, 85–94.
Leinster-Mackay, D. (1984) *The Rise of the English Prep School*, Falmer Press, Barcombe.
Le Quesne, L. (1970) 'The Headmasters' Conference between Two Peaces', *Conference*, Vol. 7, No.1, 3–12.
Lindsay, K. (1926) *Social Progress and Educational Waste*, Routledge, London.
Lowe, R. (1992) 'Education in England during the Second World War', in R. Lowe (ed.), *Education and the Second World War*, Falmer Press, London, 4–16.
Mack, E.C. (1938) *Public Schools and British Opinion, 1780 to 1860*, Methuen, London.
Mangan, J. (1981) *Athleticism in the Victorian and Edwardian Public School*, Cambridge University Press, Cambridge.
Mason, P. (1989) 'Elitism and Patterns of Independent Education', in W.L. Boyd and J.G. Cibulka (eds), *Private Schools and Public Policy: International Perspectives*, Falmer Press, Barcombe, 315–29.
Maxwell Lyte, H.C. (1911) *A History of Eton College, 1440–1910*, Macmillan, London.
McCulloch, G. (1994) *Educational Reconstruction: The 1944 Education Act and the Twenty-First Century*, Woburn Press, London.
Meisel, J.H. (1958) *The Myth of the Ruling Class: Gaetano Mosca and the 'Elite'*, University of Michigan Press, Ann Arbor.
Miliband, R. (1969) *The State in Capitalist Society*, Basic Books, New York.
Moffat, G. (1989) 'Independent Schools, Charity and Government', in A. Ware (ed.), *Charities and Government*, Manchester University Press, Manchester.
Morris, M., and C. Griggs (eds) (1988) *Education: The Wasted Years? 1973–1986*, Falmer Press, Barcombe.
Mountfield, A. (1991) *State Schools: A Suitable Case for Charity?*, The Directory of Social

Change, London.

Musgrove, F. (1970) 'Middle-Class Families and Schools, 1780–1880; Interaction and Exchange of Function between Institutions', in P.W. Musgrave (ed.), *Sociology, History and Education*, Methuen, London, 117–25.

Newsome, D. (1961) *Godliness and Good Learning*, John Murray, London.

Parkin, F. (1974) 'Strategies of Social Closure in Class Formation', in F. Parkin (ed.), *The Social Analysis of Class Structure*, Tavistock Publications, London, 1–18.

Pring, R. (1983) 'Privatisation in Education', paper prepared for RICE (Rights to Comprehensive Education), London.

Pring, R. (1986) 'Privatisation of Education', in R.Rogers (ed.), *Education and Social Class*, Falmer Press, Barcombe, 65–82.

Pring, R. (1988) 'Privatisation', *Educational Management and Administration*, Vol. 16, 85–96.

Rae, J. (1981) *The Public School Revolution: Britain's Independent Schools*, Faber & Faber, London.

Ranson, S. (1988) 'From 1944 to 1988: Education, Citizenship and Democracy', *Local Government Studies*, Vol. 14, No. 1, 1–19.

Ranson, S. (1995) 'Theorising Educational Policy', *Journal of Education Policy*, Vol. 10, No.4, 427–48.

Salter, B., and T. Tapper (1981) *Education, Politics and the State: The Theory and Practice of Educational Change*, Grant McIntyre, London.

Salter, B., and T. Tapper (1985) *Power and Policy in Education: The Case of Independent Schooling*, Falmer Press, Barcombe.

Saran, R. (1967) 'Decision-Making by a Local Education Authority', *Public Administration*, Vol. 45, 387–402.

Saran, R. (1973) *Policy-Making in Secondary Education*, Clarendon Press, Oxford.

Seldon, A. (1986) *The Riddle of the Voucher*, Institute of Economic Affairs, London.

Shilling, C. (1993) 'The Demise of Sociology of Education in Britain?', *British Journal of Sociology of Education*, Vol. 14, No. 1, 105–12.

Shrosbree, C. (1988) *Public Schools and Private Education*, Manchester University Press, Manchester.

Simon, B. (1960) *Studies in the History of Education, 1780–1870*, Lawrence & Wishart, London.

Simon, B. (1986) 'The 1944 Education Act: A Conservative Measure?', *History of Education*, Vol. 15, No.1, 31–43.

Simon, B. (1988) *Bending the Rules: The Baker 'Reform' of Education*, Lawrence & Wishart, London.

Simon, B. (1991) *Education and the Social Order, 1940–1990*, Lawrence & Wishart, London.

Simon, B. (1992) *What Future for Education?*, Lawrence & Wishart, London.

Simon, B. (1994) *The State and Education Change: Essays in the History of Education and Pedagogy*, Lawrence & Wishart, London.

Tapper, T., and B. Salter (1986) 'The Assisted Places Scheme: A Policy Evaluation', *Journal of Education Policy*, Vol. 1, No. 4, 315–30.

Tawney, R.H. (1922) *Secondary Education for All*, The Labour Party, London.

Taylor, W. (1963) *The Secondary Modern School*, Faber & Faber, London.

Thomas, H. (1994) 'Markets, Collectivities and Management', *Oxford Review of Education*, Vol. 20, No. 1, 41–56.

Thomas, H., and A. Bullock (1994) 'The Political Economy of Local Management of Schools', in S. Tomlinson (ed.), *Educational Reform and Its Consequences*, IPPR/Rivers Oram Press, London, 41–52.

Wakeford, J. (1969) *The Cloistered Elite: A Sociological Analysis of the English Public School*, Macmillan, London.

Walden, G. (1996) *We Should Know Better*, Fourth Estate, London.

Walford, G. (1986) *Life in Public Schools*, Methuen, London.

Walford, G. (1987) 'How Independent is the Independent School?', *Oxford Review of Education*, Vol. 13, No. 3, 275–96.

Walford, G. (ed.) (1989) *Private Schools in Ten Countries: Policy and Practice*, Routledge, London.

Walford, G. (1990) *Privatisation and Privilege in Education*, Routledge, London.

REFERENCES

Walford, G. (ed.) (1991) *Private Schooling: Tradition, Change and Diversity*, Paul Chapman, London.
Walford, G. (1994) *Choice and Equity in Education*, Cassell, London.
Walford, G., and S. Jones (1986) 'The Solihull Adventure: An Attempt to Reintroduce Selective Schooling', *Journal of Education Policy*, Vol. 1, No. 3, 239–53.
Wallace, R. (1981) 'The Origins and Authorship of the 1944 Education Act', *History of Education*, Vol. 10, No. 4, 283–90.
West, E.G. (1970) *Education and the State*, Institute of Economic Affairs, London.
West, E.G. (1975) *Education and the Industrial Revolution*, Batsford, London.
Wiener, M.J. (1981) *English Culture and the Decline of the Industrial Spirit, 1850–1980*, Cambridge University Press, Cambridge.
Wilkins, H.T. (1925) *Great English Schools*, Noel Douglas, London.
Wilkinson, R.H. (1964) *The Prefects: British Leadership and the Public School Tradition*, Oxford University Press, London.
Williamson, B. (1979) *Education, Social Structure and Development*, Macmillan, London.

GOVERNMENT AND PARLIAMENTARY PUBLICATIONS

Board of Education (1938) *Secondary Education with Special Reference to Grammar Schools and Technical High Schools*, HMSO, London.
Board of Education (1943) *Educational Reconstruction*, HMSO, London.
Commission Appointed to Inquire into the Revenues and Management of Certain Colleges and Schools, and the Studies Pursued and Instruction Given Therein (1864) *Report* (Clarendon Commission/Public Schools Commission), HMSO, London.
Commission Appointed to Inquire into the Revenues and Management of Certain Colleges and Schools, and the Studies Pursued and Instruction Given Therein (1864a) *Report*, Vol. II, Appendix (Clarendon Commission/Public Schools Commission), HMSO, London.
Commission on Schools not Comprised within Her Majesty's two recent Commissions on Popular Education and Public Schools (1868) *Report* (Taunton Commission), HMSO, London.
Commission on Secondary Education (1896) *Report* (Bryce Commission), HMSO, London.
Commission on the State of Popular Education in England (1861) *Report* (Newcastle Commission), HMSO, London.
Committee of Inquiry into the Education of Handicapped Children and Young People (1978) *Special Educational Needs* (Warnock Report), HMSO, London.
Committee on Public Schools (1943) *Abolition of Tuition Fees in Grant-Aided Secondary Schools, Special Report of the Committee on Public Schools* (Fleming Committee, Interim Report), MMSO, London.
Committee on Public Schools (1944) *The Public Schools and the General Educational System* (Fleming Report), HMSO, London.
Education, Arts and Home Office Subcommittee of the House of Commons Expenditure Committee (1975) *Charity Commissioners and their Accountability*, HMSO, London.
Parliamentary Select Committee on the Education of the Lower Orders (1816) *Report*, HMSO, London.
Public Schools Commission (1968) *Report* (Newsom Report), HMSO, London.
Public Schools Commission (1968a) *Report*, Vol. 2, Appendices (Newsom Report), HMSO, London.
Public Schools Commission (1970) *Report* (Donnison Report), HMSO, London.

PARLIAMENTARY DEBATES

Belstead, Lord (14 November 1972) *Hansard* (Lords), Vol. 336.
Boyson, R. (5 November 1979) *Hansard* (Commons), Vol. 973
Butler, R.A. (19 January 1944) *Hansard* (Commons), Vol. 396.
Butler, R.A. (28 March 1944) *Hansard* (Commons), Vol. 398.

Mellor, Sir J. (28 March 1944) *Hansard* (Commons), Vol. 398.
Wilkinson, E. (9 November 1945) *Hansard* (Commons), Vol. 415.
Vaizey, Lord (7 October 1976) *Hansard* (Lords) Vol. 374.

PARTY AND NON-GOVERNMENTAL PUBLICATIONS

Conservative Party (1965) *Conference*, Conservative Party, London.
Direct Grant Joint Committee (1969) *Document No. 143* (The Public Schools Commission), Direct Grant Joint Committee, London.
Harries, Gillian E.B. (ed.) (1995/96) *Independent Schools Yearbook*, A. and C. Black, London.
Headmasters Conference (1963) *Bulletin*, No.1.
Headmasters Conference (1970) *Bulletin*, No. 2.
Headmasters Conference (1979) *Bulletin*, No. 6.
HMC/SHMIS (1996) *Senior Independent Schools Scholarships*, HMC/SHMIS, Leicester.
Independent Schools Information Service (1982) *Independent Schools and the European Convention on Human Rights*, ISIS, London.
Independent Schools Information Service (1991) *Independent Schools: The Legal Case*, ISIS, London.
Independent Schools Information Service (1995) *Annual Census*, ISIS, London.
Labour Party (1980) *Private Schools: Discussion Document*, Labour Party, London.
Labour Party (1994), *Opening Doors to a Learning Society: A Policy Statement on Education*, Labour Party, London.
Labour Party (1995) *Diversity and Excellence: A New Partnership for Schools*, Labour Party, London.
National Council of Social Services (1976) *Charity Law and Voluntary Organisations* (Goodman Committee), Bedford Square Press, London.

NEWSPAPERS

Charter, D. and J. Sherman (28 February 1996) 'Blunkett Backs Fast-Track System in Comprehensives', *The Times*.
Devlin, T. (26 August 1983) 'Independent but Indebted', *The Times Educational Supplement*.
Evans, T. (9 February 1996) 'Will the Heads Play Labour's Tune?' *The Times*.
Hargreaves, D. (29 March 1996) 'It's Time to Move On', *The Times Educational Supplement*.
Jewell, D. (20 January 1992) 'The Public Service of Private Schools', *The Times*.
O'Leary, J. (4 February 1991) 'Why Charity Begins at Home', *The Times*.
O'Leary, J. (6 December 1993) 'Head's Plea: Send Us Your Daughters', *The Times*.
O'Leary, J. (11 April 1996) 'Loss of Tax on Saving Plans a Blow to Boarding Schools', *The Times*.
Skidelsky, R. (20 September 1996) 'Let Sink Schools Go Private', *The Times*.
The Times Educational Supplement (4 October 1996).
Wilby, P. (22 November 1981) 'A Parents' Guide to Private Education', *Sunday Times Magazine*.

COURT CASES

Attorney-General v. Earl of Lonsdale (1827) 1 Sim. 105
Attorney-General v. Hewer (1700) 2 Vern. 387
Brighton College v. Marriott (1926) A.C. 192–204
Income Tax Special Purposes Courts v. Pemsel (1891) A.C. 583
Jones v. Williams Amb. per Lord Camden (1767)
Morice v. Bishop of Durham (1805) 10 Ves. 522
Oppenheim and Tobacco Securities Trust Co. Ltd (1951) A.C. 297–319

Index

218